'*Working with Autistic People in the Criminal Justice and Forensic Mental Health Systems* is one of the first books that links together the perspectives from leading multidisciplinary professionals to examine the gaps that autistic offenders regularly face within the criminal justice system. An ideal guide for any practitioners to use within the forensic mental health field.'

Dr Tanya Banfield, *Head of Criminal Justice, Genius Within, UK*

'In their impressive new book Anne Sheeran and Nichola Tyler have curated a rounded, thoroughly evidenced, and immensely practical collection. Drawing on a vast array of clinical, research and experiential expertise the editors have successfully and comprehensively shown how criminal justice, mental health and learning disability services can work with, and for, people with autism, their families, carers, victims, and the public. Especially welcome were chapters on supporting the carers and staff of people with autism and on questioning people with autism in a criminal justice context. This is a collection, carefully and cogently crafted, that retains throughout an unerring focus on what works best and I recommend it to all working in the field.'

Professor Geoffrey L. Dickens, *Professor Mental Health Nursing, Centre for Applied Nursing Research, Northumbria University, UK*

'What is so pleasing about this excellent text, is that it achieves its aim of being a comprehensive handbook without losing sight of the people at the centre of it, those with autism. Centred on the British system, this handbook is nevertheless highly relevant to other jurisdictions, because of the quality of evidence the writers draw upon and the breadth of coverage of topics. It is highly recommended.'

Dr Justin Barry Walsh, *Consultant Forensic Psychiatrist, Chair, Faculty of Forensic Psychiatry Royal Australian and New Zealand College of Psychiatrists*

Working with Autistic People in the Criminal Justice and Forensic Mental Health Systems

Working with Autistic People in the Criminal Justice and Forensic Mental Health Systems: A Handbook for Practitioners is the first book to focus specifically on best practice for working with autistic people in criminal justice and forensic mental health settings. Integrating current theory, research, and clinical practice, this book provides a practical guide for multidisciplinary practitioners working with autistic people who have offended, at all stages in their pathway, regardless of the nature of offending.

The book draws together contributions from leading scholarly and clinical experts in the field of autism and forensic issues as well as the views of autistic people under the care of forensic services. Each chapter focuses on understanding the impact of autism throughout the criminal justice and forensic mental health system pathways, including how these systems are experienced by autistic people and their families and carers. Case studies and practical approaches are provided to demonstrate the application of best practice to working with autistic people in secure settings.

This book appeals to a wide audience within the fields of psychology, psychiatry, nursing, occupational therapy, speech and language therapy, as well as criminal justice staff (e.g., prison and probation), and will be the first of its kind to amalgamate theory, research, and practice in the area of autism and offending.

Nichola Tyler is a Lecturer in Forensic Psychology at Victoria University of Wellington, New Zealand. Nichola conducts research in the areas of forensic mental health, treatment evaluation, and deliberate firesetting. She has also worked in forensic settings with adult men and women who have engaged in challenging or offending behaviour.

Anne Sheeran is an NHS Clinical and Forensic Psychologist. Working within forensic mental health and prison settings, her key interest is support for autistic people and/or people with intellectual disabilities. Anne became an Approved Clinician as an early adopter of these new roles for psychologists, and is currently a full-time Responsible Clinician in both inpatient and community settings.

Working with Autistic People in the Criminal Justice and Forensic Mental Health Systems

A Handbook for Practitioners

Edited by
Nichola Tyler and Anne Sheeran

Routledge
Taylor & Francis Group

LONDON AND NEW YORK

Cover image: © Catherine McQueen/Getty Images

First published 2022
by Routledge
4 Park Square, Milton Park, Abingdon, Oxon OX14 4RN

and by Routledge
605 Third Avenue, New York, NY 10158

Routledge is an imprint of the Taylor & Francis Group, an informa business

British Library Cataloguing-in-Publication Data
A catalogue record for this book is available from the British Library

Library of Congress Cataloging-in-Publication Data
Names: Tyler, Nichola, 1987- editor. | Sheeran, Anne, 1963- editor.
Title: Working with autistic people in the criminal justice and forensic mental health systems: a handbook for practitioners / edited by Nichola Tyler and Anne Sheeran.
Description: Abingdon, Oxon ; New York, NY : Routledge, 2022. | Series: Issues in forensic psychology | Includes bibliographical references and index. |
Identifiers: LCCN 2021055653 (print) | LCCN 2021055654 (ebook) |
ISBN 9780367478285 (pbk) | ISBN 9780367478308 (hbk) |
ISBN 9781003036722 (ebk)
Subjects: LCSH: Offenders with mental disabilities. | Autistic people—
Institutional care. | Mental health services. | Forensic psychology.
Classification: LCC HV6133 .W65 2022 (print) | LCC HV6133 (ebook) |
DDC 364.3/8—dc23/eng/20220127
LC record available at https://lccn.loc.gov/2021055653
LC ebook record available at https://lccn.loc.gov/2021055654

ISBN: 978-0-367-47830-8 (hbk)
ISBN: 978-0-367-47828-5 (pbk)
ISBN: 978-1-003-03672-2 (ebk)

DOI: 10.4324/9781003036722

Typeset in Minion Pro
by codeMantra

Contents

Contributors

Regi T. Alexander is a Consultant Psychiatrist at Hertfordshire Partnership University NHS Foundation Trust and a Visiting Professor at the University of Hertfordshire. A practising clinician with research interests focusing on the forensic psychiatry of neurodevelopmental disorders, he was a member of the NICE guidelines panel on mental health in learning disability and the editor of a number of RCPsych treatment guidelines. Currently he is an Associate Dean of the Royal College of Psychiatrists, President of the Royal Society of Medicine – Intellectual Disability Section, Editor of the *Oxford Textbook of Psychiatry of Intellectual Disability*, and Convenor of RADiANT – a research consortium that brings together a large number of NHS Trusts, university academics, service users, and family members. With a particular interest in public education, he also edits *Village Voice*, an award-winning community magazine in East Anglia. In 2018, he was awarded the President's medal of the Royal College of Psychiatrists.

Clare Allely is a Reader in Forensic Psychology at the University of Salford in Manchester, UK, and is an affiliate member of the Gillberg Neuropsychiatry Centre at Gothenburg University, Sweden. Clare holds a PhD in Psychology from the University of Manchester and previously graduated with an MA (hons.) in Psychology from the University of Glasgow, an MRes in Psychological Research Methods from the University of Strathclyde, and an MSc in Forensic Psychology from Glasgow Caledonian University. Clare is also an Honorary Research Fellow in the College of Medical, Veterinary and Life Sciences affiliated to the Institute of Health and Wellbeing at the University of Glasgow. She is also an Associate of the Children's and Young People's Centre for Justice (CYCJ) at the University of Strathclyde. Clare also acts as an expert witness in criminal cases and also contributes to the evidence base used in the courts on psychology and legal issues through her published work.

Tony Attwood has been a clinical psychologist for nearly 10,000 autistic children and adults, some of whom have been seen for over 20 years. His book, *Asperger's Syndrome – A Guide for Parents and Professionals*, has sold over 450,000 copies and has been translated into over 25 languages. His subsequent book, *The Complete Guide to Asperger's Syndrome*, was published in October 2006 and is one of the primary textbooks on Asperger's syndrome.

He has been a contributor and author of over 30 peer review research papers on autism.

Will Attwood was hooked on amphetamines when he committed an armed robbery to pay a debt. Will has autism, which at that point in his life was still undiagnosed; it was while in prison, serving a three-year sentence, that he received his diagnosis. This threw light onto why so many aspects of prison life and culture had been so confusing and indeed frightening during those first few months. With the benefit of his diagnosis, Will, who has a degree in Media and Journalism, was able to chronicle his insights and experiences in his book, *Asperger's Syndrome and Jail: A Survival Guide*. He remains passionate about helping those on the autism spectrum achieve understanding and fair treatment within the criminal justice system.

Magali-Fleur Barnoux is a Lecturer in Forensic Psychology and Intellectual and Developmental Disabilities and a Chartered Psychologist at the Tizard Centre, University of Kent. Dr Barnoux completed her undergraduate degree in Psychology at the University of Leeds in 2003 and went on to complete an MSc (2010) and PhD (2015) in Forensic Psychology at the University of Kent. Dr Barnoux has worked at the Tizard Centre since 2013 and specialises in the research, assessment, and treatment of offenders with Intellectual and Developmental Disabilities. She has held a number of research and enterprise grants in the area and has extensive expertise in managing and delivering applied funded research studies within forensic settings. Dr Barnoux also undertakes consultancy work in Forensic Intellectual and Developmental Disability (e.g., training, autism assessments, expert witness work) and has collaborated with government agencies on various research projects which have informed future strategic decision-making (Home Office, Ministry of Justice).

Yvette Bates is a Senior Forensic Psychologist (HCPC Registered, BPS Chartered) with many years of experience in UK forensic settings, having worked in private prison services as autism lead. She received a Commendation from The Butler Trust in 2017 for her 'pioneering' work in this area due to its impact on practice in her local prison establishment and due to informing Government thinking. Yvette has presented at national and international conferences; her research and practice interests are in the area of being responsive to the needs of prisoners with autism.

Eddie Chaplin has extensive clinical experience in specialist mental health services for both national and local neurodevelopmental services in the community and in secure forensic services, with significant research experience in these areas.

Verity Chester has a BSc and MSc in Forensic Psychology, and is an experienced researcher, with specific interests in the offending behaviour and forensic involvement of people with developmental disabilities. Verity is the Coordinator of the Clinical Research Group in Forensic Intellectual and Developmental Disabilities (CRG-FIDD), and Network Manager for RADiANT, a clinical research network focused on intellectual/developmental disabilities. Verity is trained in the Autism Diagnostic Observation Schedule, 2nd Edition (ADOS-2) and supports the multi-disciplinary team with autism assessments. Verity is currently completing her PhD at the University of East Anglia, Norwich, and her research is investigating social information processing among autistic offenders. Verity is also the Diversity editor of *Advances in Autism*, has edited a special issue on autistic women and girls, and recently published a literature review on the presentation, recognition, and diagnosis of autism in women and girls.

Sarah Cooper is a Senior Forensic Psychologist with over 19 years of experience supporting adults with intellectual disabilities and autism. During the last six years she has worked in a low-secure forensic hospital, supporting adult male offenders with intellectual disabilities and additional complex needs, including mental health and autism. Sarah has a specialist interest in staff support procedures and restorative practices. She has introduced, developed, and led on restorative working within the service, with the aim of embedding restorative practices into the ward culture. She has presented her work at national and international conferences and begun to create a portfolio of published work.

Bethany Driver is a Trainee Clinical Psychologist at the University of East Anglia. She has numerous years of clinical experience working in both community and inpatient secure settings with adults and children with autism and intellectual disabilities. Bethany's research interests include diversity issues within clinical practice and the representation of under recognised and marginalised groups in clinical research. Bethany has contributed to research on the topic of gender and diversity within autism and has recently published a literature review on the presentation, recognition, and diagnosis of autism in women and girls.

Zoë Eastop is a Trainee Forensic Psychologist with the Kent and Medway NHS and Social Care Partnership Trust. She currently works as part of a community based forensic outreach team working with adults with a learning disability and/or autism that have engaged in offending behaviour or are at risk of offending.

Christopher Ince is a Consultant Psychiatrist, based within CNTW NHS Foundation Trust, who works within the Specialist Autism Service at

Northgate Hospital, Morpeth; this is a national referral service for those with a diagnosis of autism and significant behaviours that challenge. Dr Ince is currently Associate Medical Director (Inpatient North) and further provides input to the Newcastle Community Learning Disability Team. Dr Ince has previously worked within Forensic Learning Disability Services (Medium and Low Secure male and female) and was also a Specialist Advisor to the CQC regarding inspection of mental health and social care services. Dr Ince was a member of the CQC/DoH Expert Advisory Group for the thematic review of Restraint, Seclusion, and Segregation and further panel member for the Learning Disability Mortality Review (LeDeR) Programme.

Andy Inett is a Consultant Forensic Psychologist with over 20 years of experience of working in forensic mental health services, particularly with service users with intellectual disabilities and autism. Areas of expertise include completing detailed, structured individual risk assessments for violence, sexual offending, and firesetting; assessing personality disorders and autism; leading on community forensic outreach services; and implementation of adapted group and individual forensic psychology interventions. He regularly undertakes lecturing on forensic intellectual disability at the Institute of Psychiatry Psychology and Neuroscience (IoPPN), King's College, London, the University of Kent, and the clinical psychology doctorate at the Salomons Institute for Applied Psychology, Canterbury Christ Church University in Kent. He has also published papers, book chapters, and presented at international conferences on the use of structured risk assessments with offenders with intellectual disabilities, firesetting, and staff support and debriefing.

Claire King is a Senior Clinical Psychologist within the Forensic and Specialist Care Group at Kent and Medway NHS and Social Care Partnership Trust. Claire has a specialist interest in clinical and forensic issues related to individuals with intellectual and developmental disabilities (including autism). Claire has conducted research on the experience of being diagnosed with autism and has published research focused on individuals with autism in the criminal justice system.

Peter E. Langdon is an Honorary Consultant Clinical and Forensic Psychologist and Professor, Centre for Educational Development, Appraisal, and Research (CEDAR), University of Warwick and Brooklands Hospital, Coventry and Warwickshire Partnership NHS Trust and Herefordshire and Worcestershire Health and Care NHS. Peter completed his undergraduate degree in Psychology at Memorial University of Newfoundland. He was awarded a Lord Rothermere Fellowship and qualified as a clinical psychologist in 2000 from the Institute of Psychiatry, King's College, London. He completed his PhD at the Tizard Centre, University of Kent as an NIHR Research Fellow. He then completed an NIHR funded postdoctoral fellowship. He is a Fellow of the British Psychological Society. He has worked within secure mental healthcare services for offenders with intellectual and developmental disabilities for 20 years. His research interests fall broadly within the area of developmental psychology and include the adaptation and evaluation of psychological therapies for people with intellectual and developmental disabilities.

Michelle Mattison is an Associate Professor of Forensic Psychology at the University of Nottingham, a Registered Intermediary with the Ministry of Justice and National Crime Agency, and a Chartered Psychologist and Scientist with the British Psychological Society. Her research focuses upon vulnerability in criminal justice settings, specifically with regard to gathering and testing eyewitness evidence. As a Registered Intermediary, Michelle works with children and adults who have complex communication needs, such as autism and learning disabilities. This role involves facilitating communication with vulnerable victims and witnesses during police investigations and during criminal trial proceedings. Outside of University, Michelle trains practitioners about effective communication with children and people who have complex communication needs.

Jane McCarthy has over 20 years of experience as a Consultant Psychiatrist working with people with autism presenting across a number of services including community, outpatient, inpatient, and secure forensic service.

Clare Melvin PhD, MSc, DipPsych, BA (Hons) completed her Doctorate at the Tizard Centre, University of Kent, exploring sexual offending behaviours in individuals with autism.

David Murphy is a Chartered Forensic and Consultant Clinical Neuropsychologist based at Broadmoor Hospital, England, with over 25 years of experience working in forensic settings. In addition to forensic clinical neuropsychology, Dr Murphy has a particular interest in the assessment and management of autism in forensic services. Dr Murphy has also acted as an expert witness for several high profile cases and is an active researcher examining many aspects of autism in forensic contexts.

Glynis H. Murphy is Professor of Clinical Psychology & Disability at the Tizard Centre, University of Kent. She is a clinical and forensic psychologist, Fellow of the BPS, and Fellow of the Academy of Social Sciences. She was co-editor of JARID until 2014 and was President of IASSIDD 2008–2012. In 2013, she was awarded the Monte Shapiro prize for contributions to clinical psychology by the BPS. She has held over £2 million in research grants and has over 150 publications. Her research interests include intellectual disabilities, autism, challenging behaviour, abuse, offending, mental capacity, and the law.

Gemma Rogers is a Researcher and Assistant Psychologist within Forensic and Specialist Services in Kent and Medway NHS Social Care Partnership Trust. Gemma's research interests focus on forensic psychology and intellectual disability, mental health, and trauma. She also works clinically with male and female patients within forensic services.

Anne Sheeran is a Consultant Clinical and Forensic Psychologist. She has worked as a psychologist in secure hospitals and prisons since 1998. She is also an Approved Clinician. Anne was formerly the Professional Lead for Psychology and Psychological Therapies in the Forensic Healthcare Service at Sussex Partnership NHS Foundation Trust, where she also practised as a Responsible Clinician in a women's medium secure ward. She is currently working in a full-time Responsible Clinician Role within the Forensic Intellectual Disabilities services in Kent and Medway NHS Partnership Trust. Anne is also an Honorary Lecturer at the Centre of Research and Education in Forensic Psychology at the University of Kent. Her particular area of interest and experience is in working with people who have intellectual and developmental disabilities, and she specialises in assessment, intervention and support, and consultation, with this group.

Kirsty Taylor qualified as a Speech and Language Therapist in 1995, graduating from Reading University. She initially worked in schools for children and young people with complex neurodevelopmental and social emotional mental health needs as well as working with adults with learning disabilities and autism. In 1997, Kirsty moved to Sussex where she developed a keen interest in the communication needs of adults with learning disabilities and autism and the impact of these needs on their health and wellbeing, and subsequently behaviours which challenge. In 2012, Kirsty was recruited to introduce a new Speech and Language Therapy service within the forensic mental health service provided by Sussex Partnership Foundation NHS Trust, working as part of the multi-disciplinary teams to identify communication needs which were likely to be having an impact on the wellbeing and engagement of individuals in their recovery journey. Subsequently later, as a seconded post, Kirsty introduced Speech and Language Therapy to the Sussex liaison and diversion service when this was in its pilot stages in 2014 and continues to supervise colleagues in this now established role. At present, Kirsty supervises and works with Speech and Language Therapy colleagues within the Sussex Partnership Foundation NHS Trust forensic mental health service. Alongside this, she also continues to work in a specialist assessment and intervention service for adults with learning disabilities, many of whom have autism.

Jermaine J. A. Thompson is a dual higher trainee in Psychiatry of Learning Disability and Child and Adolescent Psychiatry, currently working in CNTW NHS Foundation Trust. He graduated from King's College, London with a Bachelor of Science in Biomedical Science before going on to study Graduate Entry Medicine at the University of Warwick. He is interested in psychopharmacology and physical health monitoring within mental health settings.

Ruth J. Tully is a Consultant Forensic Psychologist (HCPC Registered, BPS Chartered) in the UK. In practice she works with people with autism and forensic risks in prisons and other settings. Ruth is widely published in the area of forensic psychology with autism and learning disability specific publications related to diagnosis in prisons, risk, and treatment. She is particularly interested in promoting responsive violence/sexual risk assessment of people with autism, having trained hundreds of professionals in the use of structured professional judgment tools nationally and internationally.

Nichola Tyler is a Lecturer in Forensic Psychology in the School of Psychology at Victoria University of Wellington, New Zealand. Nichola's research expertise is in issues pertaining to forensic mental health, treatment evaluation, and deliberate firesetting. She has authored numerous academic articles and book chapters on offending behaviour and rehabilitation, including articles on individuals in the criminal justice system with a mental illness and/ or intellectual and developmental difficulties. Nichola also has several years of experience working in secure hospitals and prisons with men and women who have engaged in challenging or offending behaviour.

Lisa Whittingham MA, BCBA, is a PhD candidate at Brock University in the Department of Child and Youth Studies. She is also a Board-Certified Behaviour Analyst (BCBA) working with youth and adults with intellectual and developmental disabilities.

Rachel Worthington is a Chartered Psychologist and a full member of the Division of Forensic Psychology, including holding Associate Fellow status. She is also a Chartered Scientist, holds European Psychologist status, and is fully registered with the HCPC in the UK. She has an MEd in Adult Autism, is a trainer in Positive Behavioural Support (as recognised by the British Institute of Learning Disabilities), and has a Level 5 Professional Diploma in PBS. She is also trained in other standardised support mechanisms for clients such as Applied Behaviour Analysis, Person Centred Planning, the Neuroscience of Sensory Integration, Talking Mats and Makaton. She has published a number of peer reviewed articles and she has presented both nationally and internationally on working positively with people with complex needs to improve their quality of life.

Series foreword

The British Psychological Society's 2021 best practice guidelines for working with autism recognise that when there is a failure to properly understand and provide sufficient support, psychological differences can become disabilities. Outcome can be very much dependent on the availability of adequate and responsive services. The guidelines go on to conclude that there is a lack of clinical, social and educational support and that "services for individuals with autism often fail to meet their needs" (p7).

This edition goes some way to considering a response to these observations. It is also very much aligned with the aims of the *Issues in Forensic Psychology* book series which are to make forensic psychology relevant and meaningful, promote its potential to make a difference to people's lives and demonstrate how forensic psychology can contribute to and learn from other professions within the wider field of mental health. This edition has been driven by the recognition that whilst services within the criminal justice system and forensic mental health settings have developed and adapted to meet the needs of people with autism there remains a gap in our awareness and practice which this edition seeks to fill.

The editors rightly see the edition as providing a practical resource. It provides clarity in how autism is now understood and conceptualised, recognising, however, that our understanding and knowledge is still developing. It discusses the nature and significance of autism and reflects on the question of diagnosis. It has helpful contributions on the impact and significance of autism for service users, carers, staff and the families of people with autism who enter the criminal justice system or forensic mental health services. The edition is also open in its recognition that there is far more to learn and understand about the aetiology of autism and that this is continuing to evolve. It points to areas of omission such as the theme of diversity, and identifies important but unaddressed research priorities. It discusses ways to better understand and improve the experience of individuals with autism making the book practical and relevant. For example, it considers how a diagnosis of autism helps practitioners to better understand and work with an individual's offending and it provides helpful practice guidelines for how interventions can be adapted to work more effectively with people with autism.

Thought is given to the way in which particular environments might aid and assist those with autism as well as to how regimes and institutions can be adapted to better support people with autism. It explores how planning for release and discharge can be improved and the specific ways in which this can present increased risk for people with autism and how these risks can be best mitigated. A theme of the edition which is emphasised throughout is the need to understand people with autism by recognising their differences and that needs, perspectives or experiences will vary. For example, the edition presents helpful and relevant guidelines for forensic practitioners when designing and delivering interventions and recognises the importance of attending carefully to individual need, strength and preference. Another way in which the book is relevant to practitioners is in an analysis of ways in which risk assessment and formulations of risk can best be adapted for individuals with autism. It suggests how risk assessment methods can be improved to capture the particular needs and vulnerabilities of those with autism. The edition is also of considerable value in advocating and describing strategies for supporting people with autism as well discussing the role of specific support interventions which may help both the families and carers of people with autism. Recognising that certain populations are still neglected in literature, the edition considers strategies and suggestions for the management and treatment of women with autism, making recommendations for further research. Specific therapeutic initiatives involving restorative practice where being both a victim and a perpetrator can be authentically explored and addressed are also discussed.

This edition is a highly relevant practical guide. Its accessibility, relevance and value to all of those working within criminal justice and forensic mental health services make this an important and highly original contribution to the *Issues in Forensic Psychology* book series.

Richard Shuker and Geraldine Akerman
Series Editors

Reference

British Psychological Society (2021). *Working with autism: Best practice guidelines for psychologists.* www.bps.org.uk/sites/www.bps.org.uk/files/Policy/Policy%20-%20Files/Working%20 with%20autism%20-%20best%20practice%20guidelines%20for%20psychologists.pdf

Foreword

Working with Autistic People in the Criminal Justice and Forensic Mental Health Systems is a much-needed, and very well researched exploration into the increasing need for those with Autism Spectrum Disorder (ASD) to be treated with the respect, dignity, and understanding everyone deserves while incarcerated.

Having been on the inside myself, I was heartened by reading this text. It puts so much of what I experienced into context.

The Criminal Justice System (CJS) has been slow to respond to the issue of less 'visible' ailments, and often over-compensates when called to task. For example, one individual I served with went from a starting dose of 200mg quetiapine to 1200mg in two weeks, rendering him a lethargic, dull-eyed shadow of a man, someone who looked as though he belonged in a hospital, not a prison.

Over-medication, and the use of inappropriate medication (such as typical anti-psychotics and tricyclic antidepressants) is rife and is a regrettable by-product of a system which is more concerned about budgets than the people they are paid to look after. Needless to say, proven techniques such as CBT are simply not available, or at least not as accessible as is necessary.

I once put in a request to see the prison psychiatric 'team' (two people – a screener, and a psychiatrist, for a jail with 1200 inmates) and didn't see the psychiatrist for 12 weeks, by which time I had developed an eye twitch from stress. This was because I had been taken *off* my regular medication (without consult) and told I had to undergo an extensive 'consultation' process to get back *on* the medication. This inverted style of treatment means inmates will often turn to acquiring illicit substances, whether from the outside (smuggled in) or the inside (diverted medication, usually anti-psychotics).

This poses unique problems for the inmate with ASD – do they delve into the nefarious world of prison drug culture to get a proper night's rest? Or do they 'play it safe', and go through the official channels, waiting up to three months to see a doctor who may, in the end, be so unhelpful as to actually increase the sense of loneliness and helplessness?

Issues such as bullying, which can range in severity from a cell-mate dictating the 'rules' of the cell, to full-blown, repeated physical assaults (sometimes sexual in nature), can plague the inmate with ASD to the point where suicide becomes a seemingly logical response.

Talk of suicide is common, and that's why most Correctional Facilities have a Special Needs Unit (SNU) or equivalent. However, space is limited, and while some Correctional Officers (COs) are happy to facilitate improvement to an inmate's quality of life, for every CO who does this, there are three who at best won't, and at worst, relish in making life *more* difficult for the inmate.

All of the above illustrates why *Working with Autistic People in the Criminal Justice and Forensic Mental Health Systems* is a timely, necessary and progressive work.

Chapters address issues such as the prevalence of ASD within the CJS, the type of offences most likely to have been committed, the risks faced by those with ASD within the CJS, current mental health needs and, moreover, the chronic need for systemic overhaul.

Another topic raised is the potential for those with ASD to be 'verballed' by police – that is, detectives taking advantage of an individual's psychological vulnerability, including not making it clear about lawyers and the right to remain silent.

I have heard disturbing stories about police threatening suspects with violence, and worse still, making good on those threats. In addition, both police and COs are known to 'leak' false information to the prison population – taking full advantage of the misinformation grapevine which plagues jails because of boredom, anger and scapegoating. Inmates with ASD are particularly susceptible to this dubious practice.

In a perfect world, there would be an entirely separate jail for those with ASD. Although unlikely to ever happen, the more achievable changes proposed in this book would ensure inmates with ASD could be assessed and accommodated more professionally and effectively.

Inmates with ASD are at much higher risk of self-harm, usually because of their extreme exasperation at coming up against roadblock after roadblock. This applies to all inmates, but the repercussions for inmates with ASD can be much more intense.

I witnessed an inmate with ASD being pushed around (metaphorically) by the COs. Eventually, he snapped, and was relegated to the Maximum Security Unit; he was still there four months later, when I left jail for good.

Although women make up a much smaller percentage of the overall prison population, their needs are no less important, and may be more complex due to the differing manifestation of their ASD. I can only hypothesise that, judging by the level of gossip in men's prisons, it would be very difficult for a female inmate to cope with the feminine predisposition to bully through words rather than actions – often harder to deal with.

It is reassuring to know this book exists. *Working with Autistic People in the Criminal Justice and Forensic Mental Health Systems* is one more concrete step towards upgrading an archaic system – it is a relevant, well-researched conduit to facilitate this process.

Will Attwood
27 August 2021

Preface

Anne Sheeran
Nichola Tyler

A note about terminology

We acknowledge that the use of terminology such as 'condition' or 'disorder' may be seen as contentious. Further, a variety of person-first and identify-first terms are recognised and preferred by the autism community when describing autism (Kenny et al., 2016; Vivanti, 2020). In recognition of the variation and evolution of terms valued and used by autistic people, their families and carers, and professionals, we have made the editorial decision to include mixed terminology in reference to people and to autism. *This highlights the changes in terminology which have taken place in recent years, and the different preferences of autistic people. Some of the contributions do reflect a psychiatric perspective, in the context of forensic mental health systems, and the terminology used by those authors does include reference to 'autistic spectrum disorder'.* In addition, it is acknowledged that people may identify as autistic, although they are currently undiagnosed. The approaches to best practice in this handbook apply also to those who identify as autistic, awaiting diagnosis. We hope that this reflects the growing diversity in the field and that the utility of the content will not be overshadowed by semantic concerns.

Autistic people in the criminal justice and forensic mental health systems

If I break the law, I want the criminal justice system to think about autism and to know how to work well with other services.

Priority Challenge #13 – Department of Health UK, 2014

It is already some years since the publication of the document from which the above quotation is taken. The National Strategy (Department of Health and Social Care, 2021) sets out the vision for improvements in services, including for "autistic people who have been convicted of a crime to be able to get the additional support they may require to engage fully in their sentence and rehabilitation" (p.35).

Over the past decades, the presence and impact of autism has increasingly been recognised, reflected in national legislative frameworks focused on the support needs of autistic people (such as the UK *Autism Act* 2009), the (mis) representation of autistic people in popular culture, and the commissioning of specialist autism diagnostic services within health economies. Understanding the role of gender in mediating the expression and recognition of autism is also of increasing importance. At the heart of autism lies its impact on the person's relationship to the social environment (e.g., Asperger, 1991). For an autistic person, learning to understand social interaction has been described as akin to learning a second language. The Criminal Justice System (CJS) and Forensic Mental Health System (FMHS), as complex social environments with their own implicit social 'language', pose particular difficulties for autistic people and for those providing custodial and rehabilitative services to them. The pathways to offending and to recovery and desistance for autistic people also reflect the impact of the condition on the person's cognitive, emotional, and behavioural responses to the social and interpersonal world.

Despite their potentially increased risk of coming into contact with the CJS, either as a victim of crime or due to displaying challenging or offending behaviour, training on identifying, understanding, and working with autistic people is not routinely offered to professionals working across different tiers of the system (Archer & Hurley, 2013). This can have a significant impact upon all stages of the CJS. For example, characteristics of autism such as social and communication difficulties, emotional dysregulation, and difficulties in recognising the implications of their own behaviour may lead to confusion, misunderstandings, and increased anxiety and distress during the police and court process (King & Murphy, 2014; National Autistic Society, 2020). When autistic people are not identified in custody, this may impact on appropriate placement of these individuals as well as the effectiveness of care and treatment planning, and the management of vulnerability and challenging behaviour (Ashworth, 2016). As the British Psychological Society's best practice guidelines note, "Without informed guidance and support, accurate risk assessment and the management and treatment of people with autism who commit offences may cause disproportionate challenges for criminal justice agencies" (2021, p.43).

The Transforming Care agenda was developed by NHS England out of the Winterbourne View Review (Department of Health, 2012) – where the systematic and severe abuse of autistic people and/or people with intellectual disabilities was uncovered at an independent sector hospital in the UK. Transforming Care set out a programme of action to revise and improve services for people with intellectual disabilities and/or autism, including those in secure forensic hospitals, by ensuring the availability of community services to meet the needs of these individuals and in turn reducing the number of inpatient hospital beds. However, the success of Transforming Care with respect to autistic people, and in particular those in secure care, has been much debated (e.g., Marshall-Tate, Chaplin, & McCarthy, 2017; Taylor, McKinnon, Thorpe, & Gilmer, 2017; Sinclair, 2018). The need for appropriate inpatient services with clear tailored care pathways for autistic people with/without other comorbid conditions (e.g., mental illness, personality disorder) who present with high harm offending behaviour (e.g., serious violence, sexual offending, firesetting) still remains.

In response to the recent socio-political attention around the need for timely and appropriate identification, assessment and treatment of autistic people, there has been an increase in advocacy, research, and clinical practice in the area, including the development of specialist services. The driver for this handbook was the recognition from the perspective of the editors, derived from their experience in both clinical and academic settings, of the gap between the growing recognition of the particular needs of autistic people within CJS and FMHS settings, and the perception by people working in these services that they still do not always know how to 'think about autism'. The handbook draws together contributions from leading scholarly and clinical experts in the field including psychology, psychiatry, speech and language therapy, and applied behaviour analysis as well as the views of service users residing within forensic services, with the aim of providing a practical guide for multidisciplinary professionals who may come into contact with autistic people in this context.

References

Archer, N. & Hurley, E.A. (2013). A justice system failing the autistic community. *Journal of Intellectual Disabilities and Offending Behaviour*, 4(1), 53–59. doi:10.1108/JIDOB-02-2013-0003

Ashworth, S. (2016). Autism is underdiagnosed in prisoners. *BMJ*, 353, i3028. doi: 10.1136/bmj.i3028

Asperger, H. (1991). Autistic Psychopathy in Childhood. In U. Frith (Ed), *Autism and Asperger Syndrome*. Cambridge: Cambridge University Press.

Autism Act (2009). London: HMSO. Retrieved from: www.legislation.gov.uk/ukpga/2009/15/pdfs/ukpga_20090015_en.pdf

British Psychological Society (BPS) (2021). *Working with Autism: Best Practice Guidelines for Psychologists*. Retrieved from: www.bps.org.uk/sites/www.bps.org.uk/files/Policy/Policy%20-%20Files/Working%20with%20autism%20%20best%20practice%20guidelines%20for%20psychologists.pdf

Department of Health (2012). *Transforming Care: A National Response to Winterbourne View Hospital*. London. Retrieved from: https://assets.publishing.service.gov.uk/government/uploads/system/uploads/attachment_data/file/213215/final-report.pdf

Department of Health (2014). *Think Autism. Fulfilling and Rewarding Lives, the Strategy for Adults With Autism in England: An Update*. Retrieved from: https://assets.publishing.service.gov.uk/government/uploads/system/uploads/attachment_data/file/299866/Autism_Strategy.pdf

Department of Health and Social Care (2021). *The National Strategy for Autistic Children, Young People and Adults: 2021 to 2026*. Retrieved from: www.gov.uk/government/publications/national-strategy-for-autistic-children-young-people-and-adults-2021-to-2026/the-national-strategy-for-autistic-children-young-people-and-adults-2021-to-2026

Kenny, L., Hattersley, C., Molins, B., Buckley, C., Povey, C., & Pellicano, E. (2016). Which terms should be used to describe autism? Perspectives from the UK autism community. *Autism*, 20(4), 442–462. doi: 10.1177/1362361315588200

King, C. & Murphy, G.H. (2014). A systematic review of people with autism spectrum disorder and the criminal justice system. *Journal of Autism and Developmental Disorders*, 44(11), 2717–2733. doi: 10.1007/s10803-014-2046-5

Marshall-Tate, K., Chaplin, E., & McCarthy, J. (2017). Is "transforming care" failing people with autism? *Advances in Autism*, 3(2), 1–7. doi: 10.1108/AIA-10-2016-0027

National Autistic Society (2020). Autism: A guide for police officers and staff. https://www.autism.org.uk/advice-and-guidance/topics/criminal-justice/criminal-justice/professionals

Sinclair, N. (2018). Transforming care: Problems and possible solutions. *Tizard Learning Disability Review*, 23(1), 51–55. doi: 10.1108/TLDR-10-2017-0040

Taylor, J.L., McKinnon, I., Thorpe, I., & Gilmer, B.T. (2017). The impact of Transforming Care on the care and safety of patients with learning disabilities and forensic needs. *BJPsych Bulletin*, 1–4. doi: 10.1192/pb.bp.116.055095

Vivanti, G. (2020). Ask the Editor: What is the most appropriate way to talk about individuals with a diagnosis of autism? *Journal of Autism and Developmental Disorders*, 50, 691–693. doi: 10.1007/s10803-019-04280-x

Acknowledgements

We would like to extend our thanks to Christina Chronister (Editor) and Molly Selby and Danielle Dyal (Editorial Assistants) at Routledge for commissioning and supporting this project. We would also like to thank Emily Boyd for her copyediting assistance. Dr Tanya Banfield, Head of Criminal Justice at Geniuswithin, gave invaluable and refreshingly direct feedback enabling us to ensure that the language and the content reflect the aims of the handbook. Will Attwood's foreword, including a personal perspective, sets the context for those aims.

The handbook was commissioned just as the tumultuous impact of the COVID-19 pandemic was beginning. We owe enormous gratitude to the authors and their tremendous efforts to write during this time, whilst, for many, dealing with the personal impact of the pandemic and performing frontline duties. We are especially grateful to the service users who provided input and supported the project, as well as to those colleagues and service users who have contributed to our understanding of this area over the years, and to the many service users whose neurodiverse experiences and perspectives have inspired us to look at the world in a different way.

Part I
Understanding autism

Autism
Context and diagnosis
Tony Attwood

1

What is autism?

Over the years there has been a range of terms to define and describe autism, from childhood schizophrenia to Autism Spectrum Disorder (ASD). This chapter uses the term ASD to be consistent with the primary diagnostic textbook used by diagnosticians, The Fifth Edition of the Diagnostic and Statistical Manual of Mental Disorders (American Psychiatric Association (APA), 2013) and the term autistic person rather than person with autism.

The characteristics of ASD according to the Fifth Edition of the Diagnostic and Statistical Manual of Mental Disorders (DSM-5) (APA, 2013) are: persistent deficits in reciprocal social communication and social interaction; restricted, repetitive patterns of behaviour, interests or activities; and hyper- or hypo-reactivity to sensory input.

Prevalence of autism

Prevalence of autism is increasing. Current estimates are that ASD occurs in one in 44 children or around 2% of the general population (Centers for Disease Control and Prevention, 2020). Accurate figures for prevalence of autism in the Criminal Justice System (CJS) are difficult to determine but range from no over-representation (King & Murphy, 2014) to 9% (Young et al., 2017).

Aetiology of autism

Autism is a neurodevelopmental disorder with multi-factorial aetiology. Detailed analysis is beyond the scope of this chapter. Different genetic and neurological pathways to autism are emerging. In future the term 'autisms' may be used (Coleman & Gillberg, 2012), with gradual subdivision into distinct groups with different aetiologies, profiles of abilities, and prognoses.

DOI: 10.4324/9781003036722-2

Heritability is a significant factor, with estimates from twin studies ranging from 56–95% (Colvert et al., 2015; Hallmayer et al., 2011; Tick et al., 2016). Heritability is also a factor in the recurrence rate of autism within a family, currently estimated as 35% (Brian et al., 2016).

Association has been identified between autism and autoimmune disorders (Keil et al., 2010; Chen et al., 2013), prematurity (Limperopoulos, 2009) and increased parental age (over 35 at age of conception) (Gardener et al., 2009; Lampi et al., 2013).

A large meta-analysis of studies using MRI scans has indicated very little by way of qualitative differences from typical samples (Pua et al., 2017), while van Rooij et al.'s (2017) review found multiple quantitative differences in structural findings.

Level of severity

DSM-5 includes a measure of the severity of expression of ASD based on the amount of support needed in the areas of social communication and restricted, repetitive behaviours: requiring support (Level 1), substantial support (Level 2), and very substantial support (Level 3). ASD Level 1 was formerly known as Asperger's syndrome (Attwood, 2015).

Many adults have the characteristics of autism without impairment affecting daily life. However, when a crisis occurs, such as being charged with a criminal offence, the symptoms may become conspicuous, triggering a diagnostic assessment.

Deficits in reciprocal social communication

DSM-5 subdivides deficits in social-emotional reciprocity, nonverbal communication, and the development and maintenance of friendships and relationships. A diagnostic assessment will explore whether there are difficulties with reciprocal social interactions; 'reading' social cues, context, and conventions; interpreting and expressing nonverbal communication (the range of facial expressions and gestures, and the pragmatic and prosodic aspects of language); and examination of the development and maintenance of friendships and relationships from early childhood.

Theory of Mind is the ability to (meta)represent mental states in oneself and others; impairment of this ability is integral to autism (Happé, 2015), and will affect the ability to engage in reciprocal social communication, hindering the development of friendships. The autistic person may be unable to accurately identify another person's subtle emotional state, and consequently might be considered disrespectful, rude, or lacking empathy because of their failure to read nonverbal cues in others. A number of characteristics typically affect the reciprocity and quality of conversation and social interaction. These include a disarming honesty, with a tendency to make literal interpretations of what others say. There may be a limited development of the arts of persuasion, compromise, and conflict resolution, with difficulty recognising and accepting an alternative perspective. The person may be greatly confused by idioms, figures of speech, and sarcasm.

Nevertheless, there may be a strong desire to establish social connection, but with little idea of what friendship entails. This can result in a lifelong reduction in the number, depth, and duration of friendships and relationships. During early years, the autistic child may be uninterested in establishing peer friendships, having discovered aspects of life that are more enjoyable than socialising, content with long periods of solitude engaged in collecting and collating information on a special interest that may not be shared by peers. Autistic children who do want to play and engage with peers may find their attempts to increase social integration lead to rejection and ridicule and extreme vulnerability to teasing and bullying throughout childhood.

In adolescence, friendships tend to be based on complex interpersonal needs. Typical adolescents seek confidantes who can provide emotional support. At this developmental stage, the gap in social understanding and integration with peers becomes more conspicuous for autistic adolescents, who can become overwhelmed and confused by the changing and increasingly complex nature of friendship, leading to feelings of isolation, loneliness, and depression.

During adolescence and adulthood, there may be absence or delay in the development of romantic experiences, and friendships may remain limited. However, some autistic people do achieve satisfying relationships. Their partner/s may understand autism, either because they share some of the same characteristics themselves, or because they are naturally intuitive, and compassionate in understanding their autistic partner (Attwood, 2015).

Restricted, repetitive patterns of behaviour or interests and sensory sensitivity

DSM-5 (APA, 2013) subdivides restricted, repetitive patterns of behaviour into:

- repetitive motor movements
- insistence on sameness and adherence to routines
- interests that are unusual in terms of focus or intensity
- hyper- or hypo-reactivity to sensory input.

Repetitive motor movements or mannerisms, such as flapping when distressed or excited, are usually associated with ASD Level 3, or may occur in early childhood and diminish in later childhood. At all levels of autism there is an insistence on sameness and the imposition of daily routines and rituals, with considerable distress if these are changed or prevented. Routines and rituals may be mechanisms for coping with high levels of anxiety, as they are experienced as soothing and relaxing. In daily life, and in problem solving, there can be 'a one-track mind', with a lack of cognitive flexibility and a tendency to negative rumination. The cognitive profile associated with autism can also include being detail-focused, quickly identifying errors, patterns, and systems (Attwood, 2015).

There may be a history of collecting information and objects with unusual focus or intensity. Having an interest is a typical human characteristic, but in autism, the time engaged in the interest and the dominance of the interest in daily life are more intense. Interests may last for hours or decades, and adults may have several concurrent interests. A special interest has many functions, such as being a 'thought blocker' for anxiety, an energy restorative after the exhaustion of socialising, and an extremely enjoyable activity counteracting depression. Some interests involve the creation of an intricate, alternative imaginary world that is more accommodating of the characteristics of autism. Interests can also create a sense of identity and achievement, and provide opportunity for making like-minded friends, and social status in a peer group. The sense of enjoyment or euphoria associated with the interest can become almost addictive. A special interest may contribute to the development of talents in science and the arts (Fitzgerald, 2005; James, 2006).

DSM-5 includes sensory sensitivity as one of the key characteristics of autism. Research indicates that atypical sensory experience may occur in as many as 90% of autistic individuals and affects every sensory modality (Robertson & Baron-Cohen, 2017). In some cases, the person experiences a 'sensory avalanche', contributing to a meltdown or to sensory fascination (Smith & Sharp, 2013). Specific sensory experiences that are extremely aversive may form the basis of the development of a phobia (Ozsivadjian et al., 2012). We have yet to achieve an understanding of why autistic people have atypical patterns of sensory sensitivity (Crane et al., 2009; Tavassoli et al., 2014) based on neural foundations and explanations (Marco et al., 2011). Sensitivities may be to environmental stimuli unnoticed by others (such as perfume, flickering lights, or sounds). In contrast, there may be a lack of perception of low levels of ordinary bodily sensations, or pain and discomfort. Sensitivity to external sensory experiences may be heightened, alongside reduced sensitivity to internal experiences (interoception), including the perception and recognition of internal emotional states.

Alexithymia

Recent research has explored the association between autism and alexithymia – the inability to recognise and describe one's own emotions (e.g., Kinnaird et al., 2019). Alexithymia is neither exclusive to autism, nor apparent in all autistic adults. Where present, alexithymia limits the ability to distinguish and identify cognitions and bodily sensations (both positive and negative), and to translate those feelings and thoughts into a coherent narrative using a precise and subtle vocabulary, in turn increasing the difficulty for others in understanding what the autistic person is feeling. Such misunderstanding can lead to a breakdown in communication and the potential for increased agitation.

Best practice in diagnostic assessment

An autistic adult may be assessed by one or more clinicians, using a range of diagnostic instruments and interview scripts, as well as information provided by family members or friends (Attwood, 2015). There is no universally agreed exclusive diagnostic instrument. Diagnosis relies upon expert clinical opinion and information obtained from the clinician's choice of instruments (Fusar-Poli et al., 2017) (see Tables 1.1 and 1.2). Clinical guidance suggests that these assessments should be used in conjunction with other instruments that measure the characteristics of autism as defined in DSM-5 (Pugliese et al., 2015) (see Table 1.3).

The diagnostic assessment should be conducted in an 'autism friendly' environment that is quiet with no distractions. It is also important to be aware of sleepiness, hunger, and thirst, and address where possible. Some countries have national clinical guidelines outlining the expectations for a

Table 1.1 Screening instruments for autism

AQ (Autism Quotient)	Self-report measure, developed and evaluated at Cambridge University, used to screen for autism in adults (Baron-Cohen et al., 2001) 1) A brief 10-item version 2) A fuller 50-item version. A score above a cut-off indicates further assessment is warranted.
GQ-ASC (Girls Questionnaire – Autism Spectrum Condition)	Designed to identify characteristics of autism in women (Brown et al., 2020). 21-item questionnaire created with reference to research literature, autobiographies, and extensive clinical experience.

Table 1.2 Assessments to support diagnosis

ADOS-2 (The Autism Diagnostic Observation Schedule)	Internationally regarded as the principal instrument to support a diagnosis of autism in children and adults (Martin et al., 2018). Facilitates the assessment of social communication and restrictive and repetitive behaviours.
	Suitable for use with individuals with mild intellectual disability.
	It is suggested that, due to the way it was developed, the ADOS-2 is less sensitive for females and/or those with higher levels of intellectual functioning (Frigaux et al., 2019).
ADI-R (Autism Diagnostic Interview – Revised)	Comprehensive interview-based instrument covering >90 questions; collates a developmental history in relation to the diagnostic criteria for autism.
	Questions address social and communication issues, and repetitive behaviours.
	Adults may act as their own respondent. Parents/caregivers can answer on behalf of children.
RAADS-R (Ritvo Autism Asperger Diagnostic Scale – Revised)	80 items, completed by the respondent with the clinician, who explores the characteristics of autism in each statement through conversation, providing an opportunity to explain the statement in more detail and whether these have changed over time (e.g., always true and present, true when a child, only as an adult, or never true). The diagnostician provides the final rating (Ritvo et al., 2011).
MIGDAS-2 (Monteiro Interview Guidelines for Diagnosing Autism Spectrum, 2nd edition)	A less well-known assessment tool which provides qualitative descriptions of Language and Communication, Social Relationships and Emotional Responses, and Sensory Use and Interests (Monteiro & Stegall, 2018).

comprehensive diagnostic assessment, including recommended diagnostic instruments (e.g., National Institute for Health and Care Excellence (NICE) guidelines, 2012; Autism CRC, 2018).

Clinical diagnostic assessment may include additional valuable strategies that have yet to be confirmed by research. An example is for the clinician to ask, 'Who are you?' Typical adults answer after only a moment's thought, and tend to identify themselves by their relationships, social networks, and personality characteristics. An autistic adult may take some time to reply, eventually saying that they do not know, perhaps adding that this has long been a cause for introspection and rumination; or may answer by describing an identity focusing on interests and knowledge.

Diagnostic assessment can also include assessment of the person's ability to read social and nonverbal communication and contextual cues by using pictorial materials depicting social interaction and/or emotional responses with clear, subtle, or ambiguous content.

Table 1.3 Additional diagnostic procedures

- Social Responsiveness Scale 2nd Edition (Constantino, 2011)
- Adult Repetitive Behaviour Questionnaire-2 (Barrett et al., 2018)
- Sensory Perception Questionnaire (Tavassoli et al., 2014)
- Camouflaging of Autistic Traits Questionnaire (Hull et al., 2019)
  Determines whether camouflaging may have compromised the validity of diagnostic assessments
- Coventry Grid for Adults (Cox et al., 2019)
  Assists in the differentiation of autism and the effects of complex trauma

Assessment of Alexithymia

TAS-20	Toronto Alexithymia Scale (Kooiman et al., 2002).
	Three subscales:
	DIF: Difficulty Identifying Feelings
	DDF: Difficulty Describing Feelings
	EOT: Externally Orientated Thinking
	Assesses negative emotions only.
PAQ	Perth Alexithymia Questionnaire (Preece et al., 2018)
	Assesses alexithymia for both negative and positive emotions.
Interview Guide for the Diagnostic Assessment of Able Adults with Autism Spectrum Disorder	An interview guide using the DSM-5 criteria by UK Royal College of Psychiatrists (Berney et al., 2017)

Challenges to the diagnostic assessment

Adaptations to autism

There are three psychological adaptations which a person may make to having a deficit in their ability to interact socially (Attwood & Garnett, 2019). The first is to actively avoid social interactions, due to feeling overwhelmed and uncertain in social situations, aware of the risk of making a social *faux pas*. The person may be perceived as an introvert. Alternatively, the person may be highly motivated to engage socially; but due to their difficulty reading subtle social signals that regulate and moderate the reciprocity of social engagement, may be perceived as intrusive, intense, and irritating.

A third adaptation, only recently recognised in research and clinical practice, is camouflaging. The person avidly observes and analyses social interactions; they identify the social rules and conventions and successfully imitate social behaviour. This adaptation creates a superficial sociability and reciprocity that is effective but exhausting (Cook et al., 2017). It may also delay a referral for diagnostic assessment. DSM-5 states that the "symptoms must be present in the early developmental period but may not fully manifest until social demands exceed limited capacities, or may be masked by learned strategies later in life" (p.50). Research suggests 70% of autistic adults consistently use camouflaging in social situations (Cage & Troxell-Whitman, 2019).

While males are still more likely to be diagnosed with autism, the gender ratio and prevalence is changing. Autistic females are better than males at camouflaging, and more likely to use this strategy in a wider range of social situations (Hull et al., 2020). Increasingly, autism is diagnosed in adults, both male and female, who were not considered to be autistic during their childhood (issues for women are considered in Chapter 12).

Absence of informant to provide early developmental history

For childhood diagnosis, there is usually additional information from a parent about the developmental history, but this may not be available for adults. The diagnostician may seek further information from others who know the person well. If this information is not available, there will be a greater reliance on the clinician's observations and on the person's self-report. Nevertheless, a valid diagnostic assessment for autism can still be made.

Need for early identification in the CJS

Although autistic adults are not necessarily more prone to offending (Mouridsen, 2012), once in the system, the person's diagnosis will be relevant to the police and first responders (Buchan, 2020) and to the defence and prosecution in terms of criminal responsibility and criminal culpability (Freckelton & List, 2009). Autism will also be relevant in terms of sentencing, especially regarding the options of a custodial sentence or community correction. Autism may be both a mitigating and aggravating factor in sentencing (Berryessa, 2016), and judges are less likely to incarcerate due to the psychological effects of prison (Robertson & McGillivray, 2015). In addition to the problematic social context of prison (Case study 1), correctional officers and prison protocols and procedures are often rigid and may fail to accommodate the characteristics of an autistic adult. While there may be some positive attributes to prison, particularly in terms of the degree of structure and routine, and also education and training that may be available (Helverschou et al., 2009), there are nevertheless numerous challenges and pitfalls. My son, himself autistic and an ex-prisoner, has addressed many of these in a helpful and reassuring survival guide (Attwood, 2019).

There are now psychological therapy manuals specifically designed for autistic adults (Attwood & Garnett, 2016; Gaus, 2019). Within the criminal justice and forensic mental health systems, psychological therapy for mental health issues, and offence-focused interventions, will need to accommodate the particular profile of abilities and experiences of those who are autistic.

Box 1.1   Case study 1

A man in his 60s was academically gifted as a child and successful in his professional career. As an adult he had been diagnosed with ADHD, depression, and OCD, which had affected his motivation and work performance. A psychiatrist suggested he may have autism but had not conducted a formal diagnostic assessment.

The man had pleaded guilty following arrest for possession of child pornography. His defence requested a diagnostic assessment for autism from a clinical psychologist and expert opinion on whether, if present, autism was a factor relevant to the offence, and subsequent appropriate sentencing options.

The diagnosis was confirmed. The man had developed a fascination with pornography, which became a special interest, such that he began to explore, collect, and catalogue all different types of pornography (an example of a special interest serving as a thought blocker for anxiety, stress, and depression). The pornography sites became a source of sexual information, and also provided enjoyable sensory experience for someone whose depression limited his ability to experience pleasure. The interest eventually became a compulsion that was exceedingly difficult to resist due to both his OCD characteristics and his diagnosis of ADHD. His impaired Theory of Mind also meant he had difficulty identifying distress in the faces of the children in the images, which could have acted as an inhibitory mechanism for the offending.

The report made reference to research suggesting community sentencing as more appropriate than custodial sentences in such cases, and also to the mental health effects of a custodial sentence on an autistic offender. The prison environment is characterised by mistrust, distinct hierarchies of power and control, overcrowding, limited privacy, close proximity to anti-social individuals, and exposure to victimisation, violence, and hostility. Prison becomes a source of considerable stress for autistic prisoners in terms of their vulnerability, and creates and exacerbates anxiety and depression.

Box 1.2   Case study 2

The wife of a man in his 40s had identified characteristics of autism in her husband's childhood, and as a potential explanation of difficulties in their relationship. They had two adolescent children. At work he was described as a recluse, but had a reputation for talent in resolving technical issues. He told his GP that he had increased stress and responsibilities at work, and was concerned about his tax liabilities. He was also distressed by noise and chaos at home, living with teenagers. His GP prescribed SSRI medication for depression and referred him to a clinical psychologist for CBT to manage depression and episodic rage.

The psychologist noted that he rarely mentioned his own and others' emotions when describing his childhood, or his home and work life. He tended to focus on external rather than internal experiences, and was unable to describe his feelings in particular situations. He appeared to have difficulty converting his inner thoughts and feelings into speech. He described how he would have a low-level internal sensation or feeling that was unpleasant, but could not determine if the feeling was anxiety, sadness, or anger. His primary reaction was to try to suppress the unpleasant feeling with intellectual distraction or thought blocker, such as reading a technical magazine. This was an effective strategy for low-level distress, but the intensity of feeling could almost instantaneously 'explode' into either rage and destructive energy, usually directed at an object, or to suicidal ideation and actions as a means of ending the intense and overwhelming despair. He described how he could not perceive and thus foresee the imminent explosion or implosion. His wife described how she could not identify signs in his behaviour, speech, or thinking that a 'meltdown' was imminent. She feared for her safety and that of her children, and was considering applying for a domestic violence order.

After his arrest, following a serious violent incident, his defence team sought confirmation of an autism diagnosis, and clarification as to whether autism would have been a mitigating factor in his actions. The characteristics of alexithymia were confirmed, and he was subsequently diagnosed with autism following assessment.

The changing concept of autism

When I began my study of autism in the early 1970s, it was primarily associated with children and perceived as an expression of schizophrenia. Parents, clinicians, and research changed the conception of autism to an expression of a neurodevelopmental disorder. The diagnostic criteria have also changed over the last 50 years, and are still a work in progress. There will almost certainly be a DSM-6, with revised diagnostic criteria, and revised and new diagnostic instruments. It is interesting to note that the conceptualisation of autism is evolving to become an expression of neurodivergence. Autism is discovered rather than diagnosed. We are increasingly recognising that autism only becomes a disability in the context of the expectations of the neurotypical world (Happé & Frith, 2020), and this is writ large in the complex criminal justice and forensic mental health systems.

References

American Psychiatric Association (APA). (2013). *Diagnostic and Statistical Manual of Mental Disorders*, 5th edition. Washington, DC: APA.

Attwood, T. (2015). *The Complete Guide to Asperger's Syndrome – Revised*. London: Jessica Kingsley Publishers.

Attwood, T. & Garnett, M. (2016). *Exploring Depression and Beating the Blues: A CBT Self-Help Guide to Understanding and Coping with Depression in Asperger's Syndrome (ASD Level 1)*. London: Jessica Kingsley Publishers.

Attwood, T. & Garnett, M. (2019). Adaptations to autism. In *Autism in Girls* (pp. 1–16). Arlington: Future Horizons.

Attwood, W. (2019). *Asperger's Syndrome and Jail: A Survival Guide London*. London: Jessica Kingsley Publishers.

Autism CRC. (2018). *A National Guideline for the Assessment and Diagnosis of Autism Spectrum Disorders in Australia*. Retrieved from: www.autismcrc.com.au/access/

Baron-Cohen, S., Wheelwright, S., Skinner, R., Martin, J., & Clubley, E. (2001). The Autism-Spectrum Quotient (AQ): Evidence from Asperger syndrome/high functioning autism, males and females, scientists and mathematicians. *Journal of Autism and Developmental Disorders*, 31, 5–17. doi: 10.1023/A:100565341147

Barrett, S.L., Uljarevic, M., Jones, C., & Leekham, S.R. (2018). Assessing subtypes of restricted and repetitive behaviour using the Adult Repetitive behaviour Questionnaire-2 in autistic adults. *Molecular Autism*, 9(58), 1–10. doi: 10.1186/s13229-018-0242-4

Berney, T., Brugha, T., & Carpenter, P. (2017). *Royal College of Psychiatrists Interview Guide for the Diagnostic Assessment of Able Adults with Autism Spectrum Disorders (ASD)*. Retrieved from: www.asdinfowales.co.uk/resource/RC-Psych_Diagnostic-Interview-Guide-for-the-Assessment-of-Adults-with-ASD.pdf

Berryessa, C.M. (2016). Judicial attitudes regarding the sentencing of offenders with high functioning autism. *Journal of Autism and Developmental Disorders*, 46, 2770–2773. doi: 10.1007/s10803-016-2798-1

Brian, J., Bryson, S.E., & Smith, I.M. (2016). Stability and change in autism spectrum disorder diagnosis from age 3 to middle childhood in a high-risk sibling cohort. *Autism*, 20, 888–892. doi: 10.1177/1362361315614979

Brown, C.M., Attwood, T., Garnett, M., & Stokes, M.A. (2020). Am I autistic? Utility of the girl's questionnaire for Autism Spectrum Condition as an autism assessment in adult women. *Autism in Adulthood*, 2(3), 216–226. doi: 10.1089/aut.2019.0054

Buchan, A. (2020). *Autism and the Police: Practical Advice for Officers and other First Responders*. London: Jessica Kingsley Publishers.

Cage, E. & Troxell-Whitman, Z. (2019). Understanding the reasons, contexts and costs of camouflaging for autistic adults. *Journal of Autism and Developmental Disorders*, 49, 1899–1911. doi: 10.1007/s10803-018-03878-x

Centers for Disease Control and Prevention. (2021). *Data and Statistics on Autism Spectrum Disorders: Prevalence March 2020*. Retrieved from: www.cdc.gov/ncbddd/autism/data.html

Chen, M.-H., Su, T.-P., Chen, Y.-S., Hsu, J.-W., Huang, K.-L., Chang, W.-H., Chen, T.-J., & Bai, Y.-M. (2013). Comorbidity of allergic and autoimmune diseases in patients with autism spectrum disorder: A nationwide population-based study. *Research in Autism Spectrum Disorders*, 7, 205–212. doi: 10.1016/j.rasd.2012.08.008

Coleman, M. & Gillberg, C. (2012). *The Autisms*, 4th edition. New York: Oxford University Press.

Colvert, E., Tick, B., McEwen, F., Stewart, C., Curran, S.R., Woodhouse, E., Gillan, N., Hallett, V., Lietz, S., Garnett, T., Ronald, A., Plomin, R., Rijsdijk, F., Happé, F., & Bolton, P. (2015). Heritability of Autism Spectrum Disorder in a UK population-based twin sample. *JAMA Psychiatry*, 72(5), 415–423. doi: 10.1001/jamapsychiatry.2014.3028

Constantino, J.N. (2011). *Social Responsiveness Scale* (SRS-2), 2nd edition. Pearson.

Cook, A., Ogden, J., & Winstone N. (2017). Friendship motivations, challenges and the role of masking for girls with autism in contrasting school settings. *European Journal of Special Needs Education*, 33, 302–315. doi: 10.1080/08856257.2017.1312797

Cox, C., Bulluss, E., Chapman, F., Cookson, A., Flood, A., & Sharp, A. (2019). The Coventry Grid for adults: A tool to guide clinicians in differentiating complex trauma and autism. *Good Autism Practice*, 20, 76–87.

Crane, L., Goddard, L., & Pring, L. (2009). Sensory processing in adults with autism spectrum disorders. *Autism*, 13(3), 215–228. doi: 10.1177/1362361309103794

Fitzgerald, M. (2005). *The Genesis of Autistic Creativity: Asperger's syndrome and the arts*. London: Jessica Kingsley Publishers.

Freckelton, I., & List, D. (2009). Asperger's disorder, criminal responsibility and criminal culpability. *Psychiatry, Psychology and Law*, 16(1), 16–40. https://doi.org/10.1080/13218710902887483

Frigaux, A., Evrard, R., & Lighezzolo-Alnot, J. (2019). ADI-R and ADOS and the differential diagnosis of autism spectrum disorders: Interests, limits and openings. *L'Encephale*, 45(5), 441–448. doi: 10.1016/j.encep.2019.07.002

Fusar-Poli, L., Brondino, N., Rocchetti, M., Panisis, C., Provenzani, U., Damiani, S., & Politi, P. (2017). Diagnosing ASD in Adults without ID: Accuracy of the ADOS-2 and the ADI-R. *Journal of Autism and Developmental Disorders*, 47(11), 3370–3379. doi: 10.1007/s10803-017-3258-2

Gardener, M., Spiegelman, D., & Buka, S.L. (2009). Prenatal risk factors for autism: Comprehensive meta-analysis. *British Journal of Psychiatry*, 195(1), 7–14. doi: 10.1192/bjp.bp.108.051672

Gaus, V.L. (2019). *Cognitive-Behavioral Therapy for Adults with Autism Spectrum Disorder*, 2nd edition. New York: Guilford Press.

Hallmayer, J., Cleveland, S., Torres, A., Phillips, J., Cohen, B., Torigoe, T., Miller, J., Fedele, A., Collins, J., Smith, K., Lotspeich, L., Croen, L.A., Ozonoff, S., Lajonchere, C., Grether, J.K., & Risch, N. (2011). Genetic heritability and shared environmental factors among twin pairs with autism. *Archives of General Psychiatry*, 68(11), 1095–1102. doi:10.1001/archgenpsychiatry.2011.76

Happé, F. (2015). Autism as a neurodevelopmental disorder of mind-reading. *Journal of the British Academy*, 3, 197–209. doi: 10.5871/jba/003.197

Happé, F. & Frith, U. (2020). Annual Research Review: Looking back to look forward – changes in the concept of autism and implications for future research. *The Journal of Child Psychology and Psychiatry*, 61, 218–232. doi: 10.1111/jcpp.13176

Helverschou, S.B., Bakken, T.L., & Martinsen, H. (2009). The Psychopathology in Autism Checklist (PAC): A pilot study. *Research in Autism Spectrum Disorders*, 3, 179–195. doi: 10.1016/j.rasd.2008.05.004

Hull, L., Mandy, W., Lai, M.C., Baron-Cohen, S., Allison, C., Smith, P., & Petrides, K.V. (2019). Development and validation of the Camouflaging Autistic Traits Questionnaire (CAT-Q). *Journal of Autism and Developmental Disorders*, 49, 819–833. doi: 10.1007/s10803-018-3792-6

Hull, L., Lai, M-C., Baron-Cohen, S., Allison, C., Smith, P., Petrides, K.V., & Mandy, W. (2020). Gender differences in self-reported camouflaging in autistic and non-autistic adults. *Autism*, 24(2), 352–363. doi: 10.1177/1362361319864804

James, I. (2006). *Asperger's Syndrome and High Achievement: Some very remarkable people*. London: Jessica Kingsley Publishers.

Keil, A., Daniels, J.L., Forssen, U., Hultman, C., Cnattingius, S., Söderberg, K.C., Feychting, M., & Sparene, P. (2010). Parental autoimmune Diseases associated with Autism Spectrum Disorders in offspring. *Epidemiology*, 21, 805–808. doi: 10.1097/EDE.0b013e3181f26e3f

King, C. & Murphy, G.H. (2014). A systematic review of people with autism spectrum disorder and the Criminal Justice System. *Journal of Autism and Developmental Disorders*, 44(11), 2717–2733. doi: 10.1007/s10803-014-2046-5

Kinnaird, E., Stewart, C., & Tchanturia, K. (2019). Investigating alexithymia in autism: A systematic review and meta-analysis. *European Psychiatry*, 55, 80–89. doi: 10.1016/j.eurpsy.2018.09.004

Kooiman, C.G., Spinhoven, P., & Trijsburg, R.W. (2002). The assessment of alexithymia: A critical review of the literature and psychometric study of the Toronto Alexithymia Scale – 20. *Journal of Psychosomatic Research*, 53, 1083–1090. doi: 10.1016/s0022-3999(02)00348-3

Lampi, K., Hinkka-Yli-Salomäki, S., Lehti, V., Helenius, H., Gissler, M., Brown, A.S., & Sourander, A. (2013). Parental age and risk of Autism Spectrum Disorders in a Finnish national birth cohort. *Journal of Autism and Developmental Disorders*, 43(11), 2526–2535. doi: 10.1007/s10803-013-1801-3

Limperopoulos, C. (2009). Autism Spectrum Disorders in survivors of extreme prematurity. *Clinics in Perinatology*, 36, 791–805. doi: 10.1016/j.clp.2009.07.010

Marco, E.J., Hinkley, L.B.N., Hill, S.S., & Nagarajan, S.S. (2011). Sensory processing in autism: A review of neurophysiologic findings. *Pediatric Research*, 69(5), 48R. doi: 10.1203/PDR.0b013e3182130c54

Martin, C., Pepa, L., & Lord, C. (2018). DSM-5 diagnosis of Autism Spectrum Disorder. In *Assessment of Autism Spectrum Disorder*, 2nd edition. Goldstein, S. and Ozonoff, S. (eds). New York: Guilford Press.

Monteiro, M. & Stegall, S. (2018). *Monteiro Interview Guidelines for Diagnosing Autism Spectrum*, 2nd edition. Los Angeles: Western Psychological Services.

Mouridsen, S.E. (2012). Current status of research on autism spectrum disorders and offending. *Research in Autism Spectrum Disorders*, 6(1), 79–86. doi: 10.1016/j.rasd.2011.09.003

National Institute for Health and Care Excellence (NICE). (2012). *Autism Spectrum Disorder in Adults: Diagnosis and Management*. Retrieved from: www.nice.org.uk/guidance/cg142/resources/autism-spectrum-disorder-in-adults-diagnosis-and-management-pdf-35109567475909

Ozsivadjian, A., Knott, F., & Magiati, I. (2012). Parent and child perspectives on the nature of anxiety in children and young people with autism spectrum disorders: a focus group study. *Autism*, 16(2), 107–121. doi: 10.1177/1362361311431703

Preece, D.A., Becerra, R., Robinson, K., Dandy, J., & Allan, A. (2018). The psychometric assessment of alexithymia: Development and validation of the Perth Alexithymia Questionnaire. *Personality and Individual Differences*, 132, 32–44. https://doi.org/10.1016/j.paid.2018.05.011

Pua, E.P.K., Bowden, S.C., & Seal, M.L. (2017). Autism spectrum disorders: Neuroimaging findings from systematic reviews. *Research in Autism Spectrum Disorders*, 34, 28–33. doi: 10.1016/j.paid.2018.05.011

Pugliese, C.E., Kenworthy, L., Hus Bal, V., Wallace, G.L., Yerys, B.E., Maddox, B.B., White, S.W., Popal, H., Armour, A.C., Miller, J., Herrington, J.D., Schultz, R.T., Martin, A., & Gutermuth Anthony, L. (2015). Replication and comparison of the newly proposed ADOS-2, Module 4 algorithm in ASD without ID: A multi-site study. *Journal of Autism and Developmental Disorders*, 45(12), 3919–3931. doi: 10.1007/s10803-015-2586-3

Ritvo, R.A., Ritvo, E.R., Guthrie, M., Ritvo, J., Hufnagel, D.H., McMahon, W., Tonge, B., Matix-Cols, D., Jassi, A., Attwood, T., & Eloff, J. (2011). The Ritvo Autism Asperger Diagnostic Scale-Revised (RAADS-R): A scale to assist the diagnosis of autism. *Journal of Autism and Developmental Disorders*, 41(8), 1076–1089. doi: 10.1007/s10803-010-1133-5

Robertson, C.E. & McGillivray, J. (2015). Autism behind bars: A review of the research literature and discussion of key issues. *The Journal of Forensic Psychiatry and Psychology*, 26, 719–736. doi: 10.1080/14789949.2015.1062994

Robertson, C. & Baron-Cohen, S. (2017). Sensory perception and autism. *Nature Reviews Neuroscience*, 18, 671–684. doi: 10.1038/nrn.2017.112

Smith, R.S. & Sharp, J. (2013). Fascination and isolation: A grounded theory exploration of unusual sensory experiences in adults with Asperger syndrome. *Journal of Autism and Developmental Disorders*, 43(4), 891–910. doi: 10.1007/s10803-012-1633-6

Tavassoli, T., Hoekstra, R., & Baron-Cohen, S. (2014). The Sensory Perception Quotient (SPQ): Development and validation of a new sensory questionnaire for adults with and without autism. *Molecular Autism*, 5, 29. doi: 10.1186/2040-2392-5-29

Tick, B., Bolton, P., Happé, F., Rutter, M., & Rijsdijk, F. (2016). Heritability of autism spectrum disorders: A meta-analysis of twin studies. *Journal of Child Psychology and Psychiatry*, 57(5), 585–595. doi: 10.1111/jcpp.12499

Van Rooij, D., Anagnostou, E., Arango, C., Auzias G., Behrmann, M., Busatto, G.F., & Buitelaar, J.K. (2017). Cortical and subcortical brain morphometry differences between patients with autism spectrum disorder and healthy individuals across the lifespan. *American Journal of Psychiatry*, 175(4), 359–369. doi: 10.1176/appi.ajp.2017.17010100

Young, S., González, R.A., Mullens, H., Mutch, L., Malet-Lambert, I., & Gudjonsson, G. (2017). Neurodevelopmental disorders in prison inmates: Comorbidity and combined associations with psychiatric symptoms and behavioural disturbance. *Psychiatry Research*, 261, 109–115. doi: 10.1016/j.psychres.2017.12.036

Autism and mental health

Jermaine J. A. Thompson and Christopher Ince

2

Introduction

Autistic people are susceptible to the same range of psychiatric disorders as non-autistic people. It is worth noting, however, the huge fluctuations in the reported prevalence of co-morbid psychiatric conditions within the autistic population. The diagnostic criteria and assessment tools used; the individual factors of age, gender, and presence of an intellectual disability; the person's presentation; and the concept of clinician diagnostic overshadowing can all influence the presentation and recognition of co-morbidities.

It is also necessary to consider the variance in the phenomenological presentation of mental illness according to the person's level of functioning, which can impact on the ability of the individual to self-report symptomatology and assist in the gathering of relevant information, and thus inform whether a further collateral history is desirable or required, as opposed to mere observational diagnostic approach, which may increase likelihood of error. It is recognised that co-morbid psychiatric conditions are more likely to occur in the autistic population and awareness of trans-diagnostic frameworks will aid assessment and management of these co-morbidities.

It is critical to highlight the importance of allowing the necessary time to administer any assessments, the need for structured tools to be appropriately validated within the target population, and that non-specific language terms (such as the Likert scales of 'sometimes' and 'often') may in themselves be unhelpful and not take into account an individual's specific language usage and processing. Whilst validated tools are helpful, particularly in obtaining a baseline against which progression (either positive or negative) can be measured, their utility will depend upon the skills of the assessor and their further ability to ensure that the presentation of autism (particularly language, broader communication and sensory aspects, and the person's emotional literacy and ability to recognise emotional states within themselves and others) are taken into consideration.

It is also important to highlight the issue of diagnostic overshadowing and that any investigation of a reported mental illness includes the relevant

DOI: 10.4324/9781003036722-3

consideration of underlying physical health conditions and investigation where appropriate; examples include hyperthyroidism presenting as anxiety, hypothyroidism presenting as low mood and depression, and in those with a co-existing learning disability, the risks related to pain and other physical health problems that impact upon behaviours that challenge as a means of communication.

Prevalence, incidence, and epidemiology

The prevalence of one co-morbid psychiatric disorder within the adult autism population has been reported to be 33% (Neacsu, 2019); for two or more additional diagnoses, reported prevalence ranges from 54.8% (Hossain et al., 2020) to 94% (Neacsu, 2019). It is similarly noted that older adults with autism also have an overall elevated likelihood of developing a co-morbid psychiatric condition (Hand et al., 2020); when considering the prevalence of specific co-morbid disorder groups, mood disorders and anxiety disorders increase with age, whereas neurodevelopmental disorders such as Attention Deficit Hyperactivity Disorder (ADHD) decrease with age (Houghton et al., 2017). The low prevalence in the adult and older adult populations reflects a previous lack of awareness of ADHD within this cohort and suggests an attribution of symptoms to other conditions such as bipolar disorder. However, it is hypothesised that the prevalence of co-existing neurodevelopmental disorders will increase with better recognition, particularly of ADHD, especially in the adult population.

The commonest co-morbidities are mood disorders (35.9%) and anxiety disorders (37.2%) (Hand et al., 2020) followed by cognitive and psychotic disorders; disorders of personality (based upon the criteria within ICD-10; World Health Organization, 1992), despite being more difficult to recognise and diagnose, still occur within the autistic population in up to 3.1% (Hand et al., 2020). There is concern that the broadened criteria for Disorders of Adult Personality, as set out within DSM-5 (American Psychiatric Association (APA), 2013), may lead to an increase in diagnosis of such conditions; the impact upon treatment and access to appropriate services, and risk of more pejorative labelling, remains to be seen.

Pharmacological interventions

Psychotropic medication is commonly prescribed where there are co-morbid diagnoses, with 58.9% of autistic patients being prescribed a form of psychotropic medication (Buck et al., 2014). Psychotropic polypharmacy is also used, with

35% to 59% of the autistic population being prescribed two or more psychotropic medications (Buck et al., 2014; Houghton et al., 2017). Antidepressants are the most common psychotropic medication prescribed due to their role in pharmacological management of mood and anxiety disorders. However, there is also a significant proportion of autistic people, varyingly reported as being between 20% and 40% (Buck et al., 2014; Houghton et al., 2017), who do not take any psychotropic medications, which highlights the importance of robust multi-factorial formulation, and the relevance, as set out within the current National Institute for Health and Care Excellence Guidelines (NICE, 2016), of behavioural and psychological therapies as first line interventions in managing the phenotypic presentation of autism, other mental disorders, and the interface between them (Buck et al., 2014; Houghton et al., 2017).

In response to the historical over-use of psychotropic medication for people with autism (and Intellectual Disability) for management of 'behaviours that challenge', in 2016 NHS England launched the STOMP-LD (Stopping Over-Medication of People with a Learning Disability, Autism or Both) programme in partnership with VODG (Voluntary Organisations Disability Group) following research by Public Health England (Mehta, 2019) that estimated:

> on an average day in England, between 30,000 and 35,000 adults with a learning disability, autism or both are taking a prescribed antipsychotic, an antidepressant or both without appropriate clinical indications (psychosis or affective/anxiety disorder). A substantial proportion of people with a learning disability, autism or both who are prescribed psychotropic drugs for behavioural purposes can safely have their drugs reduced or withdrawn.

Secondary care services are now beginning to criticise the usage of medication prescriptions alongside General Practice, which is addressing the issues of medication initiation. There is also the reduction in appropriate social care, education, training, and other vocational opportunities, and the widespread absence of specialist community teams for autistic people who do not have a learning disability. The move to community teams with a broader 'neurodevelopmental' remit will hopefully address the shortfall in access to appropriate specialist care. However, within England and Wales areas of deficient practice remain.

Autism and anxiety disorders

Anxiety disorders can have atypical presentations and there may be close overlap of symptoms with the diagnostic criteria and characteristics of autism. For example, it can be difficult to differentiate between repetitive behaviours that occur as a component of a preoccupation or restricted pattern of interests associated with autism, as opposed to those of Obsessive-Compulsive Disorder (OCD). Similarly, an aversion to dogs may be as a result of a true phobic disorder, or linked to sensory aspects of autism (such as noise or texture) or the intrinsic anxiety due to the animal's unpredictability.

Accordingly, diagnostic overshadowing is unfortunately common when looking at anxiety disorders and autism together (Kerns et al., 2014); careful consideration of the relevant history will usually point to the prevailing problem. Using the examples in the previous paragraph, in cases where distress (ego-dystonia) accompanies the completion of the repetitive behaviours, this is likely to indicate an OCD picture. Similarly, a previous traumatic experience with dogs usually signals a phobic disorder (although the identifying trauma may appear negligible and thus be less easily recognised as a setting event).

Within the adult autism population, the lifetime prevalence of any anxiety disorder ranges from 35% to 50%, with 17% to 37% currently experiencing a single anxiety disorder (Ezell, 2019; Hollocks et al., 2018). For multiple simultaneous anxiety disorders, the prevalence is reported to be approximately 30% in terms of meeting current diagnostic criteria (Ezell, 2019); however, there is little information on the prevalence of specific combinations of disorders – see Hollocks et al.'s (2018) summary of pooled estimates of current and lifetime prevalence of a range of anxiety disorders (Social Phobia, OCD, Panic, Generalised Anxiety Disorder, Phobia, and PTSD).

As stated already, OCD is of interest within the autistic population due to overlapping symptomatology, including repetitive behaviours of a narrowed repertoire, intrusive recurrent thoughts, and inflexibility to routines and presence of 'intensity'. Careful examination of the relevant symptoms is required when trying to differentiate between the two conditions, paying particular attention to the aim of the behaviour, the emotional impact/outcome, intensity of the behaviour, and even the content of the behaviour (Jacob, 2009; Postorino, 2017). Clinicians should also be careful to not pathologise aspects of autism that objectively appear to impact upon presentation or behaviour, but are actually mechanisms for self-soothing, self-stimulation, anxiety reduction, and other outcomes that are similarly positive and thus functional to the individual.

Screening tools for anxiety disorders are a valid method of determining the presence of a co-morbid disorder, in addition to a clinical history and mental state examination (MSE). Structured assessments such as the Structured Clinical Interview for DSM IV Axis 1 Disorders (SCID) (Lugnegård et al., 2011; Spain, 2016) or self-report scales, such as the Depression Anxiety Stress Scale (Park, 2020), are both validated means of detecting anxiety disorders within the autistic population. However, the necessity for careful consideration of both the measures used and their relevance for the autistic person who is taking part in the assessment cannot be over-emphasised.

In terms of intervention, and aside from self-management strategies that address self-stimulation, desensitisation, communication skills, and functional avoidance, it is important to explore whether there are underpinning specific stressors to address. These may include difficulties with the unpredictability of social interaction, changes to social interaction demands (such as changing peer group), and anxiety as a consequence of social rejection and bullying. Prevention of engagement in preferred or repetitive behaviours (particularly if used as a self-management strategy), or sensory aversions, may also serve as significant stressors.

Psychological interventions for anxiety within the autistic population are primarily Cognitive Behavioural Therapy (CBT) (e.g., Gaus, 2011), however, the majority of evidence regarding CBT is from studies with high functioning autistic children and adolescents (Sukhodolsky, 2013; Ung et al., 2015). It is important to note when looking at the available evidence whether 'anxiety as a component of autism' or an identified anxiety disorder is being studied and consideration should also be given to the manner in which the therapy is being delivered. Common modifications to content and delivery (White et al., 2018) include addressing autism core symptoms, increasing focus on developing emotional insight, and psychoeducation on the relationship between autism and anxiety. Mindfulness Behavioural Interventions (MBIs) are also currently being explored for treatment of anxiety, due to their benefits of increasing tolerance and self-management (Semple, 2019); however, there is currently limited evidence.

Pharmacological management of anxiety disorders will vary depending on the type of disorder and the clinical presentation of the patient. In broad terms, the NICE CG142 Guidance recommends reference to usual clinical guidelines for treatment of any specific mental illness. It should be noted that it is crucial to explain the expected time course for effectiveness of medication and to explain and monitor the impact of side effects, which may include cognitive and somatic features which may actually increase the subjective level of anxiety or distress. The guidance confirms that the recommended management of OCD is a combination of CBT and Selective Serotonin Reuptake Inhibitors (SSRIs); while there is limited evidence for behavioural treatment of OCD within the autistic population (Weston et al., 2016), pharmacological treatments are more established but often confer a higher 'risk' due to the increased doses of SSRIs that are required and the subsequent increased susceptibility to behavioural activation and other associated side effects of SSRIs, such as impulsivity, sensory hyperacuity, and insomnia.

Autism and mood disorders

Similar to anxiety disorders, mood disorders can cause significant impairment to baseline social and cognitive functioning, which may be impaired in those with autism. Both unipolar and bipolar disorders are associated with increased risks which can lead to severe consequences such as social isolation, accumulation of debt, self-harm, and suicide (Hudson, 2019). Given that autistic people may present with behavioural impairments, it is important to recognise and treat mood disorders at an earlier stage to prevent exacerbation of these behaviours.

Within the autistic population, the lifetime prevalence of a unipolar illness is 23–61%, with up to 37% currently experiencing an illness (Hollocks et al., 2018; Hudson, 2019); for bipolar illness, the current prevalence ranges from 6 to 21% (Hollocks et al., 2018). Depressive and bipolar disorders are more likely to be diagnosed at a younger age in autistic people compared to those without autism (Kirsch, 2019), suggesting that screening at younger ages may be a useful tool in identifying mood disorders; this also highlights the need for the provision of services across the age range. This further highlights the need for appropriate services within both primary and secondary care, and a recognition that the externally observed severity of the intrinsic depressive disorder may not meet the criteria for Community Mental Health Teams, but the presence of co-morbid autism requires this level of expertise, both in terms of diagnosis, and also the development of an appropriate management plan.

In terms of diagnosis, depressive disorders are characterised by impairment of independence, adaptive functioning, social integration, and communication; thus, an exacerbation of existing difficulties may be evident rather than the emergence of a novel set of symptoms. This again highlights the relevance of baseline assessment and the benefit of a collateral history. It is also necessary to take a detailed history to examine the relevance of predisposing, presenting, and perpetuating factors (the '5P model'; Macneil, 2012) given the likelihood of multiple factors such as isolation, bullying and other social difficulties, negative self-comparisons with non-autistic peers (e.g., regarding employment and relationship status), and the tendency toward negative thinking and rumination which may be a characteristic cognitive feature associated with the underlying autism. Formulation including social factors will influence the development and delivery of a treatment plan, both in the acute phase and longer-term (Chandrasekhar, 2015).

Pharmacological treatment of bipolar illness for autistic people will again broadly follow standard treatment guidelines. In the acute phase, this will consist of mood stabilisers as the first choice, particularly second-generation antipsychotics, which can reduce the behavioural and the psychotic symptoms (Vannucchi et al., 2014), with adjunct bio-psychosocial interventions regarding protective factors, adaptive functioning, mitigation of relevant stressors and high expressed emotion, and additional strategies to minimise any adverse effects from medication, such as potential weight gain.

Autism and schizophrenic spectrum disorders

Schizophrenia spectrum disorders (SSDs) and autism have an important historical connection; before the notion of SSD and autism as separate conditions, as theorised by Rutter (1972) and Kolvin (1971) in the 1970s, SSD and autism were always thought of as a continuum. Bleuler (1950) initially described autism as a form of schizophrenia. Despite the current clear distinction between the two disorders described in current diagnostic manuals, SSD and autism were, historically, frequently researched together due to the high rate of heritability and similar genetic components of both disorders.

Misidentification of symptoms between autism and SSD may cause diagnostic uncertainty. For example, unusual beliefs which may be related to a person's interests and cognitive style may be confused with the delusional ideas of SSD; inflexibility and rigidity of thought content within autism can be confused with delusional conviction seen in SSD; challenges to differential diagnosis are compounded by difficulties in social communication in both disorders. More recent research further confirms the presence of grandiose and paranoid delusional beliefs in some autistic people (i.e., without SSD) with associations with social anxiety and self-consciousness (Abell & Hare, 2005). The 'self-talk' which an autistic person may use as a conscious or unconscious strategy for processing their experiences may be mistaken for response to auditory hallucinations. Conversely, diagnostic overshadowing may prevent clinicians from exploring whether the contents of thought and perception reflect the presence of a psychotic illness when the person being assessed is known, or thought, to be autistic. Profound consequences in terms of distress, loss of functioning, and distress for families can result in such cases, and the presence of active psychotic symptoms may also be linked to increased risk of harm to self and others.

The prevalence of schizophrenia within the autistic population is reported to be 6.4% to 9.5% (De Giorgi et al., 2019; Lugo Marín, 2018); when comparing prevalence between those with autism and without, autistic people were 3.5 times more likely to have a diagnosis of schizophrenia (Zheng et al., 2018)

Treatment of schizophrenia within the autistic population will not vary from the guidance for those without autism, however confirmation of diagnosis is essential in terms of appropriate access to a relevant treatment pathway. Conversely, given that people with schizophrenia have an elevated risk of mortality (Saha et al., 2007), the burden of which is partially due to the risk associated with antipsychotic medication, additional care must be taken when managing SSD in autistic people – this compounds the acknowledged elevated risk of mortality in autism compared to the general population (Mouridsen, 2008).

Autism and disorders of feeding and eating (FED)

Diagnostic frameworks dealing with the nosology of disordered feeding and eating have undergone an expansion in numerous ways within the change in the respective classificatory systems; these are of particular importance to autistic people. While it is possible for autistic people to be diagnosed with a more characteristic FED such as anorexia nervosa or bulimia nervosa, the inclusion of more novel disorders, such as Avoidant Restrictive Food Intake Disorder (ARFID), has provided a greater understanding of feeding and eating difficulties within the autistic population. This will inform more specific and guided management of co-morbid FED and autism in the future.

The literature concerning co-morbid FED and autism is meagre, with the majority of research exploring autistic traits within females with an existing diagnosis of anorexia nervosa. The majority of FEDs are diagnosed in females, which can prove problematic when developing studies or looking into current evidence, given that autism is harder to diagnose within the female population (Loomes, 2017). Despite this, the limited evidence shows that 6.4% of autistic people have a diagnosis of anorexia nervosa (Nickel, 2019) and a diagnosis of autism confers a five-fold lifetime increased risk of developing anorexia nervosa (Koch, 2015).

It is well known that autistic people may present with selective or 'picky' eating, which is often linked to sensory sensitivities to texture, smell, or taste. Food selectivity can be common in children but there is growing evidence that it can occur within adulthood (Kinnaird, 2019). Since the identification of ARFID, there has been an increasing interest in its connection to autism, due to the overlap with selective eating (Dovey et al., 2019). The presence of a narrowed repertoire of food intake due to sensory aspects is included within the DSM-5 diagnostic criteria for ARFID; however, the additional presence of sequelae from rigid beliefs regarding food intake, the presence of selective eating, and subsequent nutritional deficiency and/ or weight loss, alongside a significant anxiety component such as a fear of choking, is needed to distinguish ARFID and merits further examination, both in terms of diagnostic relevance and selection of an appropriate treatment modality.

The core principles of management of feeding and eating disorders can be encompassed within a biopsychosocial approach. Despite variation within the aetiology and presentation of the range of FED, key treatments including correction of any blood abnormalities, restoration of physical health (as opposed to weight gain, which those with anorexia may find challenging as a concept), increasing repertoire of food intake, and psychotherapeutic work, will be universally applicable and all play a role in improving the patient's condition. Any psychotherapeutic work will need to be adapted for autistic people; however, it could also be that selective eating may persist and that changes to the food regime may still have to incorporate sensory sensitivities to avoid any undue distress.

Autism and disorders of adult personality

There is an increasing focus on autistic people who present to services in a manner that, at a cursory level, suggest the presence of a Disorder of Adult Personality – particularly relevant for women, who may attract a diagnosis of Emotionally Unstable Personality Disorder (EUPD) as a consequence of 'masking' behaviours, social naivety, and broader interpersonal difficulties. Studies suggest that autism should be considered as a differential diagnosis, particularly in cases of atypical presentation and persistent suicidality in women with EUPD characteristics (Bringmann & Maidman, 2019).

Autistic people who have a history of contact with the criminal justice system are at similar risk of diagnosis misattribution, with Dissocial or Paranoid Personality Disorder or, in more extreme cases, a formal diagnosis of psychopathy. It is recognised that there are certain autistic traits, including fixed interests, rigid thinking patterns, unusual sensory interests, and difficulties in emotional reciprocity, which may increase the risk of offending behaviour, especially when they are associated with criminal or violent themes; similar careful evaluation of the developmental history is key and allows for appropriate treatment to be modified accordingly.

The Psychopathy Checklist-Revised (PCL-R) (Hart et al., 1992) is a rating scale to assess for the presence of psychopathy by probing interpersonal, affective, lifestyle, and antisocial aspects. Evidence from a study with young offenders found that those with autism scored significantly higher in the affective component of the PCL-R, which suggests a similar lack of empathy 'traditionally' present in those with psychopathy (Hofvander et al., 2019). However, there is a clearer distinction between autism and psychopathy in terms of deficits within subtypes. There is some evidence that autistic people may have difficulties with cognitive empathy but appear to have intact emotional empathy, whereas those with psychopathy are thought to have the opposite; difficulties with emotional empathy but not cognitive empathy (e.g., Grant, 2018). Careful assessment by clinicians experienced in working with autistic people is required where there are questions about severe personality disturbance. The issues of autism and offending are discussed in Chapter 4.

Conclusion

Autistic people are at risk of co-morbid mental health problems and may present with distressing symptoms and experiences which require careful exploration to avoid misdiagnosis, and to ensure that the appropriate treatment pathway is identified. In forensic settings, this is crucial both in terms of mental health recovery for the person with autism, and to enable engagement with interventions related to risk reduction and rehabilitation.

References

Abell, F., & Hare, D. J. (2005). An experimental investigation of the phenomenology of delusional beliefs in people with Asperger syndrome. *Autism*, 515–531. doi: 10.1177/1362361305057857

American Psychiatric Association (APA). (2013). *Diagnostic and statistical manual of mental disorders (5th ed.)*. Artlington, VA. https://doi.org/10.1176/appi.books.9780890425596

Bleuler, E. (1950). *Dementia praecox or the group of schizophrenias*. International Universities Press.

Bringmann, S. A., & Maidman, P. A. (2019). Diagnosis of autism spectrum disorder in women with suicidality and characteristics of borderline personality disorder. *Tijdschrift voor psychiatrie*, 121–125. PMID: 30793273

Buck, T. R., Viskochil, J., Farley, M., Coon, H., McMahon, W. M., Morga, J., & Bilder, D. A. (2014). Psychiatric comorbidity and medication use in adults with autism spectrum disorder. *Journal of Autism and Developmental Disorders*, 3063–3071. doi: 10.1007/s10803-014-2170-2

Chandrasekhar, T. (2015). Challenges in the diagnosis and treatment of depression in autism spectrum disorders across the lifespan. *Dialogues in Clinical Neuroscience*, 17(2), 219–227. doi: 10.31887/DCNS.2015.17.2/tchandrasekhar

De Giorgi, R. D., De Crescenzo, F., D'Alò, G. L., Pesci, N. R., Di Franco, V., Sandid, C., & Armando, M. (2019). Prevalence of non-affective psychoses in individuals with autism spectrum disorders: a systematic review. *Journal of Clinical Medicine*, 8(9), 1304. doi:10.3390/jcm8091304

Dovey, T. M., Kumari, V., Blissett, J., & Mealtime Hostage Parent Gang (2019). Eating behaviour, behavioural problems and sensory profiles of children with Avoidant/Restrictive Food Intake Disorder (ARFID), autistic spectrum disorders or picky eating: Same or different? *European Psychiatry*, 61, 56–62. doi:10.1016/j.eurpsy.2019.06.008

Ezell, J. H. (2019). Prevalence and predictors of anxiety disorders in adolescent and adult males with autism spectrum disorder and fragile X syndrome. *Journal of Autism and Developmental Disorders*, 1131–1141. doi:10.1007/s10803-018-3804-6

Gaus, V. (2011). Cognitive behavioural therapy for adultd with autism spectrum disorder. *Advances in Mental Heath and Intellectual Disabilities*, 5(5), 15–25. https://doi.org/10.1108/20441281111180628

Grant, T. F. (2018). Criminal responsibility in autism spectrum disorder: A critical review examining empathy and moral reasoning. *Canadian Psychology*, 59(1), 65–75. doi:10.1037/cap0000124

Hand, B. N., Angell, A. M., Harris, L., & Arnstein Carpenter, L. (2020). Prevalence of physical and mental health conditions in Medicare-enrolled, autistic older adults. *Autism*, 24(3), 755–764. doi:10.1177/1362361319890793

Hart, S. D., Hare, R. D., & Harpur, T. J. (1992). The Psychopathy Checklist—Revised (PCL–R): An overview for researchers and clinicians. In J. C. Rosen & P. McReynolds (Eds.), *Advances in Psychological Assessment,* Vol. 8, (pp. 103–130). Plenum Press. https://doi.org/10.1007/978-1-4757-9101-3_4

Hofvander, B. B., Bering, S., Tärnhäll, A., Wallinius, M., & Billstedt, E. (2019). Few differences in the externalizing and criminal history of young violent offenders with and without autism spectrum disorders. *Frontiers in Psychiatry,* 10, 911. https://doi.org/10.3389/fpsyt.2019.00911

Hollocks, M. J., Lehr, J. W., Magiati, I., Meiser-Stedman, R., & Brugha, T. S. (2018). Anxiety and depression in adultd with autism spectrum disorder: a systematic review and meta-analysis. *Psychological Medicine,* 49, 559–572. doi:10.1017/S0033291718002283

Hossain, M. M., Khan, N., Sultana, A., Ma, P., McKyer, E. L. J., Ahmed, H. U., & Purohit, N. (2020). Prevalence of comorbid psychiatric disorders among people with autism spectrum disorder: An umbrella review of systematic reviews and meta-analyses. *Psychiatry Research,* 287, 112922. doi:10.1016/j.psychres.2020.112922

Houghton, R. O., Ong, R. C., & Bolognani, F. (2017). Psychiatric comorbidities and use of psychotropic medications in people with autism spectrum disorder in the United States. *Autism Research,* 2037–2047. doi:10.1002/aur.1848

Hudson, C. L. (2019). Prevalence of depressive disorders in individuals with autism spectrum disorder: A meta-analysis. *Journal of Abnormal Child Psychology,* 47(1), 165–175. doi:10.1007/s10802-018-0402-1

Jacob, S. L.-W. (2009). Autism spectrum and obsessive-compulsive disorders: OC behaviors, phenotypes and genetics. *Autism Research,* 2(6), 293–311. doi:10.1002/aur.108

Kerns, C. M., Kendall, P. C., Berry, L … & Herrington, J. (2014). Traditional and atypical presentations of anxiety in youth with autism spectrum disorder. *Journal of Autism and Developmental Disorders,* 44, 2851–2861. doi: 10.1007/s10803-014-2141-7

Kinnaird, E. N. (2019). Eating as an autistic adult: An exploratory qualitative study. *PLoS One,* 14(8), 1–17. doi: 10.1371/journal.pone.0221937

Kirsch, A. C. (2019). Association of comorbid mood and anxiety disorders with autism spectrum disorder. *JAMA Paediatrics,* 174(1), 63–70. doi: 10.1001/jamapediatrics.2019.4368

Koch, S. L. (2015). Autism spectrum disorder in individuals with anorexia nervosa and in their first- and second-degree relatives: Danish nationwide register-based cohort-study. *British Journal of Psychiatry,* 206, 401–407. doi: 10.1192/bjp.bp.114.153221

Kolvin, I. (1971). Psychoses in childhood – a comparative study. In M. Rutter (Ed.), *Infantile Autism Concepts, Characteristics and Treatment* (pp. 7–26). London: Churchill.

Loomes, R. H. (2017). What is the male to female ration in autism spectrum disorder? A systematic review and meta-analysis. *Journal of the American Academy of Child and Adolescent Psychiatry,* 56(6), 466–474. doi: 10.1016/j.jaac.2017.03.013

Lugnegård, T., Hallerbäck, M. U., & Gillberg, C. (2011). Psychiatric comorbidity in young adults with a clinical diagnosis of Asperger syndrome. *Research in Developmental Disabilities,* 32(5), 1910–1917. https://doi.org/10.1016/j.ridd.2011.03.025

Lugo Marín, J. A.-F. (2018). Prevalence of schizophrenia spectrum disorders in average-IQ adults with autism spectrum disorders: A meta-analysis. *Journal of Autism and Developmental Disorders,* 48, 239–250. doi:10.1007/s10803-017-3328-5

Macneil, C. A. (2012). Is diagnosis enough to guide interventions in mental health? Using case formulation in clinical practice. *BMC Medicine,* 10, 111. https://doi.org/10.1186/1741-7015-10-111

Mehta, H. (2019). *Psychotropic Drugs and People with Learning Disabilities or Autism.* Public Health England. Retrieved from: www.gov.uk/government/publications/psychotropic-drugs-and-people-with-learning-disabilities-or-autism

Mouridsen, S. E.-H. (2008). Mortality and causes of death in autism spectrum disorders: an update. *Autism*, 12(4), 403–414. doi:10.1177/1362361308091653

Neacsu, R. D. (2019). P.810 Asperger syndrome and associated co-morbidities over a 14 year timespan. *European Neuropsychopharmacology*, 29(6), S539. doi:10.1016/j.euroneuro.2019.09.675

National Institute for Health and Care Excellence (NICE). (2016). *CG142 – Autism Spectrum Disorders in Adults: Diagnosis and Management*. Retrieved from: www.nice.org.uk/guidance/cg142/resources/autism-spectrum-disorder-in-adults-diagnosis-and-management-pdf-35109567475909

Nickel, K. (2019). Systematic review: Overlap between eating, autism spectrum, and attention-deficit/hyperactivity disorder. *Frontiers in Psychiatry*. doi:10.3389/fpsyt.2019.00708

Park, S. H. (2020). Validation of the 21-item Depression, Anxiety, and Stress Scales (DASS-21) in individuals with autism spectrum disorder. *Psychiatry Research*, 291, 113300. https://doi.org/10.1016/j.psychres.2020.113300

Postorino, V. K. (2017). Anxiety disorders and obsessive-compulsive disorder in individuals with autism spectrum disorder. *Current Psychiatry Reports*, 19, 92. doi:10.1007/s11920-017-0846-y

Rutter, M. (1972). Childhood schizophrenia reconsidered. *Journal of Autism and Childhood Schizophrenia*, 2(4), 315–337.

Saha, S., Chant, D., & McGrath, J. (2007). A systematic review of mortality in schizophrenia: Is the differential mortality gap worsening over time? *Archives of General Psychiatry*, 64(10), 1123–1131. doi:10.1001/archpsyc.64.10.1123

Semple, R. J. (2019). Yoga and mindfulness for youth with autism spectrum disorder: Review of the current evidence. *Child and Adolescent Mental Health*, 24(1), 12–18. doi:10.1111/camh.12295

Spain, D. D. (2016). Social anxiety in adult males with autism spectrum disorders. *Research in Autism Spectrum Disorders*, 32, 13–23. doi:10.1016/j.rasd.2016.08.002

Sukhodolsky, D. G. (2013). Cognitive-behavioral therapy for anxiety in children with high-functioning autism: A meta-analysis. *Pediatrics*, 132(5), e1341–e1350. doi:10.1542/peds.2013-1193

Ung, D. S., Sells, R., Small, B. J., & Storch, E. A. (2015). A systematic review and meta-analysis of cognitive-behavioral therapy for anxiety in youth with high functioning autism spectrum disorders. *Child Psychiatry and Human Development*, 46, 533–547. doi:10.1007/s10578-014-0494-y

Vannucchi, G. M., Massi, G., Toni, C., Dell'Osso, L., Erfurth, A., & Perugi, G. (2014). Bipolar disorder in Adults with Asperger's syndrome: A systematic review. *Journal of Affective Disorders*, 168, 151–160 doi:10.1016/j.jad.2014.06.042

Weston, L., Hodgekins, J., & Langdon, P. E. (2016). Effectiveness of cognitive behavioural therapy with people who have autistic spectrum disorders: A systematic review and meta-analysis. *Clinical Psychology Review*, 49, 41–54. https://doi.org/10.1016/j.cpr.2016.08.001

White, S. W., Simmons., G. L., Gotham, K. O., Conner, C. M., Smith, I. C., Beck, K. B., & Mazefsky, C. A. (2018). Psychosocial treatments targeting anxiety and depression in adolescents and adults with autism spectrum disorder: Review of the latest research and recommended future directions. *Current Psychiatry Reports*, 20(10), 82. doi: 10.1007/s11920-018-0949-0

World Health Organization (1992). *The ICD-10 Classification of Mental and Behavioural Disorders: Clinical Descriptions and Diagnostic Guidelines*. Retrieved from: www.who.int/classifications/icd/en/bluebook.pdf

Zheng, Z. Z., Zheng, P., & Zou, X. (2018). Association between schizophrenia and autism spectrum disorder: A systematic review and meta-analysis. *Autism Research*, 11(8), 1110–1119. doi: 10.1002/aur.1977

Receiving a diagnosis of autism in adulthood

3

Claire King and
Gemma Rogers

Introduction

Increased awareness of autism in the last few decades has created a "lost generation" of individuals who remain undiagnosed until adulthood (Lai & Baron-Cohen, 2015), which means they are unlikely to receive the support they might need (Huang et al., 2020; Lewis, 2016a). When considering individuals with autism in the criminal justice system, we know that they are no more likely to offend than those without autism (King & Murphy, 2014). Although there is no reliable data for the prevalence of people with autism within the criminal justice and forensic mental health systems, research suggests that it is higher in prison (Young et al., 2017) and in secure psychiatric settings (Tromans et al., 2018) than in the community. However, it is also likely that there is an undiagnosed population in the criminal justice system (Vinter et al., 2020).

Although autism does not predispose an individual to commit a crime, it may contribute towards the circumstances leading to an offence; for example, a fixed interest manifesting as a sexual preoccupation (Vinter et al., 2020). Autism can also act as an antecedent to mental health difficulties, which can precipitate offending behaviour (de la Cuesta, 2010). Autistic people can appear to have little empathy (Baron-Cohen & Wheelwright, 2004), and whilst this is more likely to be a difficulty with social communication of emotions rather than a lack of experiencing empathy (Poquerusse et al., 2018), it can have problematic consequences, including harsher treatment and sentencing (Vinter et al., 2020).

Despite the title of this book, it is not possible to focus this chapter solely on the experience of receiving a diagnosis of autism as an adult within the criminal justice and forensic mental health systems, as there is not enough research in this area. The recent increase in awareness and diagnosis of autism (Leedham et al., 2020) has correlated with an expansion of research exploring the experiences of people receiving an autism diagnosis in adulthood (Huang et al., 2020; Jones et al, 2014; Leedham et al., 2020; Lewis, 2016a; Stagg & Belcher, 2019), but research has failed to capture the experiences of those within the criminal

DOI: 10.4324/9781003036722-4

justice system. Instead, this chapter focuses on what the wider research tells us about the experiences of people receiving a diagnosis of autism in adulthood, as well as what current forensic service users who have received an autism diagnosis in adulthood tell us about their experiences, before making suggestions as to how the experience and outcomes for autistic people who receive a diagnosis in adulthood within forensic settings can be improved.

The first author's doctoral thesis explored the experiences of adults receiving a diagnosis of autism in the community (King, 2015), which included a literature review and interviews with people who had received their diagnosis in adulthood. The literature review was recently updated by the second author. In addition, interviews were completed with service users in forensic mental health settings to explore their experiences of receiving their diagnosis[1] whilst in these services. Four main themes emerge from the literature and King's (2015) research, and similar themes were found when interviewing forensic service users. Each of these themes will be discussed in more detail in this chapter.

The search for an explanation for the experience of difference

A common experience of autistic people is a sense of feeling different from other people, often from a young age, with many reporting experiences of not fitting in (Huang et al., 2020; Leedham et al., 2020; Portway & Johnson, 2005; Punshon et al., 2009; Sandell et al., 2013; Wylie, 2014), feeling different from others (Lewis, 2016a; Vinter et al., 2020), feelings of stigma (Lewis, 2017), and that something was wrong with them (MacLeod & Johnston, 2007). People describe feeling "alien" and of "being a different type of human" (p.353, Stagg & Belcher, 2019).

Box 3.1   Case study: James

James, age 28, was admitted to a secure psychiatric unit following a conviction for arson. James experienced childhood abuse and has made attempts to end his life. He received a diagnosis of autism as a child, which was reassessed and confirmed following admission, as there was uncertainty about the validity of the earlier diagnosis.

During interview, James expressed his view that staff make assumptions about him based on stereotyped views of autism. He said that this "makes me feel like a freak" and that he thinks that staff hold him to "lower standards" than he is capable of. James worries that other people think he is using his diagnosis as an excuse for his behaviour and feels misunderstood a lot of the time.

[I felt] "alone, misunderstood, not listened to" (James)
"I'm just different from everyone else" (David)

Without the context of an autism diagnosis within which to make sense of this experience, participants in King's (2015) study looked elsewhere for an explanation. Often, the explanation that appeared to make most sense to them and other people was that they were to blame for this difference. This experience is also described in the literature, with participants in Punshon et al.'s (2009) study describing a process of internalising other people's ideas on how to explain their difficulties in the absence of any other framework within which to do this. Ideas from others were often negative and participants came to understand themselves as "lazy" or "weird and strange" (p.276, Punshon et al., 2009).

"[I told my mother] I'm being bullied and the reaction was (...) oh you been teasing again" (Harry)
   "After a while you start to feel that it is an issue with you because everyone else seems to be getting on quite nicely and you're not" (Nicole)

In addition, autistic people often put great effort into "pretending to be normal" or camouflaging (Lai et al., 2017). Unsuccessful attempts to establish oneself as "normal" can result in feelings of exhaustion and unhappiness and support internalised beliefs of being fundamentally "defective" or "wrong" (p.139, Leedham et al., 2020). It has also been suggested that camouflaging can contribute towards a delay in diagnosis as a person's difficulties can be overlooked by clinicians (Leedham et al., 2020).

The literature suggests that social pressures to conform and difficulty making sense of one's experiences of difference can also lead to mental health difficulties (Huang et al., 2020; Leedham et al., 2020; Portway & Johnson, 2005; Tani et al., 2012). Autistic adults are reported to experience increased rates of co-morbid mental health difficulties (Ghaziuddin & Zafar, 2008; King & Murphy, 2014; Lin & Huang, 2017). In addition, women diagnosed with autism in adulthood also report experiences of bullying and sexual victimisation (Bargiela et al., 2016; Kanfiszer et al., 2017).

Experiences of the diagnostic process

Research suggests that people experience frustrations with the length of time the diagnostic process takes, with experiences of being misdiagnosed (Punshon et al., 2009) and insufficient time allocated to the diagnostic process and post-diagnostic discussion (Huang et al., 2020; Jones et al., 2014).

"It was kind of a long process to get that diagnosis, which kind of frustrates me (...) my college were prepared to give me help and extra time and I couldn't get it done, because of the fact I didn't have the diagnosis" (Ryan)

The exception to these experiences can be found in Sandell et al.'s (2013) study, in which participants were actively involved in the diagnostic process. This study will be explored in more detail later in the chapter.

After years of negative experiences, a lack of trust of health care professionals is often reported by people with autism (Punshon et al., 2009). Lewis (2016b, 2017) discusses the plight of individuals who struggled to describe their symptoms and report a fear of not being believed by health care professionals. Additionally, the inherent power imbalance that often exists between a service user and a clinician is likely to create further anxiety. In criminal justice or forensic mental health services, this power imbalance is even more explicit, as service users are often detained against their will, and the clinician is seen as part of the system that detains them (Simms-Sawyers et al., 2020).

"There's a bit of frustration also (...) what has seeing all of the different mental health people over the years really been about?" (Nicole)

Receiving a formal diagnosis is described as a difficult, potentially life changing experience. The importance of the post-diagnostic period for those receiving an autism diagnosis has been well documented (Bargiela et al., 2016; Huang et al., 2020; Jones et al., 2014; Lewis, 2016a; Powell & Acker, 2016) and this should be seen as a key time for support and intervention. Connecting with a peer community provides opportunity to establish new relationships and improve previous ones which can establish a sense of belonging and acceptance after a lifetime of feeling different from others (Arnold et al., 2020; Lewis, 2017; Punshon et al., 2009). However, the literature suggests that services to support this are lacking and without clear pathways (Arnold et al., 2020; Crane et al., 2018; Huang et al., 2020; Jones et al., 2014; Lewis, 2017).

Diagnosis of autism as an explanation for self

"It wasn't big shocking news" (Dennis)

Although often expected, the experience of receiving a diagnosis of autism can be an emotional one. Diagnosis provides an opportunity to attach meaning to the experience of not fitting in, giving a name to the previously unknown (King, 2015; Leedham et al., 2020: Lewis, 2016b). Research suggests that this validates feelings of difference, leading to relief (Arnold et al., 2020; Huang et al., 2020;

Jones et al., 2014; Leedham et al., 2020; Vinter et al., 2020) and exoneration from the blame for their previous difficulties (Punshon et al., 2009). Diagnosis provides an opportunity to reframe longstanding interpersonal, social, and sensory difficulties (Arnold et al., 2020; Huang et al., 2020; Jones et al., 2014; Leedham et al., 2020; Vinter et al., 2020) and provides an opportunity to let go of the search of how to explain one's differences (Stagg & Belcher, 2019).

> *"Because it explains why I am why I am. Why I'm so annoying. Why I do what I do"* (Dennis)
> *"When it had felt like I'm an alien on another planet, well that's because in some ways that's the case"* (Nicole)

However, diagnosis can also generate grief, adjustment in identity, and for some people, re-experiencing of traumatic memories (Leedham et al., 2020). Research suggests that once given a diagnosis of autism, individuals may experience a process of coming to terms with it. Initially it may be difficult to accept (MacLeod & Johnston, 2007) and people may feel frustration or anger at the length of time taken to receive their diagnosis (Arnold et al., 2020; Jones et al., 2001; Jones et al., 2014). Over time people find a way to accommodate the diagnosis into their understanding of themselves (Huws & Jones, 2008). Some people consider their diagnosis a relief (Jones et al., 2014; Vinter et al. 2020), and experience increased self-esteem (Jones et al., 2001) and self-acceptance (Sandell et al., 2013), but others continue to dislike their diagnosis (Huws & Jones, 2008).

> *"Those immediate reactions (of shock) were very close and personal but as life has gone by since then (…) I look at things in a different light"* (George)
> *"I can cope with things a lot better, and I smile at myself when I'm finding that I'm having to do things in a certain way and realise that kind of, the reason why in the past its always felt good to do, to brush my teeth in exactly the same way is because, maybe it's an Asperger's thing"* (Nicole)

Box 3.2   Case study: Dennis

Dennis, age 42, was admitted to a secure psychiatric unit from prison. He has several convictions for violent crimes. Dennis experienced significant trauma as a child. He received a diagnosis of a mild learning disability as a child. He received a diagnosis of autism whilst detained within a secure hospital.

During his interview, Dennis spoke of struggling to make sense of his difficulties during his early years. He said that both he and other mental health professionals who worked with him had suspected for some time that he may be autistic, but this was not properly assessed. Dennis expressed mixed views about his diagnosis, saying that he believes it helps others to understand him, but also that "it is just a label". He feels that other people assume that those with autism are "stupid" and worries that some people may use his autism as an excuse for his offending behaviour.

Diagnosis of autism as an explanation for others

"It helps everyone to understand me" (Dennis)

Receiving a diagnosis of autism provides people with a way to communicate to others about their experiences or difficulties. However, choosing whether to disclose their diagnosis to other people can often be a dilemma for autistic individuals because of concerns about possible reactions (King, 2015; Punshon et al., 2009).

"I've had people say to me, 'that's not your diagnosis'" (Nicole)

Leedham et al.'s (2020) research suggests that individuals disclosing an autism diagnosis experience a range of reactions from their family. Some individuals experienced patronising or negative reactions from their families, including denial of the diagnosis, whilst others' families were relieved as it absolved them from blame. Some individuals found that their family were not surprised and had long been aware of their difficulties and diagnosis invited others to accept their differences.

"My dad doesn't even believe it (autism) is a condition" (Ryan)
"I would rather people didn't know but, in some contexts, it helps, gives insight into my understanding of certain topics" (James)

Whilst knowledge of autism in the public arena is increasing, many stereotypes of people with autism continue to prevail. As well as experiences of bullying (Huws & Jones, 2008), the forensic service users interviewed also spoke about experiences of mental health and criminal justice system professionals making assumptions about their abilities and difficulties, based on the diagnosis of autism rather than fully understanding them as a person.

"[The staff] are always asking 'can you manage that?', 'is it too noisy in here for you?'. They look at general things about autism and assume it's going to affect [me] massively" (James)

There was also a concern from the forensic service users that assumptions are made about their offending behaviour and their ability to rehabilitate based on stereotyped views.

"... this (offending behaviour) happened before, so it will happen in the future"
(James)
"Maybe some people using it just to excuse my crimes, excuse my behaviour"
(Dennis)

How can we improve the experience and outcomes of adults who receive a diagnosis of autism in the criminal justice and forensic mental health system?

Improving the experience of the diagnostic process

There is an obvious need to improve the diagnostic process for all adults seeking an autism diagnosis (Huang et al., 2020; Jones et al., 2014). Research and the service user voice reveal a common theme of stereotyping and stigma, likely due to limited awareness of the diversity of autism (Vinter et al., 2020). Professional preconceptions about autism, power imbalances, and misunderstanding can serve as barriers to diagnosis, and to the care and support needed, which in turn could lead to declining mental health (Leedham et al., 2020), and potentially longer sentences or misplacement within the criminal justice system (Vinter et al., 2020). Timely recognition and skilled assessment and diagnosis is needed to effectively assess risk, understand potential links to offending behaviour, and offer appropriate services.

Due, in part, to diminished autism service provision past adolescence (Jones et al., 2014), lack of autism screening and assessment measures in the criminal justice system, and limited opportunity to implement these, many people remain undiagnosed. As noted previously, without the proper diagnosis and support, this may lead to inappropriate assessment, legal decisions, and clinical intervention (Murrie et al., 2002). Without the proper support, it is also possible that for some, their autism (diagnosed or not) played a part in their offence and that, had they been able to access adequate and timely support, the offending behaviour may have been avoided. Developing and validating screening measures that can be used within forensic populations and using these routinely within the criminal justice and forensic mental health services would allow for better identification of people with undiagnosed autism so that appropriate assessment, diagnosis, and support can be provided.

Diagnosis of autism in adulthood can be complex, given that current assessment tools usually require a detailed developmental history, something typically difficult to access during adulthood. This can be even more difficult to obtain for individuals in the criminal justice system, as many will have complicated histories, including trauma, abuse, and co-morbid substance misuse and mental health difficulties (Shulman et al., 2020). Even if the person is in contact with their primary caregivers, it is often not possible to get an accurate or detailed developmental interview and so the assessor may have to rely on self-report information. Clinicians responsible for identifying, assessing, and diagnosing autism within the criminal justice and forensic mental health systems should be experienced and skilled in formulating how complex life experiences can impact a person within the context of possible autism. It is important that autism symptoms are not misunderstood as challenging behaviour or mental health difficulties and that clinicians avoid missing a diagnosis of autism because an individual's experiences do not fit the "classic" symptoms of autism. It is equally important that people are not given false diagnoses of autism when their experiences might be better understood within an alternative formulation or diagnosis.

A shift towards a model in which service users and autistic people are active participants in the planning and delivery of services is essential for creating person centred services. Sandell et al. (2013) explored people's experiences of receiving a diagnosis of autism or Attention Deficit Hyperactivity Disorder (ADHD) at a Swedish neuropsychiatric clinic in which active participation in the diagnostic process is key. Clients were actively involved in validating and discussing assessment results, could accept or decline their diagnosis, select post-diagnostic services that they thought would be helpful, and suggest other services that might not already be offered. This approach was found to be a positive experience for people receiving a diagnosis of autism as adults, in which they felt heard and respected, although the authors acknowledge that more research is required on this approach before wider recommendations can be made.

Availability of post-diagnostic support

Access to post-diagnostic support can be beneficial for anyone receiving a diagnosis of autism in adulthood, as it supports the process of coming to terms with the diagnosis and integrating it into one's existing sense of self, as well as reducing mental health difficulties and improving quality of life (Jones et al., 2014). Many people benefit from formal support with this process (Arnold et al., 2020; Crane et al., 2018; Stagg & Belcher, 2019), whilst others may benefit from access to peer networks (Bargiela et al., 2016). Post-diagnostic support services are currently scarce in the UK and many autistic adults lack access to them (Huang et al., 2020; Jones et al., 2014).

Such support would likely be even more beneficial for people who receive their diagnosis of autism within the criminal justice or forensic mental health system. Individuals in these systems are more likely than those in the general population to have mental health difficulties and have experienced childhood trauma (Tyler et al., 2019). It is suggested, then, that those people with more complex and traumatic life experiences would benefit more from support when re-evaluating their personal history.

Adults with autism can often 'fall through the gap' of the services available. They may not meet the criteria for either mental health or learning disability teams and as a result can be left with no support (Jones et al., 2014). Clearer pathways, which include post-diagnostic support for those without a co-morbid diagnosis of mental health difficulties or learning disability, are needed to ensure that more people are not lost to this gap in services. It is also important that, following discharge from criminal justice or forensic mental health services, individuals receive support required for their needs associated with autism, and not only with offending. This may mean specific teams for autistic people with offending histories, or effective partnership between community forensic and autism teams.

Staff training

Although the research into staff's understanding of autism within the criminal justice and forensic mental health system is limited, the benefit of increased autism awareness among prison staff through events such as Autism Awareness Week has been evidenced (Vinter et al., 2020). Increased autism awareness is paramount for both the criminal justice and forensic mental health systems, through training and also through establishing autism friendly environments, designed and delivered in collaboration with autistic people.

It is evident from both the literature and from service user interviews described in this chapter that many staff hold stereotyped views of autistic people, which can impact negatively on the support they are able to provide. Repeating a quote by professor of special education Stephen Shore (Lime Network, 2018), who has a diagnosis of autism, James said:

"When you've met one person with autism you've met one person with autism"

Services should ensure that all staff have adequate training in working with autistic people to improve the experiences of these service users.

Although knowledge and awareness of autism is improving, much is to be done to better understand and improve the experiences of individuals who receive a diagnosis of autism in the criminal justice or forensic mental health system. Staff training, active participation of service users in service development, and improved pathways for assessment and post-diagnostic support are some ways in which services can improve the experiences of autistic adults within these systems. In addition, it is essential that more research on the experience of those who receive their diagnosis of autism in the criminal justice and forensic mental health systems is carried out, in order to better understand their experiences and improve the services and support available.

Acknowledgements

With thanks to Suzie Lemmey and Anne Sheeran for support and assistance, particularly with carrying out interviews with forensic service users. Thanks also to each of the service users who have been involved in this chapter, by giving their time and sharing their experiences with us.

Note

1 Names and identifying details have been changed where case studies or quotations from service users are used.

References

Arnold, R. C., Huang, Y., Hwang, Y. I., Richdale, A., Troller, J. N., & Lawson, L. P. (2020). "The single most important thing that has happened to me in my life": Development of the Impact of Diagnosis Scale – Preliminary Revision (IODS-PR). *Autism in Adulthood*, 2(1), 34–41. doi: 10.1089/aut.2019.0059

Bargiela, S., Steward, R., & Mandy, W. (2016). The experiences of late-diagnosed women with autism spectrum conditions: An investigation of the female autism phenotype. *Journal of Autism & Developmental Disorders*, 46(10), 3281–3294. doi: 10.1007/s10803-016-2872-8

Baron-Cohen, S. & Wheelwright, S. (2004). The empathy quotient: An investigation of adults with Asperger syndrome or high functioning autism and normal sex differences. *Journal of Autism and Developmental Disorders*, 34(2), 163–175. doi: 10.1023/B:JADD.0000022607.19833.00

Crane, L., Batty, R., Adeyinka, H., Goddard, L., Henry, L. A., & Hill, E. L. (2018). Autism diagnosis in the United Kingdom: Perspectives of autistic adults, parents and professionals. *Journal of Autism and Developmental Disorders*, 48(11), 3761–3772. doi: 10.1007/s10803-018-3639-1

de la Cuesta, G. (2010). A selective review of offending behaviour in individuals with autism spectrum disorders. *Journal of Learning Disabilities and Offending Behaviour*, 1(2), 47–58. doi: 10.5042/jldob.2010.0419

Ghaziuddin, M. & Zafar, S. (2008). Psychiatric comorbidity of adults with autism spectrum disorders. *Clinical Neuropsychiatry*, 5, 9–12. doi: 10.1007/s10803-012-1679-5

Huang, Y., Arnold, S. R. C., Foley, K., & Trollor, J. N. (2020). Diagnosis of autism in adulthood: A scoping review. *Autism*, 24(6), 1311–1327. doi: 10.1177/1362361320903128

Huws, J. C. & Jones, R. S. (2008). Diagnosis, disclosure and having autism: An interpretative phenomenological analysis of the perceptions of young people with autism. *Journal of Intellectual and Developmental Disability*, 33, 99–107. doi: 10.1080/13668250802010394

Jones, L., Goddard, L., Hill, E. L., Henry, L. A., & Crane, L. (2014). Experiences of receiving a diagnosis of autism spectrum disorder: A survey of adults in the United Kingdom. *Journal of Autism and Developmental Disorders*, 44(12), 3033–3044. doi: 10.1007/s10803-014-2161-3

Jones, R., Zahl, A., & Huws, J. (2001). First-hand accounts of emotional experiences in autism: A qualitative analysis. *Disability & Society*, 16, 393–401. doi: 10.1080/09687590120045950

Kanfiszer, L., Davies, F., & Collins, S. (2017). 'I was just so different': The experiences of women diagnosed with an autism spectrum disorder in adulthood in relation to gender and social relationships. *Autism*, 21(6), 1–9. doi: 10.1177/1362361216687987

King, C. (2015). *How do people understand the role that a diagnosis of an Autism Spectrum Condition plays in their identity? An interpretative phenomenological analysis.* Unpublished doctoral thesis, University of Surrey, Guildford, UK.

King, C. & Murphy, G. H. (2014). A systematic review of people with autism spectrum disorder and the criminal justice system. *Journal of Autism and Developmental Disorders*, 44(11), 2717–2733. doi: 10.1007/s10803-014-2046-5

Lai, M. C. & Baron-Cohen, S. (2015). Identifying the lost generation of adults with autism spectrum condition. *The Lancet*, 1013–1027. doi: 10.1016/s2215-0366(15)00277-1

Lai, M. C., Lombardo, M. V., Ruigrok, A. N. V., Chakrabarti, B., Auyeung, B., Szatmari, P., & Baron-Cohen, S. (2017). Quantifying and exploring camouflaging in men and women with autism. *Autism*, 21(6), 690–702. doi: 10.1177/1362361316671012

Leedham, A., Thompson, A. R., Smith, R., & Freeth, M. (2020). 'I was exhausted trying to figure it out': The experiences of females receiving an autism diagnosis in middle to late adulthood. *Autism*, 24(1), 135–146. doi: 10.1177/1362361319853442

Lewis, L. F. (2016a). Realizing a diagnosis of autism spectrum disorder as an adult. *International Journal of Mental Health Nursing*, 25(4), 346–354. doi: 10.1111/inm.12200

Lewis, L. F. (2016b). Exploring the experience of self-diagnosis of autism spectrum disorder in adults. *Archives of Psychiatric Nursing*, 30(5), 575–580. doi: 10.1016/j.apnu.2016.03.009

Lewis, L. F. (2017). A mixed methods study of barriers to formal diagnosis of autism spectrum disorder in adults. *Journal of Autism and Developmental Disorders*, 47(8), 2410–2424. doi: 10.1007/s10803-017-3168-3

Lime Network. (2018, March 22). *Leading perspectives on disability: A Q&A with Dr. Stephen Shore*: Lime Network. Retrieved from: www.limeconnect.com/opportunities_news/detail/leading-perspectives-on-disability-a-qa-with-dr-stephen-shore

Lin, L. Y. & Huang, P. C. (2017). Quality of life and its related factors for adults with autism spectrum disorder. *Disability Rehabilitation*, 41(8), 896–903. doi: 10.1080/09638288.2017.1414887

MacLeod, A. & Johnston, P. (2007). Standing out and fitting in: A report on a support group for individuals with Asperger syndrome using a personal account. *British Journal of Special Education*, 34, 83–88. doi: 10.1111/j.1467-8578.2007.00460.x

Murrie, D. C., Warren, J. I., Kristiansson, M., & Dietz, P. E. (2002). Asperger's syndrome in forensic settings. *International Journal of Forensic Mental Health*, 1(1), 59–70. doi: 10.1080/14999013.2002.10471161

Poquerusse, J., Pastore, L., Dellantonio., S., & Esposito, G. (2018). Alexithymia and autism spectrum disorder : A complex relationship. *Frontiers in Psychology*, 9, 1196. doi: 10.3389/fpsyg.2018.01196

Portway, S. M. & Johnson, B. (2005). Do you know I have Asperger's syndrome? Risks of a non-obvious disability. *Health, Risk & Society*, 7(1), 73–83. doi: 10.1080/09500830500042086

Powell, T. & Acker, L. (2016). Adults' experiences of an Asperger syndrome diagnosis: Analysis of its emotional meaning and effect on participants' lives. *Focus on Autism and Other Developmental Disabilities*, 31(1), 72–80. doi: 10.1177/1088357615588516

Punshon, C., Skirrow, P., & Murphy, G. (2009). The 'not guilty verdict': Psychological reactions to a diagnosis of Asperger syndrome in adulthood. *Autism*, 13, 265–283. doi: 10.1177/1362361309103795

Sandell, C. Kjellberg, A., & Taylor, R. R. (2013). Participating in diagnostic experience : Adults with neuropsychiatric disorders. *Scandinavian Journal of Occupational Therapy*, 20, 136–142. doi: 10.3109/11038128.2012.741621

Shulman, C., Esler, A., Morrier, M. J., & Rice, C. E. (2020). Diagnosis of autism spectrum disorder across the lifespan. *Child and Adolescent Psychiatric Clinics of North America*, 29(2), 253–273. doi: 10.1016/j.chc.2020.01.001

Simms-Sawyers, C., Miles, H., & Harvey, J. (2020). An exploration of perceived coercion into psychological assessment and treatment within a low secure forensic mental health service. *Psychiatry, Psychology and Law*, 27(4), 578–600. doi: 10.1080/13218719.2020.1734981.

Stagg, S. D. & Belcher, H. (2019). Living with autism without knowing: Receiving a diagnosis in later life. *Health Psychology and Behavioral Medicine*, 7(1), 348–361. doi: 10.1080/21642850.2019.1684920

Tani, M., Kanai, C., Ota, H., Yamada, T., Watanabe, H., Yokoi, H., & Iwanami, A. (2012). Mental and behavioural symptoms of person's with Asperger's syndrome: Relationships with social isolation and handicaps. *Research in Autism Spectrum Disorders*, 6(2), 907–912. doi: 10.1016/j.rasd.2011.12.004

Tromans, S., Chester, V., Kiani, R., Alexander, R., & Brugha, T. (2018). The prevalence of autism spectrum disorders in adult psychiatric inpatients: a systematic review. *Clinical Practice and Epidemiology in Mental Health*, 14, 177–187. doi:10.2174/1745017901814010177

Tyler, N., Miles, H. L., Karadag, B., & Rogers, G. (2019). An updated picture of the mental health needs of male and female prisoners in the UK: Prevalence, comorbidity, and gender differences. *Social Psychiatry and Psychiatric Epidemiology*, 54, 1143–1152. doi:10.1007/s00127-019-01690-1

Vinter, L. P., Dillon, G., & Winder, B. (2020). 'People don't like you when you're different': Exploring the prison experiences of autistic individuals. *Psychology, Crime & Law*. doi:10.1080/1068316X.2020.1781119

Wylie, P. (2014). *Very late Asperger syndrome (autism spectrum disorder): How seeking a diagnosis in adulthood can change your life*. Philadelphia, PA: Jessica Kingsley.

Young, S., Gonzalez, R. A., Mullens, H., Mutch, L., Malet-Lambert, I., & Gudjonsson, G. (2017). Neurodevelopmental disorders in prison inmates: Comorbidity and combined associations with psychiatric symptoms and behavioural disturbance. *Psychiatry Research*, 261, 109–115. doi: 10.1016/j.psychres.2017.12.036

Part II
Forensic issues

Autism and offending behaviour
4

Eddie Chaplin and
Jane McCarthy

Prevalence of autism and offending

Research on crime and autism is still in its infancy, only emerging in the latter part of the last century. To date, there is little research into the prevalence of autism and offending with estimates occurring in highly specific samples. This has made providing accurate estimates more difficult for reasons including a lack of uniformity in diagnostic procedures to make comparisons, and the poor evidence available relating to reliability and validity of measures employed in forensic settings to assess people with autism.

There is often a lack of awareness and understanding about autism by clinical staff, outside of specialist services, making identification of those who have offended with autism more difficult. Further, there have been changes to our understanding of autism (e.g., diagnostic criteria have changed) and the absence of a developmental history for individuals in forensic settings may also make diagnosis more challenging (Mandell et al., 2012). However, there is no evidence to suggest that people with autism offend more than the general population, although evidence suggests that they are overrepresented in forensic populations (Payne et al., 2020).

Early research concentrating on case reports (e.g., Chesterman & Rutter, 1993), have often aimed to understand the nuances associated with autism and offending. The first study to examine the prevalence of autism within an offender population was by Scragg and Shah (1994) which showed an overrepresentation of adults with autism in a high secure hospital. More studies have followed with improved sampling methods, increased sample sizes, and comparison groups (Cheely et al., 2012; Helverschou et al., 2015; Kumagami & Matsuura, 2009; Mourisden et al., 2008; Woodbury-Smith et al., 2006). However, few quality studies include unbiased autistic and comparison samples (King & Murphy, 2014), uniformity in diagnostic procedures, and reliable and valid measures of autism (Chaplin et al., 2013), limiting the conclusions we can make. Other studies may be overinclusive, with self-report or screening tools often used as a proxy for caseness and therefore artificially

DOI: 10.4324/9781003036722-6

inflating the rates of autism. Thus, estimations of the prevalence of autism in forensic populations can vary widely between studies from 2.7% to 26% (King & Murphy, 2014). This compares to an estimated 3.6% for those with psychotic illness and 10–48% for individuals with substance misuse in prisons (Fazel et al., 2016). It is worth noting that the majority of studies to date tend to concentrate on males and rarely address the issue of ethnicity. As most studies occurred in either hospital or custodial settings, or with individuals screened for psychiatric assessment by the Courts, they are unable to address the prevalence of offending in the overall autistic population. Variations in approaches to diagnosis can be seen, with some studies using file note review as a proxy for diagnosis, some using a clinical assessment, and more recent studies using structured diagnostic tools such as ASDI and ADOS-G.

Autism and types of crime

Autistic people who offend comprise a small and generally poorly understood group (see Table 4.1). Offences by those with autism can reflect complexity of individual clinical presentation and context. Studies have reported different crime rates for specific offences and offending profiles (see Table 4.1). A Norwegian study of all individuals with autism examined by forensic psychiatric services (n = 48) reported 44% had committed violent crimes, 25% sex offences, 17% vandalism (including arson), 10% theft or robbery, and 4% fraud (Helverschou et al., 2015). The types of crimes were not related to autism subtype and 56% had no previous convictions. Fifty-two per cent reported knowing their victims and 88% of crimes were deliberately planned. An inpatient study of 138 patients in a forensic intellectual disability (ID) hospital in England found that although the 42 (30%) patients with autism had lower rates of conviction for violent offences, 13 (30.1%) vs. 50 (50.1%), sex offences, 5 (11.9%) vs. 36 (37.5%), and arson, 2 (4.8%) vs. 12 (12.5%), there were higher rates of incidents of verbal aggression and aggression towards people and property, requiring physical intervention, 3.86 (8.24%) vs. 1.82 (4.04%) (Esan et al., 2015).

Increasingly, autism has drawn media attention having been associated with novel, unusual, or serious crimes (Chaplin et al., 2013), including cybercrime (Ledingham & Mills, 2015), stalking (Mercer & Allely, 2020), serial killing and mass murder (Allely & Faccini, 2017). Examples include Gary McKinnon, Nikolas Cruz, and Brandon Fleury (see the following case studies).

Media coverage has in some instances suggested, inaccurately, that crimes are attributable to the person's autism, and fueled negative stereotypes.

Table 4.1 Association of autism symptoms and characteristics with offending

Type of offence	Summary
Arson/ Firesetting	Firesetting may be impulsive or instrumental. Motivation to set fires can include revenge, entertainment, criminal gain (insurance), ideology, difficulty coping with change. Some autistic firesetters may have a special interest in fire or fire engines and have a childhood history of firesetting. Like some other firesetters, they may also set fires out of anger, to gain revenge on people. Aside from case studies, there have been relatively few studies on firesetting. A high secure psychiatric hospital study in England, that screened all patients, reported six. (1.5%) had a diagnosis of autism, of these, one had an index offence of arson (Scragg & Shah, 1994). In another high secure psychiatric hospitals study, individuals with autism were compared to an uncertain group (where diagnosis could not be clarified) and a non-autistic group. Those in the autistic group and uncertain group (16%) were more likely to have arson as an index offence, compared to 5% in the non-autistic group (Hare et al., 1999).
	A study of 126 adolescents referred for forensic psychiatric interview found 16 had committed arson, and 15 had either PDD or autism. Sixty-three per cent of those with a PDD-NOS or autism committed arson (Siponmaa et al., 2001). [Pervasive Developmental Disorder/Pervasive Developmental Disorder – Not Otherwise Specified were terms used for subtypes of autism included in earlier versions of DSM.] A Swedish study compared characteristics with other violent offenders; those who had been convicted of arson were likely to have substance use disorders, personality disorders and psychoses, and more likely to have autism (Enayati et al., 2008)
Cybercrime	Several high-profile cases (see case studies on pp. 48 and 49 for the cases of Gary McKinnon and Brandon Fleury). In a study of 290 internet users (23 who self-reported to be autistic) with no previous contact with the criminal justice system, 122 reported to be involved in cybercriminal activity with 4% increased adjusted odds of having carried out at least one cyber-dependent criminal activity with each unit increase in Autism Quotient score (Payne et al., 2019). Cyber-dependent crime, the authors conclude, may represent an area that distinguishes high autistic-trait non-autistic groups from autistic groups, with a diagnosis of autism associated with a decreased risk of committing cyber-dependent crime.
Mass shooting Serial killers	A study of 75 mass shooter cases reported strong evidence of autism in 8% and a further 16 cases (21%) showed some indications of autistic traits (Allely & Faccini, 2017). These findings need to be interpreted with caution and not used to stigmatise those with autism.
Domestic abuse	A Swedish register study of intimate partner violence (IPV) leading to arrest used an autistic sample of 9,529 and general population controls. Finding of psychiatric conditions, except autism, was associated with increased risk of IPV against women. The rate of IPV against women was 0.1% for men with autism (Yu et al., 2019).
Drug offences	Drug use may be for pleasure, to gain new experiences, or to reduce levels of anxiety, and may, in some instances, be to please or impress others. There is increasing evidence from population studies that the problem is greater than is currently acknowledged. A Swedish study compared 26,986 individuals with an autism diagnosis and 1,349,300 non-ASD matched individuals. Of the autistic group, 3.4% (n = 913) had a substance use disorder diagnosis, compared to 0.8% (n = 10,789) (Butwicka et al., 2017). Evidence from prison studies suggests that drug-taking is becoming more common than previously for offenders with autism and other neurodevelopmental disorders (McCarthy et al., 2019).

(continued)

Type of offence	Summary
Sex offences	Explanations of sexual offending by autistic individuals include a lack of theory of mind and not being able to interpret the intentions of others, problems with social functioning and engagement, lack of understanding of social rules relating to relationships, lack of role models, poor sex education, and gaining information from unreliable sources such as tv or social media. Obsession with individuals or pornography can increase this risk. Attention and motivation of those who sexually offend or engage in inappropriate behaviour will often differ and can include fetishes on parts of the body, types of clothing and materials, or being attracted to a particular individual. However, one study found that only two of the 12 who had committed sexual offences were identified as having special interests related to their sexual offending (Sondenaa et al., 2014). Nevertheless, it is important to consider whether these and other vulnerabilities associated with autism increase the risk of sexual offending.
	A recent systematic review reported that a higher prevalence of those with autism had contact with the criminal justice system as a result of sexual offending (Allely, 2016). The evidence for sex offending is variable and data is influenced by the study population, age, and setting. For example, 60% (22) of a US sample of 37 adolescent males in a state facility undergoing sex offender treatment met the criteria for autism (Sutton et al., 2012). In contrast, a national Swedish study of 422 participants found only two participants with an autism diagnosis had received a conviction for a sexual offence (Långström et al., 2009).
Stalking	Stalking associated with autism has been explained by poor education/inability to read cues leading to perseverative patterns of cognition, linked to clumsy or inappropriate behaviours that are, or are perceived as, sexually threatening. There is currently little research apart from case studies. Mercer and Allely (2020) offer the following recommendations for interventions: intensive socio-sexual interventions to improve social interaction skills and romantic relationship functioning in individuals with autism.
	Mullen et al. (1999) identified five stalking typologies (Rejected; Intimacy Seeking; Incompetent Suitor; Predator and Resentful). It has been reported that those who stalk strangers and acquaintances often have additional mental health diagnoses, with psychosis significantly associated with increased duration of stalking behaviour and personality disorder more likely to have stalked multiple times with psychopathology associated with more persistent and recurrent stalking behaviour (McEwan & Strand, 2013).
Terrorism	To date, there have been few studies or reports on autism and terrorism or indication that autism is overrepresented in the population convicted of terror offences. There are many behaviours and offences associated with terrorism including: carrying out a terrorist attack, downloading, collecting, and sharing of information that supports terrorism; inciting or encouraging terrorism; membership/support of terrorist organisations (Al-Attar, 2019). The wide variation of offence types means that motives and maintaining factors will widely differ.
	Seven facets of High Functioning Autism were put forward to be considered during the interview of autistic terrorist suspects (Al-Attar, 2019), which are briefly described as follows:

1. Circumscribed interests – interest in terrorist groups, ideologies, and the execution of terror offences.

2. Rich vivid fantasy and impaired social imagination – fantasies may be compelling and offer sensory reward and link strongly to circumscribed interests. They may offer relief from anxiety and offer excitement.
3. Need for order, rules, rituals, routine, and predictability – "push" and "pull" factors have been seen in some radicalisation. "Push" factors can make individuals susceptible to radicalisation and ameliorate the distressing demands placed on them by a disorderly, unpredictable society where rules are not applied always as intended. As a result, the individual is unable to cope with the perceived moral chaos and social disorder. Terror groups will often put themselves forward and offer concrete solutions and act as pull factors.
4. Obsessionality, repetition, and collecting – individuals may collect propaganda and understand materials in great detail. Although motivation may not be terror-related, technically a terror offence is being committed.
5. Social interaction and communication difficulties – autistic interviewees may describe their terrorist crimes and their ideology in very graphic, matter of fact terms and provide unsolicited excessive and gratuitous detail outside of what is tolerable. How this is expressed may be in a flat or excited manner, and with the interviewee taking over the interview due to a lack of reciprocal interaction.
6. Cognitive styles – planning, cognitive flexibility, working memory, theory of mind, central coherence, and empathy were all identified as cognitive factors that may play a role in offending.
7. Sensory processing – including hypersensitivity/hyposensitivity, and visual processing strengths. Materials including websites, flags, uniforms, and terror attacks may serve sensory needs as much as they serve ideological objectives. Visual propaganda may have a powerful effect on the offender's mindset and such effects should be explored.

Violence against the person	Specific factors that may influence violent offences instigated by autistic individuals have been put forward, including social impairments such as inappropriate social approach or reciprocity and appearing insensitive to others or communication, being misread or misreading communication from others, and attributing negative intentions to non-threatening behaviour. Restricted interests and ritualistic behaviours can lead to frustration, anxiety, lack of control, or confusion. Experiences such asocial rejection, bullying, holding a grudge, feeling wronged, and seeking revenge can also increase risk of aggression and violent acts.
	Risk for violent behaviour is no greater in autistic adults and is significantly reduced when commonly comorbid conditions that are associated with violent behaviour are controlled for. Risk of violence is increased when people have psychotic symptoms or disorders, even though most people with a psychotic disorder are not violent (Del Pozzo et al., 2018).

Traditionally studies on autism and crime have focused on violence against the person, sexual offending, and, to a certain extent, firesetting. Existing evidence indicates that people with autism may commit more crimes against

Box 4.1   Case study: The case of Gary McKinnon

In 2002, over a 13-month period between February 2001 and March 2002, Gary McKinnon, a Scottish Systems administrator, was accused of the "biggest military computer hack of all time" causing $900,000 in damages. It was alleged he hacked into 97 US military and NASA computers and left a message saying, "Your security is crap". McKinnon admitted hacking into the US computers, saying he was on a "moral crusade" to find classified documents about Unidentified Flying Objects (UFOs). McKinnon faced extradition and a sentence of between six months and six-and-a-half years in prison. In 2003, he rejected a plea offer to serve between six to 12 months at a low-security US facility, followed by a transfer back to the UK for six-months parole.

The next decade was spent fighting extradition. He argued he feared that he would be sent to Guantanamo Bay. It was not until 2008 that he was diagnosed with Asperger's syndrome, a suggestion put forward following television coverage of McKinnon. McKinnon was described in the media as being obsessed with finding the truth; however, he was socially naïve, unable to read social situations or context and respond appropriately. This inability to develop an awareness of what others are thinking and to automatically interpret situations and events, and to understand social consequences, has been called mindblindness.

His extradition was ordered in 2006. McKinnon appealed this decision in the High Court, the House of Lords, and European Court of Human Rights. The psychiatric opinion was that without his support networks he was at risk of suicide if extradited. He had also now been found to be suffering from depression and paranoid ideas, which the High Court judge took into account before eventually blocking the extradition. The Director of Public Prosecutions ruled McKinnon would not face charges in the UK – ten years after the initial offence. The case saw the Home Secretary introduce the "forum bar" for similar future cases, which allows judges to block extradition when not in the interests of justice. This would be used for the first time with another person with Asperger's syndrome, Lauri Love, who was accused of a series of hacks between 2012–2013 into the computer systems of the FBI, the US Army, the Missile Defense Agency, and the Federal Reserve. He faced a prison sentence for life in the United States. Love was also diagnosed with depression. The court ruled that extradition would not be in his best interests and that he should be tried in the UK.

> **Box 4.2 Case study: The cases of Nikolas Cruz and Brandon Fleury**
>
> On Valentine's Day, 2018, Nikolas Cruz, a 19-year-old former student at Marjory Stoneman Douglas High School in Florida, opened fire with a semi-automatic rifle killing 17 people and injuring 17 others before fleeing the scene by blending in with other students leaving the building to escape the danger. He was arrested later at a fast-food outlet. Previous psychiatric examination had reported Mr. Cruz had depression, autism, and attention deficit hyperactivity disorder (ADHD). There were signs consistent with autism such as social isolation, social withdrawal, lack of social skills, and excessive interest (in guns), which fuelled hostility from public and peers towards him when seen with other behaviours not associated with autism, such as social media posts of dead animals and bragging that he had killed them, posts about school shootings, and videos of him cutting himself.
>
> A timeline of possible risk factors up to the shooting can be accessed at www.washingtonpost.com/graphics/2018/national/timeline-parkland-shooter-nikolas-cruz/
>
> Despite his mental health and neurodevelopmental history, when this volume was published, Mr. Cruz faced the death penalty.
>
> Associated with the shooting is another case of 22-year-old, Brandon Fleury, described as on the autism spectrum, who was sentenced to more than five years in prison following a conviction for three counts of cyberstalking and one count of transmitting a kidnapping threat to the families of the school shooting victims. Using aliases including Nikolas Cruz and Ted Bundy over 13 Instagram accounts he left various messages including "Did you like my Valentines gift? I killed your friends." www.independent.co.uk/news/world/americas/parkland-shooting-stalker-brandon-fleury-cyberstalking-prison-a9373371.html.

the person such as violence; however, they commit fewer types of other offences such as driving and drug-related offences (Melvin et al., 2019).

Characteristics and clinical features of individuals with autism who offend

Factors that independently increase the likelihood of offending in individuals with autism are similar to the general population (i.e., mental disorder, substance abuse, unemployment, being young, male gender, and

low socioeconomic status). Often, in an attempt to understand the motivation for offending, core symptoms of autism are proposed in explanation
including:

- cognitive impairment and rigidity,
- theory of mind, lack of empathy,
- impaired executive functioning,
- impaired central cohesion,
- the inability to appreciate the consequences and impact of their
  actions on others (Murphy, 2010),
- poor planning and perspective taking,
- impulsivity and anxiety,
- exploitation,
- excessive honesty,
- difficulty understanding social cues,
- comorbid conditions (Haw et al., 2013),
- idiosyncratic rationalisation/explanations,
- obsessions,
- social naiveté,
- revenge,
- social misunderstandings (Helverschou et al., 2015),
- circumscribed interests (Woodbury-Smith et al., 2010),
- disruption to routines (Chaplin et al., 2013).

It is also the case that some of these symptoms may be protective and reduce
the likelihood of offending, therefore it is also important to take into account
the uniqueness of individual presentation. For example, those who socially
isolate may avoid exposure to situations where offending might occur; those
who adhere to social rules and laws may seek to avoid law-breaking (King &
Murphy, 2014).

Autism in itself is not associated with convictions for violent offences once
co-occurring diagnoses are taken into account and treated (Heeramun et al.,
2017). There is a paucity of research concentrating on individual symptoms or
symptom clusters of autism as contributory factors to offending (Browning &
Caulfield, 2011). In a case-control study examining the relationship between
circumscribed interests and offending, the interests of 21 individuals with
high functioning autism (HFA) who had offended were compared, to those
of a control group of 23 non-offenders with HFA (Woodbury-Smith et al.,
2010). The authors found that although the "offending" group was more likely
to have violent interests (4/21), there was no relationship between individual
interests and offence-type. In terms of precipitating factors (i.e., events that
precede the offending behaviour), social rejection, bullying, sexual rejection,

family conflict, changes in circumstances, and bereavement have all been reported for individuals with autism (Allen et al., 2008). These findings indicate that interpersonal factors and life events are important considerations in understanding the person with autism who offends.

Conclusion

There are no definitive statistics on the overall rates of offending by individuals with autism compared to the wider population. Current consensus on the limited evidence indicates people with autism do not commit more offences but may be overrepresented within specific forensic populations. There is evidence from both case studies and the media that those with autism may be more likely to commit certain offences such as computer-related crimes that are associated with core deficits. An association with novel and serious crimes has resulted in people with autism receiving disproportionate media coverage. This adverse coverage and reporting of crime is stigmatising and distracts from the issue of the care and treatment of this group within the Criminal Justice System.

Although research has examined offence types and prevalence, there is a need for more focused research using improved methodology for assessment in forensic and custodial settings, specifically involving women and those from different ethnic backgrounds, along with studies that use comparison groups. Further research is required on how the core symptoms of autism interlink with comorbid conditions resulting in offending behaviour to support the practitioner in decision making and approaches to treatment and future risk management.

References

Al-Attar, P. Z. (2019). Interviewing terrorism suspects and offenders with an autism spectrum disorder. *International Journal of Forensic Mental Health*, 17(4), 321–337. doi: 10.1080/14999013.2018.1519614

Allely, C. S. (2016). Sexual offending and autism spectrum disorders. *Journal Of Intellectual Disabilities and Offending Behaviour*, 7(1), 35–51. doi:10.1108/jidob-09-2015-0029

Allely, C., & Faccini, L. (2017). A conceptual analysis of individuals with an autism spectrum disorder engaging in mass violence. *Journal of Forensic and Crime Studies*, 1(1), 1–5.

Allen, D., Evans, C., Hider, A., Hawkins, S., Peckett, H., & Morgan, H. (2008). Offending behaviour in adults with Asperger syndrome. *Journal of Autism and Developmental Disorders*, 38(4), 748–758. doi: 10.1007/s10803-007-0442-9

Browning, A., & Caulfield, L. (2011). The prevalence and treatment of people with Asperger's syndrome in the criminal justice system. *Criminology & Criminal Justice*, 11(2), 165–180. https://doi.org/10.1177/1748895811398455

Butwicka, A., Langstrom, N., Larsson, H., Lundstrom, S., Serlachius, E., Almqvist, C., . . . & Lichtenstein, P. (2017). Increased risk for substance use-related problems in autism spectrum disorders: A population-based cohort study. *Journal of Autism and Developmental Disorders*, 47(1), 80–89. doi: 10.1007/s10803-016-2914-2

Chaplin, E., McCarthy, J., & Underwood, L. (2013). Autism spectrum conditions and offending: An introduction to the special edition. *Journal of Intellectual Disabilities and Offending Behaviour*, 4(1/2), 5–8. https://doi.org/10.1108/JIDOB-05-2013-0012

Cheely, C. A., Carpenter, L. A., Letourneau, E. J., Nicholas, J. S., Charles, J., & King, L. B. (2012). The prevalence of youth with autism spectrum disorders in the criminal justice system. *Journal of Autism and Developmental Disorders*, 42(9), 1856–1862. doi: 10.1007/s10803-011-1427-2

Chesterman, P., & Rutter, S. C. (1993). Case report: Asperger's syndrome and sexual offending. *The Journal of Forensic Psychiatry*, 4(3), 555–562. https://doi.org/10.1080/09585189308408222

Del Pozzo, J., Roché, M. W., & Silverstein, S. M. (2018). Violent behavior in autism spectrum disorders: Who's at risk? *Aggression and Violent Behavior*, 39, 53–60. doi:10.1016/j.avb.2018.01.007

Enayati, J., Grann, M., Lubbe, S., & Fazel, S. (2008). Psychiatric morbidity in arsonists referred for forensic psychiatric assessment in Sweden. *The Journal of Forensic Psychiatry & Psychology*, 19(2), 139–147. https://doi.org/10.1080/14789940701789500

Esan, F., Chester, V., Gunaratna, I. J., Hoare, S., & Alexander, R. T. (2015). The clinical, forensic and treatment outcome factors of patients with autism spectrum disorder treated in a forensic intellectual disability service. *Journal of Applied Research in Intellectual Disabilities*, 28(3), 193–200. https://doi.org/10.1111/jar.12121

Fazel, S., Hayes, A. J., Bartellas, K., Clerici, M., & Trestman, R. (2016). Mental health of prisoners: Prevalence, adverse outcomes, and interventions. *The Lancet Psychiatry*, 3(9), 871–881.

Hare, D., Gould, J., Mills, R., & Wing, L. (1999). *A preliminary study of individuals with autistic spectrum disorders in three special hospitals in England*. National Autistic Society. Retrived from: www.nas.org.uk/content/1/ c4/38/68/3hospitals.pdf

Haw, C., Radley, J., & Cooke, L. (2013). Characteristics of male autistic spectrum patients in low security: Are they different from non-autistic low secure patients? *Journal of Intellectual Disabilities and Offending Behaviour*, 4(1/2), 24–32. https://doi.org/10.1108/JIDOB-03-2013-0006

Heeramun, R., Magnusson, C., Gumpert, C. H., Granath, S., Lundberg, M., Dalman, C., & Rai, D. (2017). Autism and convictions for violent crimes: Population-based cohort study in Sweden. *Journal of the American Academy of Child and Adolescent Psychiatry*, 56(6), 491–497. e492. https://doi.org/10.1016/j.jaac.2017.03.011

Helverschou, S. B., Rasmussen, K., Steindal, K., Sondanaa, E., Nilsson, B., & Nottestad, J. A. (2015). Offending profiles of individuals with autism spectrum disorder: A study of all individuals with autism spectrum disorder examined by the forensic psychiatric service in Norway between 2000 and 2010. *Autism*, 19(7), 850–858. doi: 10.1177/1362361315584571

King, C., & Murphy, G. H. (2014). A systematic review of people with autism spectrum disorder and the criminal justice system. *Journal of Autism and Developmental Disorders*, 44(11), 2717–2733. doi: 10.1007/s10803-014-2046-5

Kumagami, T., & Matsuura, N. (2009). Prevalence of pervasive developmental disorder in juvenile court cases in Japan. *Journal of Forensic Psychiatry & Psychology*, 20(6), 974–987. doi: 10.1080/14789940903174170

Långström, N., Grann, M., Ruchkin, V., Sjöstedt, G., & Fazel, S. (2009). Risk factors for violent offending in autism spectrum disorder: A national study of hospitalized individuals.

Journal of Interpersonal Violence, 24(8), 1358–1370. https://doi.org/10.1177/08862 60508322195

Ledingham, R., & Mills, R. (2015). A preliminary study of autism and cybercrime in the context of international law enforcement. *Advances in Autism*, 1(1), 2–11. https://doi.org/10.1108/AIA-05-2015-0003

Mandell, D. S., Lawer, L. J., Branch, K., Brodkin, E. S., Healey, K., Witalec, R., . . . & Gur, R. E. (2012). Prevalence and correlates of autism in a state psychiatric hospital. *Autism*, 16(6), 557–567. https://doi.org/10.1177/1362361311412058

McCarthy, J., Chaplin, E., Forrester, A., Underwood, L., Hayward, H., Sabet, J., . . . & Murphy, D. (2019). Prisoners with neurodevelopmental difficulties: Vulnerabilities for mental illness and self-harm. *Criminal Behaviour and Mental Health*, 29(5–6), 308–320. https://doi.org/10.1002/cbm.2132

McEwan, T. E., & Strand, S. (2013). The role of psychopathology in stalking by adult strangers and acquaintances. *Australian and New Zealand Journal of Psychiatry*, 47(6), 546–555. doi:10.1177/0004867413479408

Melvin, C., Malovic, A., & Murphy, G. H. (2019). Autism and offending. In *A Clinician's Guide to Mental Health Conditions in Adults with Autism Spectrum Disorders: Assessment and Interventions*. London: Jessica Kingsley Publishers.

Mercer, J. E., & Allely, C. S. (2020). Autism spectrum disorders and stalking. *Journal of Criminal Psychology*, 10(3), 201–218. doi:10.1108/jcp-01-2020-0003

Mourisden, S. E., Rich, B., Torrben, R., & Nedergaard, N. J. (2008). Pervasive developmental disorders and criminal behaviour: A case controlled study. *International Journal of Offender Therapy and Comparative Criminology*, 52(2), 196–205. https://doi.org/10.1177/0306624X07302056

Mullen, P. E., Pathé, M., Purcell, R., & Stuart, G. W. (1999). Study of stalkers. *American Journal of Psychiatry*, 156(8), 1244–1249.

Murphy, D. (2010). Understanding offenders with autism-spectrum disorders: What can forensic services do? Commentary on … Asperger syndrome and criminal behaviour. *Advances in Psychiatric Treatment*, 16(1), 44–46. https://doi.org/10.1192/apt.bp.109.006775

Payne, K.-L., Maras, K., Russell, A. J., & Brosnan, M. J. (2020). Self-reported motivations for offending by autistic sexual offenders. *Autism*, 24(2), 307–320. https://doi.org/10.1177/1362361319858860

Payne, K.-L., Russell, A., Mills, R., Maras, K., Rai, D., & Brosnan, M. (2019). Is there a relationship between cyber-dependent crime, autistic-like traits and autism? *Journal of Autism and Developmental Disorders*, 49(10), 4159–4169. doi: 10.1007/s10803-019-04119-5

Scragg, P., & Shah, A. (1994). Prevalence of Asperger's syndrome in a secure hospital. *The British Journal of Psychiatry*, 165(5), 679–682. https://doi.org/10.1192/bjp.165.5.679

Siponmaa, L., Kristiansson, M., Jonson, C., Nyden, A., & Gillberg, C. (2001). Juvenile and young adult mentally disordered offenders: the role of child neuropsychiatric disorders. *The Journal of the American Academy of Psychiatry and the Law*, 29(4), 420–426. PMID: 11785613

Sondenaa, E., Helverschou, S. B., Steindal, K., Rasmussen, K., Nilson, B., & Nottestad, J. A. (2014). Violence and sexual offending behavior in people with autism spectrum disorder who have undergone a psychiatric forensic examination. *Psychological Reports*, 115(1), 32–43. doi:10.2466/16.15.PR0.115c16z5

Sutton, L. R., Hughes, T. L., Huang, A., Lehman, C., Paserba, D., Talkington, V., . . . & Marshall, S. (2012). Identifying individuals with autism in a state facility for adolescents adjudicated as sexual offenders. *Focus on Autism and Other Developmental Disabilities*, 28(3), 175–183. doi:10.1177/1088357612462060

Woodbury-Smith, M., Clare, I., Holland, A., & Kearns, A. (2006). High functioning autis-
    tic spectrum disorders, offending and other law-breaking: Findings from a commu-
    nity sample. *The Journal of Forensic Psychiatry & Psychology*, 17(1), 108–120. https://doi.
    org/10.1080/14789940600589464
Woodbury-Smith, M., Clare, I., Holland, A. J., Watson, P. C., Bambrick, M., Kearns, A., &
    Staufenberg, E. (2010). Circumscribed interests and 'offenders' with autism spectrum disor-
    ders: a case-control study. *The Journal of Forensic Psychiatry & Psychology*, 21(3), 366–377.
    https://doi.org/10.1080/14789940903426877
Yu, R., Nevado-Holgado, A. J., Molero, Y., D'Onofrio, B. M., Larsson, H., Howard, L. M., &
    Fazel, S. (2019). Mental disorders and intimate partner violence perpetrated by men towards
    women: A Swedish population-based longitudinal study. *PLoS Medicine*, 16(12), e1002995.
    https://doi.org/10.1371/journal.pmed.1002995

Questioning autistic people

5

Police and courts

*Michelle Mattison and
Clare Allely*

Introduction

Contact with the criminal justice system can be a challenging experience. This experience can be particularly challenging for people with autism (Allely & Cooper, 2017). Adolescents and adults with autism have frequent contact with police (see Rava et al., 2017; Salerno & Schuller, 2019; Tint et al., 2017). Studies have also found that members of the autism community (i.e., parents and adults with autism) have expressed dissatisfaction regarding their experiences with criminal justice professionals (e.g., Crane et al., 2016; Helverschou et al., 2017).

While it's important to remember that no two people with autism have exactly the same profile and needs, there are a range of characteristics which are commonly presented. These characteristics centre around (i) social interaction and communication and (ii) restricted and repetitive behaviours, and can adversely affect communication during investigative interviews and court proceedings. Early identification of autism by criminal justice professionals is crucial.

Characteristics of autism which can affect communication in the CJS

Theory of Mind (ToM) and alexithymia

It is well-established that many individuals with autism find it challenging to appreciate the subjective experiences of others – typically referred to as an impaired Theory of Mind (ToM) (e.g., Baron-Cohen et al., 1985; Hobson, 1993). Someone with an impaired ToM will have difficulties in recognising and understanding that someone else has different thoughts, desires, beliefs and intentions to themselves. In criminal justice processes, this can be challenging because a person with autism may not understand the purpose or importance of questioning from the police or the courts' perspective. Lack of ToM can lead some criminal justice professionals to perceive that an individual with

DOI: 10.4324/9781003036722-7

autism has no interest in the process of the investigative interview or during the court proceedings, and/or perceive them as being arrogant (Archer & Hurley, 2013). Such challenges may result in a perceived lack of cooperation or understanding about the content and detail needed in response to questions. This is discussed more under the '*Verbal and non-verbal communication*' section later in this chapter.

Impairment in ToM can also mean that individuals with autism may not display outward expressions of empathy which, for suspects and defendants, may be incorrectly interpreted and perceived by criminal justice professionals as being evidence of culpability or lack of remorse. Similarly, research has suggested that many people with autism have difficulty identifying and describing their own emotions, and in being able to distinguish feelings from the bodily sensations of emotional arousal (e.g., Berthoz & Hill, 2005; Hill et al., 2004). This is typically referred to as 'alexithymia'. In some instances, the presence of alexithymia can make an individual appear to be lacking in emotion towards others. Like impairment in ToM, alexithymia may be perceived as a lack of remorse. It is important to recognise that inappropriate or unexpected expression may not be indicative or reflective of what a person with autism is actually feeling or thinking (Allely & Cooper, 2017).

Sensory processing

Many individuals with autism experience differences in processing sensory information across the range of modalities including sound, sight, touch and smell (Crane et al., 2009). These differences can range from *hyper*sensitivity (acute, heightened or excessive sensitivity) including strong reactions to sounds which are loud and 'impulsive' or sudden (e.g., fire alarms, the passing of a loud motorbike on the road, vacuum cleaners), bright or fluorescent lights, the touch of others or one's own clothes (e.g., texture of the material or the label on clothes) and strong smells (e.g., strong cooking smells, perfume, car fumes), to *hypo*sensitivity, including the inability to orient to sounds and 'dampened' or apparent lack of response to pain (see Allely, 2013).

As highlighted by Crane and colleagues (2009), individuals with autism can experience general sensory overload. General sensory overload is not specific to a particular sensitivity (e.g., lighting *or* sounds), and can involve sensitivity to multiple modalities (i.e., lighting *and* sound). Particular sensory sensitivities can lead to significant distress, which is referred to as a 'sensory overload' (e.g., Jones et al., 2003; Pellicano & Burr, 2012; Bogdashina, 2016). Sensory overload can result in the presentation of challenging or self-injurious behaviour as well as adverse effects on communication (Pellicano, 2013).

Being present in unfamiliar settings such as police stations and courts can trigger sensory overload which can lead to a negative experience or a poor level of engagement. In some forensic situations, it is possible that these reactions are misinterpreted as indications of guilt or deliberate acts of anti-social behaviour (e.g., Debbaudt, 2002; Murphy, 2018).

Verbal and non-verbal communication

People with autism may present with a unique or diverse manner of verbal communication (Klin et al., 2005; Foster, 2015). For instance, speaking in a monotonous voice with little or no variation in prosodic features including: speech rate and rhythm, pitch/fundamental frequency, loudness, intensity, duration and pause/silence (McCann & Peppé, 2003). Differences can also be evident in the use of gestures, personal space, timing (e.g., difficulties with turn-taking during a conversation with another person), topic selection and difficulties with understanding non-literal language, metaphors, irony, sarcasm or humour (Allely & Cooper, 2017).

Some individuals with autism may have difficulties with the pragmatic aspects of language and expression of significant interests, and may not be understood or could be misinterpreted by criminal justice professionals (Cea, 2014). For instance, during an investigative interview or court proceedings, a person with autism may suddenly shift the topic of the discussions to a topic that is something that they want to talk about (which may be a preoccupation or restricted interest, see Allely & Cooper, 2017), and it may be challenging to interrupt the discourse. This behaviour of switching or focusing the topic of conversation to something that is of personal interest may appear evasive in a criminal justice setting; sometimes leading to questions about credibility and culpability. Alternatively, an individual with autism may respond at great length and with substantial amounts of detail. This may generate information that is not relevant to the question or the case but, importantly, it may cause increased fatigue.

Impairment in non-verbal social communication is a recognised characteristic in persons with autism, with many finding making and maintaining eye contact with others challenging. This can lead some criminal justice professionals to question the veracity and reliability of evidence provided and may be associated with shame, guilt and culpability (Allely & Cooper, 2017). However, it is crucial to note that many individuals with autism who have difficulty in making and/or maintaining eye contact may avert their gaze because it helps to minimise sensory overload.

Very often, individuals with autism also have significant processing speed weaknesses, and this can be exacerbated during high stakes situations

(Kroncke et al., 2016). During criminal justice proceedings, many individuals with autism require additional time in order to process verbal information that is presented and to provide an answer to a question that has been asked of them (Crane & Maras, 2018; Murphy, 2018).

Overall, practitioners should recognise that "the language and questions directed at an individual with autism may require particular attention and preparation" (Murphy, 2018, p. 315).

Compliance and suggestibility

Compliance and suggestibility are two important factors to consider in the context of the criminal justice system. While both factors are related, there are important distinctions to note. Compliance refers to the tendency of an individual to outwardly agree or assent to propositions while internally disagreeing. Alternatively, suggestibility refers to an individual's internal acceptance of information, particularly when recalling information. This definition refers to suggestibility more generally, rather than investigative suggestibility. Within a forensic context, such as an investigative interview context, suggestibility is a potential vulnerability during questioning. For instance, an individual who is significantly suggestible may be vulnerable to leading questions and interrogative pressure (e.g., Gudjonsson, 2018).

Studies have found that individuals with autism may display greater levels of compliance, eagerness to please and avoidance of confrontation (e.g., North et al., 2008; Chandler et al., 2019; Freckelton, 2013). Therefore, individuals with autism are at increased risk of complying with procedural pressures. In a police interview or court setting this may result in the individual making statements which are erroneous and self-incriminating (Gudjonsson, 2003) or respond compliantly to the requests and demands of the interviewer (e.g., not requesting a break), even though they do not actually hold this information as being true (Maras & Bowler, 2012). It has also been reported that individuals with autism may be particularly fearful of figures in authority who place them under what they experience as pressure by their authoritarian manner and their style or nature of questioning (Freckelton & Selby, 2009; Freckelton, 2011). It has been suggested that impairments in social communication, which frequently result in increased levels of social anxiety (e.g., Kuusikko et al., 2008), may be an explanation for why individuals with autism could be more predisposed towards compliance and a desire to please the interviewer (Maras & Bowler, 2012).

Numerous studies have found that, while persons with autism may be more vulnerable to risk factors for increased compliance, differences are not always evident in terms of suggestibility (Maras & Bowler, 2012; McCrory

et al., 2007; North et al., 2008). In a police investigative interview or court setting, higher risk of compliance may result in the individual with autism being
pressured into agreeing to a statement in order to terminate the interview or
proceedings sooner (Gudjonsson, 2003).

Memory and recall

Investigative interviews primarily rely on interviewees' ability to freely
recall event information in a coherent and detailed manner. This is supported with the use of open questioning styles, such as "tell me what you've
come to talk to me about today". While cued recall in persons with autism
is generally found to be unimpaired and comparable to persons without
autism (Bennetto et al., 1996; Gardiner et al., 2003), free recall is often
diminished, where people with autism perform at lower levels than typically developed people, especially on tasks that provide no retrieval support
(see Bowler, Gardiner, & Grice, 2000; Mattison et al., 2015; 2018; Smith
et al., 2007, but also see Henry et al., 2017).

Overall, people with autism present with a unique memory profile, with
strengths and weaknesses in various abilities (Bennetto et al., 1996; Boucher
& Bowler, 2008). There is evidence to suggest that memory deficits or impairment may exist in individuals with autism, increasing vulnerability during
investigative interviews (e.g., Bowler et al., 1997; Bigham et al., 2010; Boucher
et al., 2012; Maister et al., 2013). Specifically, many individuals with autism
experience difficulty in consciously recollecting past events, and may have a
tendency to rely on feelings of familiarity to guide their memory much more
than individuals without autism (e.g., Bowler, Gardiner, Grice, & Saavalainen,
2000; Maras & Bowler, 2012; Johnson et al., 2018). Deficits in 'source monitoring' abilities are also apparent (Bowler et al., 2004; Bennetto et al., 1996; Hala
et al., 2005), which means that somebody with autism may have difficulty
keeping track of and recalling where and when information was learned.

Many people with autism have enhanced semantic memory (general
knowledge) and memory for details which are non-social in nature (such as
objects and surroundings) but exhibit impaired or poor episodic memory –
in other words, memory for specific events (Crane & Goddard, 2008; Bigham
et al., 2010). Episodic recall can not only take longer for persons with autism,
but some people may recall fewer events overall, or may recall fewer social
details of an event (e.g., relating to people and actions, which are usually
of interest to criminal proceedings) (e.g., Goddard et al., 2007; Crane et al.,
2012). These differences can result in the need for more prompting in order
to retrieve specific episodes (Crane & Maras, 2018). For example, a person
with autism may be able to remember that their sister usually throws things

when she gets angry (semantic memory), but they may be unable to remember a specific example of this, such as the particular day and time that their sister came home from work earlier than usual, was really angry because her boyfriend had just broken up with her and she threw a frying pan (episodic memory). In such a situation, it may be that the individual with autism is able to remember some elements of the event but not temporal markers such as when it happened. There is increasing evidence that disorders in timing and/or time perception may possibly be a key feature, or cause, of some of the behavioural and cognitive impairments exhibited in individuals with autism (e.g., Allman & DeLeon, 2009; Allman et al., 2011; Allman, 2011). This difficulty can make a suspect or defendant with autism appear to be uncooperative and even non-responsive when they are being questioned by criminal justice practitioners (Kroncke et al., 2016). When questioning a victim or witness, this diversity in memory recall may result in a case not proceeding due to insufficient evidence or a lack of cohesion. It is therefore crucial that criminal justice practitioners have an awareness of memory and recall differences in people with autism.

Key recommendations when questioning an individual with autism in forensic contexts

An overview of key recommendations to support questioning of individuals with autism in forensic contexts is presented in Table 5.1. Professionals should carefully and appropriately plan investigative interviews and court proceedings which involve a person with autism. With appropriate consent, professionals should try to obtain information that might inform understanding of an individual's communication needs. Professionals should also

Table 5.1 Checklist for interviewing individuals with autism

Areas for consideration	Key recommendations
Theory of Mind (ToM)	• Allow additional time to build rapport and to establish trust; • Where possible, provide (in advance) photographs of relevant persons, rooms and buildings; this will help to build rapport and familiarity; • Where appropriate, actively explain thoughts, beliefs and intentions of others; • Provide clear information about the function and purpose of the interaction/procedure; • When possible, provide clear information about the timing of schedules (e.g., what will happen and when) – do not assume prior knowledge; • Actively check understanding by asking the person to explain in their own words.

Sensory processing	• Carefully consider the environment where questioning will take place; • Gather information about any hypersensitivities that the individual may have; • Ask the person themselves or someone who knows them (e.g., friends, relatives); • Where possible, arrange for pre-interview visits to the interview venue and/or pre-trial visits to the court; • Ask if anything in the room is causing any discomfort (e.g., fans, strip lights, direct eye contact) or distracting with their ability to focus; • When possible, make appropriate adaptations to settings; • Allow the individual to bring an appropriate sensory comfort item to reduce anxiety and manage hypersensitivity.
Verbal and non-verbal communication	• Where possible, plan questions in advance; • Questions should be kept concise to avoid overloading; • Allow more time to process and comprehend questions and for answers to be provided; • Ask questions which are framed in the correct tense and do not make reference to a past event as if in the present (e.g., "Now you are in the street and looking at the house"); • Use clear language – avoid questions which may be leading and ambiguous in interpretation; • Use literal language. Questions that use metaphors, sarcasm or that are non-literal and need some degree of inference, insinuation, deduction or abstractive extrapolation should be avoided; • Avoid negatives and double negatives (e.g., "You would not disagree with that interpretation, David, would you?" or "Is it not the case that he did not go outside?"); • Avoid questions consisting of multiple parts (e.g., "On the night of January 30th were you in the park, and on the following morning did you see Dennis?"); • Support the individual to stay on topic by being clear about exactly what you need to know (e.g., "Now, I'm going to ask you about…" "Now, we're just going to talk about…"); • If an individual has difficulties with verbal communication and safety allows it, the use of a laptop or pen and paper for the individual to respond to questions should be considered; • Adopt an accepting and understanding response to unexpected or unusual repetitive forms of verbal and non-verbal communication.
Compliance	• Actively monitor and facilitate the person's need for breaks; • Phrase questions in a non-leading way, paying particular attention to questions which are phrased as statements (e.g., "So you saw him enter the restaurant?"). Such questions may not be recognised by someone with autism as something that can be disagreed with; • Questions need to be direct and the use of 'tags' should be avoided (such as asking the following question, "You went to the flat, didn't you?").
Memory and recall	• Be aware of the challenges that a person with autism may have when trying to recall information about past events – some details may be easier to recall, and others challenging; • Allow additional time for recall; • Support recall by providing additional prompts with careful questioning; • Prior to questioning, explore the use of appropriate visual aids. For some people with autism, these can scaffold recall and reduce anxiety.

determine whether the individual has any additional neurodevelopmental and/or co-morbid mental health needs. Numerous studies have found that, in individuals with autism, psychiatric co-morbidities are common in those who become involved with the criminal justice system (see Murphy, 2018 and Chapter 2 of this book). In some countries, provisions exist which can enable more effective communication and participation for people with autism in criminal justice proceedings. Such provisions include the use of 'Appropriate Adults' and 'intermediaries'.

In England and Wales, Appropriate Adults work with police suspects who are considered to be vulnerable. An Appropriate Adult's duty is to ensure that a vulnerable suspect is aware of their rights whilst detained, and to facilitate communication during an investigative interview. The provision has attracted some academic and political controversy, due to the differences in how this provision is applied. For instance, it is mandatory in England and Wales that juvenile suspects are appointed an appropriate adult, but it is not mandatory for vulnerable adults. The research evidence regarding the overall effectiveness of this provision is scarce (for an overview, see Medford et al., 2003).

Intermediaries are specialists who can conduct a communication assessment of a person with autism (who may be a victim, witness, suspect or defendant – eligibility varies across countries). These assessments allow for bespoke recommendations to be provided to criminal justice professionals. As part of the role, an intermediary may facilitate communication during an investigative interview and during trial proceedings (see Cooper & Mattison, 2017 for more details). To date, the only empirical evidence which concerns autism and the use of intermediaries did not reveal statistically significant benefits of the provision in terms of event recall when children with autism took part in mock investigative interviews (Henry et al., 2017). However, Collins et al. (2017) found that the intermediary provision improved mock jurors' perceptions of young witnesses' testimony and the quality of cross-examination. Nonetheless, research evidence is still emerging, and the provision is perceived positively in terms of enabling access to justice.

Conclusion

- Individuals with autism can experience considerable difficulties in being able to understand police and court demands, while simultaneously struggling to be understood by practitioners working in those settings;
- Autism can affect memory and recall of past events;
- Gathering information about the person's individual communication needs will inform appropriate adaptations to venues and processes;
- Careful planning of police and court questioning is critical.

References

Allely, C. S. (2013). Pain sensitivity and observer perception of pain in individuals with autistic spectrum disorder. *The Scientific World Journal*. doi:10.1155/2013/916178

Allely, C. S., & Cooper, P. (2017). Jurors' and judges' evaluation of defendants with autism and the impact on sentencing: A systematic Preferred Reporting Items for systematic reviews and meta-analyses (PRISMA) review of autism spectrum disorder in the courtroom. *Journal of Law and Medicine*, 25(1), 105–123. PMID: 29978627

Allman, M. J. (2011). Deficits in temporal processing associated with autistic disorder. *Frontiers in Integrative Neuroscience*, 5, 2. doi: 10.3389/fnint.2011.00002

Allman, M. J., & DeLeon, I. G. (2009). No time like the present: Time perception in autism. *Causes and Risks for Autism*, 65–76. ISBN: 978-1-60456-861-5

Allman, M. J., DeLeon, I. G., & Wearden, J. H. (2011). Psychophysical assessment of timing in individuals with autism. *American Journal on Intellectual and Developmental Disabilities*, 116(2), 165–178. doi: 10.1352/1944-7558-116.2.165

Archer, N., & Hurley, E. A. (2013). A justice system failing the autistic community. *Journal of Intellectual Disabilities and Offending Behaviour*, 4(1/2), 53–59. https://doi.org/10.1108/JIDOB-02-2013-0003

Baron-Cohen, S., Leslie, A. M., & Frith, U. (1985). Does the autistic child have a "theory of mind"? *Cognition*, 21(1), 37–46. https://doi.org/10.1016/0010-0277(85)90022-8

Bennetto, L., Pennington, B. F., & Rogers, S. J. (1996). Intact and impaired memory function in autism. *Child Development*, 67, 1816–1835. https://doi.org/10.1111/j.1467-8624.1996.tb01830.x

Berthoz, S., & Hill, E. L. (2005). The validity of using self-reports to assess emotion regulation abilities in adults with autism spectrum disorder. *European Psychiatry*, 20(3), 291–298. https://doi.org/10.1016/j.eurpsy.2004.06.013

Bigham, S., Boucher, J., Mayes, A., & Anns, S. (2010). Assessing recollection and familiarity in autistic spectrum disorders: Methods and findings. *Journal of Autism and Developmental Disorders*, 40(7), 878–889. doi: 10.1007/s10803-010-0937-7

Bogdashina, O. (2016). *Sensory perceptual issues in autism and Asperger syndrome: different sensory experiences-different perceptual worlds*. London: Jessica Kingsley Publishers. ISBN: 1784501794, 9781784501792

Boucher, J., & Bowler, D. M. (Eds.). (2008). *Memory in autism*. Cambridge: Cambridge University Press.

Boucher, J., Mayes, A., & Bigham, S. (2012). Memory in autistic spectrum disorder. *Psychological Bulletin*, 138(3), 458–496. https://doi.org/10.1037/a0026869

Bowler, D. M., Gardiner, J. M., & Berthollier, N. (2004). Source memory in adolescents and adults with Asperger's syndrome. *Journal of Autism and Developmental Disorders*, 34, 533–542. https://doi.org/10.1007/s10803-004-2548-7

Bowler, D., Gardiner, J., & Grice, S. (2000). Episodic memory and remembering in adults with Asperger syndrome. *Journal of Autism and Developmental Disorders*, 30(4), 295–304. https://doi.org/10.1023/A:1005575216176

Bowler, D. M., Gardiner, J. M., Grice, S. J., & Saavalainen, P. (2000). Memory illusions: False recall and recognition in adults with Asperger's syndrome. *Journal of Abnormal Psychology*, 109, 663–672. https://doi.org/10.1037/0021-843X.109.4.663

Bowler, D. M., Matthews, N. J., & Gardiner, J. M. (1997). Asperger's syndrome and memory: Similarity to autism but not amnesia. *Neuropsychologia*, 35, 65–70. https://doi.org/10.1016/S0028-3932(96)00054-1

Cea, C. N. (2014). Autism and the criminal defendant. *St. John's Law Review*, 88(2), 495. Retrieved from: https://scholarship.law.stjohns.edu/lawreview

Chandler, R. J., Russell, A., & Maras, K. L. (2019). Compliance in autism: Self-report in action. *Autism*, 23(4), 1005–1017. https://doi.org/10.1177/1362361318795479

Collins, K., Harker, N., & Antonopoulos, G. A. (2017). The impact of the registered intermediary on adults' perceptions of child witnesses: Evidence from a mock cross examination. *European Journal on Criminal Policy and Research*, 23(2), 211–225. https://doi.org/10.1007/s10610-016-9314-1

Cooper, P., & Mattison, M. (2017). Intermediaries, vulnerable people and the quality of evidence: An international comparison of three versions of the English intermediary model. *The International Journal of Evidence & Proof*, 21(4), 351–370. https://doi.org/10.1177/1365712717725534

Crane, L., & Goddard, L. (2008). Episodic and semantic autobiographical memory in adults with autism spectrum disorders. *Journal of Autism and Developmental Disorders*, 38(3), 498–506. https://doi.org/10.1007/s10803-007-0420-2

Crane, L., Goddard, L., & Pring, L. (2009). Sensory processing in adults with autism spectrum disorders. *Autism*, 13(3), 215–228. https://doi.org/10.1177/1362361309103794

Crane, L., & Maras, K. (2018). General memory abilities for autobiographical events in adults with autism spectrum disorder. In J. L. Johnson, G. S. Goodman, & P. C. Mundy (Eds.), *The Wiley handbook of memory, autism spectrum disorder, and the law* (pp. 146–178). Hoboken, NJ: Wiley Blackwell. https://doi.org/10.1002/9781119158431.ch8

Crane, L., Maras, K. L., Hawken, T., Mulcahy, S., & Memon, A. (2016). Experiences of autism spectrum disorder and policing in England and Wales: Surveying police and the autism community. *Journal of Autism and Developmental Disorders*, 46(6), 2028–2041. https://doi.org/10.1007/s10803-016-2729-1

Crane, L., Pring, L., Jukes, K., & Goddard, L. (2012). Patterns of autobiographical memory in adults with autism spectrum disorder. *Journal of Autism and Developmental Disorders*, 42(10), 2100–2112. https://doi.org/10.1007/s10803-012-1459-2

Debbaudt, D. (2002). *Autism, advocates and law enforcement professionals: Recognising and reducing risk situations for people with autism spectrum disorders*. London: Jessica Kingsley Publishers.

Foster, S. (2015). Autism is not a tragedy…ignorance is: Suppressing evidence of Asperger's syndrome and high-functioning autism in capital trials prejudices defendants for a death sentence. *Lincoln Memorial University Law Review*, 2(9). Retrieved from: https://digitalcommons.lmunet.edu/cgi/viewcontent.cgi?referer=https://scholar.google.com/&httpsredir=1&article=1043&context=lmulrev

Freckelton, I. (2011). Autism spectrum disorders and the criminal law. In M-R. Mohammadi (Ed.), *A comprehensive book on autism spectrum disorders*. IntechOpen. doi: 10.5772/975

Freckelton, I. (2013). Autism spectrum disorder: Forensic issues and challenges for mental health professionals and courts. *Journal of Applied Research in Intellectual Disabilities*, 26(5), 420–434. https://doi.org/10.1111/jar.12036

Freckelton, I. R., & Selby, H. (2009). *Expert evidence: Law, practice, procedure and advocacy (6th Edition)*. Australia: Thomson Reuters.

Gardiner, J. M., Bowler, D. M., & Grice S. J. (2003). Further evidence of preserved priming and impaired recall in adults with Asperger's syndrome. *Journal of Autism and Developmental Disorders*, 33, 259–269. https://doi.org/10.1023/A:1024450416355

Goddard, L., Howlin, P., Dritschel, B., et al. (2007). Autobiographical memory and social problem-solving in Asperger syndrome. *J Autism Dev Disord*, 37, 291–300. doi 10.1007/s10803-006-0168-0

Gudjonsson, G. H. (2003). *The psychology of interrogations and confessions: A handbook*. New York: John Wiley & Sons. doi: 10.1002/9780470713297

Gudjonsson, G. H. (2018). Interrogative suggestibility. In G. H. Gudjonsson (Ed.), *The psychology of false confessions: Forty years of science and practice* (pp. 51–61). London: Wiley. ISBN: 978-1-119-31568-1

Hala, S., Rasmussen, C., & Henderson, A. M. (2005). Three types of source monitoring by children with and without autism: The role of executive function. *Journal of Autism and Developmental Disorders*, 35(1), 75–89. https://doi.org/10.1007/s10803-004-1036-4

Helverschou, S. B., Steindal, K., Nøttestad, J. A., & Howlin, P. (2017). Personal experiences of the Criminal Justice System by individuals with autism spectrum disorders. *Autism*, 22(4), 460–468. https://doi.org/10.1177/1362361316685554

Henry, L. A., Crane, L., Nash, G., Hobson, Z., Kirke-Smith, M., & Wilcock, R. (2017). Verbal, visual, and intermediary support for child witnesses with autism during investigative interviews. *Journal of Autism and Developmental Disorders*, 47(8), 2348–2362. https://doi.org/10.1007/s10803-017-3142-0

Hill, E., Berthoz, S., & Frith, U. (2004). Brief report: Cognitive processing of own emotions in individuals with autistic spectrum disorder and in their relatives. *Journal of Autism and Developmental Disorders*, 34(2), 229–235. https://doi.org/10.1023/B:JADD.0000022613.41399.14

Hobson, R. P. (1993). *Autism and the development of mind*. Hove, UK: Erlbaum.

Johnson, J. L., Goodman, G. S., & Mundy, P. C. (2018). Autism spectrum disorder, memory, and the legal system: Knowns and unknowns. *The Wiley Handbook of Memory, Autism Spectrum Disorder, and the Law*. Hoboken, NJ: Wiley.

Jones, R. S., Quigney, C., & Huws, J. C. (2003). First-hand accounts of sensory perceptual experiences in autism: A qualitative analysis. *Journal of Intellectual and Developmental Disability*, 28(2), 112–121. https://doi.org/10.1080/1366825031000147058

Klin, A., Pauls, D., Schultz, R., & Volkmar, F. (2005). Three diagnostic approaches to Asperger syndrome: Implications for research. *Journal of Autism and Developmental Disorders*, 35(2), 221–234. https://doi.org/10.1007/s10803-004-2001-y

Kroncke, A. P., Willard, M., & Huckabee, H. (2016). Forensic assessment for autism spectrum disorder. In *Assessment of Autism Spectrum Disorder* (pp. 345–373). Cham: Springer.

Kuusikko, S., Pollock-Wurman, R., Jussila, K., Carter, A. S., Mattila, M.-L., Ebeling, H., Pauls, D. L., & Moilanen, I. (2008). Social anxiety in high-functioning children and adolescents with autism and Asperger syndrome. *Journal of Autism and Developmental Disorders*, 38, 1697–1709. https://doi.org/10.1007/s10803-008-0555-9

Maister, L., Simons, J. S., & Plaisted-Grant, K. (2013). Executive functions are employed to process episodic and relational memories in children with autism spectrum disorders. *Neuropsychology*, 27(6), 615–627. https://psycnet.apa.org/doi/10.1037/neu0000069

Maras, K. L., & Bowler, D. M. (2012). Brief report: Suggestibility, compliance and psychological traits in high-functioning adults with autism spectrum disorder. *Research in Autism Spectrum Disorders*, 6(3), 1168–1175. https://doi.org/10.1016/j.rasd.2012.03.013

Mattison, M. L., Dando, C. J., & Ormerod, T. C. (2015). Sketching to remember: Episodic free recall task support for child witnesses and victims with autism spectrum disorder. *Journal of Autism and Developmental Disorders*, 45(6), 1751–1765. https://doi.org/10.1007/s10803-014-2335-z

Mattison, M., Dando, C. J., & Ormerod, T. C. (2018). Drawing the answers: Sketching to support free and probed recall by child witnesses and victims with autism spectrum disorder. *Autism*, 22(2), 181–194. https://doi.org/10.1177/1362361316669088

McCann, J., & Peppé, S. (2003). Prosody in autism spectrum disorders: A critical review. *International Journal of Language and Communication Disorders*, 38(4), 325–350. https://doi.org/10.1080/1368282031000154204

McCrory, E., Henry, L. A., & Happé, F. (2007). Eye-witness memory and suggestibility in children with Asperger syndrome. *Journal of Child Psychology and Psychiatry*, 48(5), 482–489. https://doi.org/10.1111/j.1469-7610.2006.01715.x

Medford, S., Gudjonsson, G. H., & Pearse, J. (2003). The efficacy of the appropriate adult safeguard during police interviewing. *Legal and Criminological Psychology*, 8(2), 253–266. http://dx.doi.org/10.1348/135532503322363022

Murphy, D. (2018). Interviewing individuals with an autism spectrum disorder in forensic settings. *International Journal of Forensic Mental Health*, 17(4), 310–320. https://doi.org/10.1080/14999013.2018.1518939

North, A. S., Russell, A. J., & Gudjonsson, G. H. (2008). High functioning autism spectrum disorders: An investigation of psychological vulnerabilities during interrogative interview. *The Journal of Forensic Psychiatry and Psychology*, 19(3), 323–334. https://doi.org/10.1080/14789940701871621

Pellicano, E. (2013). Sensory symptoms in autism: A blooming, buzzing confusion? *Child Development Perspectives*, 7(3), 143–148. https://doi.org/10.1111/cdep.12031

Pellicano, E., & Burr, D. (2012). When the world becomes 'too real': A Bayesian explanation of autistic perception. *Trends in Cognitive Sciences*, 16(10), 504–510. https://doi.org/10.1016/j.tics.2012.08.009

Rava, J., Shattuck, P., Rast, J., & Roux, A. (2017). The prevalence and correlates of involvement in the criminal justice system among youth on the autism spectrum. *Journal of Autism and Developmental Disorders*, 47(2), 340–346. https://doi.org/10.1007/s10803-016-2958-3

Salerno, A. C., & Schuller, R. A. (2019). A mixed-methods study of police experiences of adults with autism spectrum disorder in Canada. *International Journal of Law and Psychiatry*, 64, 18–25. https://doi.org/10.1016/j.ijlp.2019.01.002

Smith, B. J., Gardiner, J. M., & Bowler, D. M. (2007). Deficits in free recall persist in Asperger's syndrome despite training in the use of list-appropriate learning strategies. *Journal of Autism and Developmental Disorders*, 37, 445–454. doi: 10.1007/s10803-006-0180-4

Tint, A., Palucka, A. M., Bradley, E., Weiss, J. A., & Lunsky, Y. (2017). Correlates of police involvement among adolescents and adults with autism spectrum disorder. *Journal of Autism and Developmental Disorders*, 47(9), 2639–2647. https://doi.org/10.1007/s10803-017-3182-5

Supporting autistic people in prisons

Yvette Bates and Ruth J. Tully

6

Introduction

The National Institute for Health and Clinical Excellence (NICE, 2012) highlighted that the needs of autistic people in prisons need recognising, stating that "Individuals with autism may have contact with the criminal justice system, either as victims of crime or offenders, and it is important that their needs are recognised" (p.4). It would be easy to assume from this that there is some sort of record or easy way of finding out the prevalence of autism in forensic settings. However, the formal prevalence rates of autism in the prison population remain unclear; with limited research having been completed, and what has occurred focusing on highly specific samples (Talbot, 2008; Chaplin et al., 2013). One problem with identifying people with autism is that screening and formal assessment is not routine and indeed can be hard to access, notwithstanding some important challenges to the effective diagnostic assessment of an adult in prison.

The identification of prisoners with autism is essential for ensuring their health and emotional well-being, as well as enabling their ability to reduce their risk of re-offending. Indeed, Robinson et al. (2012) note that the early identification of prisoners with autism would enable appropriate care to be provided, and risk of future offending to be more effectively assessed and managed. Prison-based diagnostic assessment, the prison environment and vulnerabilities, as well as the provided (and required) prison-based support for people with autism, will be discussed.

Prison screening and assessment

Despite recognition that autism is 'hidden' in forensic settings (Ashworth & Tully, 2016), routes to diagnosis and funding/resource allocation for differential assessments are not straightforward. There is no routine standardised screening/assessment undertaken at any stage of the Criminal Justice System process in the UK to determine the presence (and extent) of autism (Michna &

DOI: 10.4324/9781003036722-8

Trestman, 2016). This poses difficulty for prioritisation of people who may require further assessment.

The Bradley Report (2009), whilst not focusing on individuals with autism specifically, highlighted the need for better screening services to be available upon arrival at prison in order to provide a greater continuity of care as people enter and leave prison (Department of Health, 2009). A lack of suitable assessment tools is often cited as a reason for the absence of screening services (Archer & Hurley, 2013; Underwood et al., 2013). Staff and researchers have attempted to bridge this gap; for example, attempts have been made to develop a prison specific screening tool for autism based on the structure of the Asperger Syndrome (and high functioning autism) Diagnostic Interview (ASDI; Gillberg et al., 2001). This tool was designed by researchers in association with 'Research Autism' (Brugha et al., 2007) and requires Prison Officers, as informants, to complete the assessment based on their knowledge of the prisoner's functioning. Research in Scotland found a statistically significant correlation between the screening tool and the full ASDI, and good levels of specificity of the screening tool. However, sensitivity was shown to be low and therefore its routine use was not recommended (Robinson et al., 2012; Underwood et al, 2013). Whilst the informant completing the screening tool was required to know the prisoner well, this was set at a minimum time period of only one week; therefore, the level of knowledge that the informants had in relation to the identification of autism was a likely limitation of the study and effectiveness of the tool. Indeed, prison (and other Criminal Justice) staff can have limited awareness and understanding of autism (McCarthy et al., 2015) which is likely to affect recognition that a person may need support. This therefore will likely affect staff contribution to assessments, which may involve them having noticed characteristics associated with autism. In addition, unpublished research utilising this assessment tool identified that there were challenges with staff differentiating between autism and personality traits, likely impacting on the findings of the assessment tool (Bates et al., 2014).

Although we do not consider establishing causality to be strictly necessary, since understanding the person and their needs is more important, sometimes establishing factors associated with a diagnosis of autism (or other condition) can explain some elements of the person's presentation (or even their offending behaviour) and open up 'doors' to specialist services which can provide tailored support. Therefore, accurate diagnosis is critical.

NICE guidelines highlight the importance of recognising potential indicators of autism amongst adults and undertaking appropriate assessments to reach a diagnosis (NICE, 2012). These guidelines suggest that for adults with possible autism who are not understood to have a moderate or severe learning disability, consideration should be given to using the Autism-Spectrum

Quotient – 10 items (AQ-10; Allison et al., 2012). If a score of six or above is obtained on this tool, or if there are concerns around autism based on clinical judgement of past history, then it is recommended that a comprehensive assessment is undertaken. However, it is our experience that the AQ-10 can often miss people who may lack insight into their presentation or may minimise their problems (which can occur for a variety of reasons), and it can also 'screen in' those who may endorse items when objectively the item may not apply. Therefore, with any screen, assessor knowledge and experience are key to appropriate application and interpretation.

NICE (2012) defines a comprehensive assessment as including elements of diagnosis, needs, and risk and that such assessments should be undertaken by:

> professionals who are trained and competent, be team based and draw on a range of professionals and skills, where possible involve a family member, partner, carer or other informant or use documentary evidence (such as school reports) or current and past behaviour.
>
> (p.18)

It is recommended that formal assessment tools be utilised to inform complex cases as a part of a comprehensive assessment undertaken by experienced clinicians who can also rule out other reasons for the development of apparently autistic traits (Cox et al., 2019). See Chapter 1 for an overview of assessment tools for autism.

Within prisons, there are recognised challenges to the undertaking of such assessments, including the often limited availability of an 'in house' screening and/or assessment pathway, lack of trained professionals, limited resources, and potential funding issues. Further, the cost of formal training and assessment materials can be high and where the budget for an assessment sits (e.g., healthcare, prison psychology, or offender management units) is often an issue of internal debate with the accepted answer often lying with the rationale for the assessment (e.g., to inform parole processes, or responsivity within/suitability for interventions, or mental health assessment). In addition, autism diagnosis may not be part of the everyday practice of clinicians (e.g., psychologists) in prison. Therefore, assessments may be outsourced which can add further cost and time to the process.

Where diagnostic assessment can be provided, issues arise when attempting to gather behavioural information, due to the way in which this may have been documented within prison, as well as practical problems in finding and involving an informant/carer to contribute to the developmental history part of the assessment process, as required in the administration of the Autism Diagnostic Interview – Revised (ADI-R; Le Couteur et al., 2003) or Diagnostic

Interview for Social and Communication Disorders (DISCO; Wing, 2006) (see Chapter 1 for an overview). Many adults in prison are of an age where their parent/carer is sadly deceased, have had unsafe adults in their lives who would not be appropriate to inform the assessment, or they may have been in many foster or local authority care placements without a consistent caregiver who can provide detailed developmental history. Where there is no informant, this places even more importance on collateral information such as childhood medical and social records. However, accessing these, often many years after records were compiled, can sometimes be difficult or impossible. Therefore, in prisons, diagnostic assessment is complex. Assessors in our experience do their best to try to overcome these challenges as much as possible and to accept and highlight any limitations to their diagnostic opinion within their report. Despite these complexities, there are a number of opportunities where appropriate assessments and identification could take place, including in reception, during healthcare appointments, education, or psychology assessments for programmes (Myers, 2004). However, there continues to be a need for the development and validation of appropriate prison specific screening tools, and at least the formal inclusion of currently recommended screening tools alongside assessor clinical judgement, as well as, where required, the wider availability of a clear and accessible formal assessment pathway.

Prison environment/vulnerabilities

Regardless of whether their autism is recognised and/or diagnosed, autistic individuals face unique challenges in the prison setting. Simply receiving a prison sentence can be more challenging for individuals with autism than those without, due to the inherent disruption this will cause to their established community routines, social support, and social care packages that may be in place. As part of their autism, individuals often have rigid routines for their day which can provide them with stability and predictability. Disruption to these routines, whether due to the imposition of a prison sentence itself, and/or the changeability of prison regimes beyond the control of the individual, can be highly distressing (Cashin & Newman, 2009). In our experience, prisons can sometimes work well for people with autism in the sense that some elements of the regime have a predictable pattern which can provide comfort for autistic people (e.g., McAdam, 2012) who have reported they have enjoyed a firm routine and been able to cope (Helverschou et al., 2017). However, prisons have to (necessarily) adapt to risks and regime interruptions which may mean that planned and usually routine activities are cancelled without warning, or an individual may be forced to change employment role in the prison. Emergencies can occur which are disruptive for all concerned.

Even when the regime has been running smoothly, the mere anticipation that things might suddenly change can be anxiety provoking for individuals with autism. Coping with regime and routine change has been highlighted as being a particular concern of prisoners with autism (e.g., Vinter et al., 2020). This was further highlighted during the Coronavirus pandemic in 2020, at which time prison regimes effectively had to shut down and in-person social visits were stopped, causing distress to many prisoners but especially those with autism for the reasons already described.

Relational elements of the prison environment can also be challenging due to social, communication, and imagination difficulties associated with autism. The person's presentation can also increase vulnerability to bullying, exploitation, and isolation (e.g., Cashin & Newman, 2009; McAdam, 2012). It may be hard to make friends, and therefore life may be lonely. The prison environment can also be chaotic and volatile. This can be more difficult for someone with autism to cope with, and they may be more likely to get into confrontation with others, linked to cognitive and emotional differences or challenges (Michna & Trestman, 2016). Autistic people may be (and feel) misunderstood by other prisoners and staff and anxious about engaging with other people (de la Cuesta, 2010) which may result in self-isolation and exacerbate loneliness. Further, social isolation or anxiety around other people may be linked to offending risk for some, depending on their offence and specific manifestation of risk indicators. These issues may also/instead be specific to their autism and therefore not easy to change or manage.

The sensory profile differences of autistic people can affect their social responsivity (Crasta et al., 2019). Research exploring the experience of prisoners with autism indicates that too much noise, or something as everyday as the sound of another prisoner whistling in a corridor, can ruin the autistic individual's day because of the sensory aspect of this noise and their subjective experience of it (Vinter et al., 2020). Individuals who might in the community have been able to successfully avoid aversive noises or other sensory experiences are unable to exert the same control in prison, which can be very distressing. Whether caused by hypersensitivity or hyposensitivity to sensory stimuli, this can be particularly challenging for those in prison (Higgs & Carter, 2015) who may experience distress in response to stimuli unnoticed by others. These may arise from environmental or systemic factors that cannot easily be changed. However, we consider that we have a duty to be aware of such issues and make efforts to make changes based on the individual's responsivity needs.

Coping skills and problem-solving techniques that people with autism have developed in their usual environments are interrupted and sometimes simply not possible to apply in a prison environment. In the community it is possible to use strategies such as listening to music, or having a wide range of distraction and calming techniques, in order to help manage stress and deal with strong emotions positively. In prison these strategies and methods are often unavailable, difficult to obtain, or not available at the right time to help the person cope. This might be simply due to being detained or locked in their room at a time they need access to a particular strategy or outside space to help them to cope, or security reasons may mean that they cannot engage in a specific useful activity. Added to this comes the distress and disruption that result from the lack of opportunity for an autistic individual to engage with their specific special interest (often identified as being a preoccupation or "*borderline obsessions*" (Vinter et al., 2020)), which might otherwise help to reduce anxiety or maintain mental well-being (Allely, 2015).

An environmental challenge frequently encountered in prisons is related to multi-agency working. Multi-agency working is a useful and necessary approach when working with people with a history of offending, but also brings challenges including professions who may not fully understand each other's roles, and professions who have different understanding of the same condition (i.e., autism). Specifically, in prison, there are prison employed staff and also seconded healthcare staff (e.g., NHS or private healthcare providers), who both work with the same individuals to meet their broad needs. Although training can be (and is) provided to address these needs, there remains a lack of knowledge about autism in the criminal justice system (Helverschou et al., 2017). Staff members with limited knowledge of autism may misunderstand undesirable behaviours and wrongly interpret this as intentional misbehaviour (Michna & Trestman, 2016). It is imperative that behaviour is understood in context in order to be able to support and help the person manage it. If we don't understand someone's needs, it is inevitably much more difficult to be able to meet those needs and help them reduce their risk of re-offending and progress through the prison system.

Even when knowledge gaps are dealt with, information sharing and communication remains a challenge. Healthcare and prison records are kept on separate systems; non-healthcare prison staff, appropriately, cannot access health records due to patient confidentiality, without consent of the person. If an autism diagnosis was made prior to imprisonment or by the healthcare team, then unless the prisoner raises this with prison staff, or they are otherwise aware of what to look out for, they may be unaware of the need for relevant information, inhibiting their ability to respond to the needs of people in prison.

The lack of formal screening for autism results in staff being unable to take difficulties in coping into consideration, and as a result when individuals react badly, negatively, or persist with what are often seen as problem behaviours, they can be labelled as a 'problem prisoner' when they instead are a person with additional unmet needs (Archer & Hurley, 2013). This can in turn result in inappropriate treatment recommendations being made in relation to risk reduction. For example, simple emotion regulation intervention may be recommended when the issue is about sensory processing and resultant behaviour.

Support

Specialist support and consultancy in custody

Whether related specifically to autism or other comorbid issues, such as learning disability or mental health conditions, some autistic persons in custody may benefit from being assessed for suitability for transfer to a forensic secure hospital rather than a prison. However, it is our experience that many individuals with autism will not be considered suitable for transfer to hospital under the *Mental Health Act* (1983) and will therefore be managed and supported with their rehabilitation within the mainstream prison estate.

However, with increased understanding, prison staff can adapt the environment to make some of the sensory issues associated with prison life more bearable. This is not always easy in a restricted environment. Even something as simple as a quiet area/safe space, as suggested by Vinter et al. (2020), is not simple to plan in a prison. However, with time and care, the implementation of such space could provide significant benefits. In an ideal world, a full Occupational Therapy and Speech and Language Therapy assessment for each autistic person in prison would inform adaptations and requirements based on sensory, communication, and practical needs. Input from the education department related to any specific learning difficulties such as dyslexia can also be of great help. However, in our experience, such comprehensive and specialist assessments are not always present or possible to commission. In the absence of this specialist advice, we consider that consultancy from the prison psychology department, if they have the expertise, should be sought. There are also general adjustments and environmental adaptations which can be considered such as ensuring that:

- "communal areas are uncluttered and ordered environments with clearly defined spaces and clear visual clues that enable confident movement from one area to another";
- "each autistic person is enabled to self-regulate sensory input, e.g. by wearing ear defenders or being able to retreat to a quiet place";
- "each autistic person is supported to cope with changes in routine, such as cancellations of sessions or staff changes";
- "prison officers know what triggers may cause each autistic person to become anxious, angry or upset, and how to avoid the triggers".

(Examples summarised from: National Autistic Society, n.d.)

Prison-based risk assessment and interventions

It is acknowledged that undertaking risk assessments with individuals with autism can be challenging and it has been proposed that there is a need for good practice guidelines for assessing risk within this population (see Chapter 9). However, with appropriate risk assessments, we can potentially establish and formulate the treatment needs of an individual in relation to risk focused intervention. Prisons pose unique challenges when it comes to risk assessment and offending behaviour programmes.

Offending behaviour programmes for people with autism are discussed in Chapter 8 of this book. However, it is important to note that within prisons, a number of group-based accredited offending behaviour interventions are delivered aimed at reducing re-offending. These interventions target treatment needs relating to a variety of offence types. Positively, there is no specific exclusion criterion for individuals with autism, rather a more strength-based approach focused on individual responsivity, needs, and engagement.

At this time, there are no accredited offending behaviour programmes specifically designed for individuals with autism available within prisons internationally. In our experience, if autism/autistic traits are recognised and well understood, and appropriate support is available, then an individual can potentially participate in mainstream accredited intervention, or benefit from an alternative of one to one intervention if available. Where this is not the case, the issue of autism is still at risk of remaining a 'hidden crisis' (Ashworth & Tully, 2016). Prisons are beginning to recognise the need for prison-based autism specialist services, with HMP Wakefield developing the first such service in the form of the Mulberry Unit. Such initiatives are positive but are a drop in the ocean compared to the actual need for specialist and informed services in prisons.

Autism Accreditation in England and Wales

According to the National Autistic Society (2019), Autism Accreditation is the:

> UK's only autism specific quality assurance programme of support and development for all those providing services to autistic people. Achieving accreditation proves that an organisation is committed to understanding autism and setting the standard for autism practice.

It has been suggested that the successful implementation of these standards is likely to lead to reduced distress for people with autism and improved engagement with rehabilitative and day to day prison processes (Lewis et al., 2015). Whilst this process is specific to the UK, these standards could be considered good practice and have the potential to be implemented internationally.

Currently, in England and Wales, there are few establishments that have formally achieved accreditation, and progress in working towards accreditation can be hindered by limited resources and other emergency operational issues becoming a necessary priority. However, we would encourage that this initiative should be a commitment taken on by all prisons in order to ensure awareness of autism amongst both staff and prisoners. The standards embedded within the accreditation process encourage a multi-disciplinary approach, focusing on residential, education, and health initiatives aimed at supporting individuals with autism whilst in custody. For each area, four specific 'topics' are identified: commitment and consultation, understanding the autistic person, enabling the autistic person, and positive outcomes for the autistic person. We believe this is a crucial initiative.

Strategy

Having a formal strategy in place to ensure the identification and assessment of individuals with autism/autistic traits and the provision of appropriate support is of benefit to prisons. Underlying the strategy would be increased communication across all departments in order to adopt a multi-disciplinary approach, including healthcare, psychology and programmes, residential, education, and also the equalities team members.

Staff awareness training for all 'prisoner facing' staff is essential in improving outcomes for individuals with autism and should therefore form an important part of any formal strategy. Jordan (1999) highlights that prison staff should have at least an 'adequate understanding' of autism. Awareness training has been shown to increase staff knowledge and confidence in working with people with autism in the justice system (Ashworth & Tully, 2017). Archer & Hurley (2013) recommend a tiered autism awareness training for all CJS (Criminal Justice System) staff, with those prison staff who may need to implement interventions (e.g., healthcare, education, and Probation staff), benefitting from more specialist training. Whilst this is beginning to take place within some prisons, this training is not widely available or a mandatory requirement for all prison staff. There is also benefit in providing awareness training to prisoners who are in formalised peer-supporting roles within the prison.

This strategy could helpfully form the foundation and give structure to the process of working towards and achieving Autism Accreditation. Whilst there is national guidance on managing prisoners with additional needs or various diagnoses, there needs to be local focus on taking these issues forward, and prisons need to also be able to take into account their local prison population when strategy and policy planning.

Conclusion

The prevalence of autism in prisons is difficult to estimate, linked to lack of routine screening and specialist diagnostic assessment. The absence of a pathway is concerning as it may lead to lack of appropriate support and intervention for those who need it, the consequences of which may not be limited to personal distress, but could link to re-offending, or prolonged imprisonment. Awareness of autism in prisons is improving, but there is a long way to go. We recommend that priority for investment and focus should include:

- Prevalence research informed by introduction of routine screening;
- Access to a suitable assessment pathway consistent with NICE guidelines;
- Increased awareness of autism across all areas, especially when assessing suitability for offence-focused/psychological interventions;
- Interventions specifically designed for prisoners with autism;
- Mandatory tailored staff awareness training for all prisoner-facing staff;
- A formal strategy at national and local level;
- Environmental adaptations where possible based on analysis of sensory effects;
- National policy supporting routine sharing of best practice between prisons.

These points are beginning to come into focus in prisons, but momentum is easily lost where there are a multitude of challenges every day for staff and prisoners to deal with. However, we hope that these recommendations would improve the experiences and access for prisoners with autism, with resulting positive effect on successful resettlement and long-term desistance from offending.

References

Allely, C. S. (2015). Experiences of prison inmates with autism spectrum disorders and the knowledge and understanding of the spectrum amongst prison staff: A review. *Journal of Intellectual Disabilities and Offending Behaviour*, 6(2), 55–67. doi: 10.1108/JIDOB-06-2015-0014

Allison, C., Auyeung, B., & Baron-Cohen, S. (2012). Towards brief 'red flags' for autism screening: The short Autism Spectrum Quotient and the short Quantitative Checklist for autism in toddlers in 1000 cases and 3000 controls. *Journal of American Academy of Child and Adolescent Psychiatry*, 51, 202–212. doi: 10.1016/j.jaac.2011.11.003

Archer, N. & Hurley, E. S. (2013). A justice system failing the autistic community. *Journal of Intellectual Disabilities and Offending Behaviour*, 4(1/2), 53–59. doi: 10.1108/JIDOB-02-2013-0003

Ashworth, S. & Tully, R. J. (2016). ASD in forensic settings: Hidden populations still experience the 'diagnosis crisis'. *British Medical Journal.* doi: 10.1136/bmj.i3028

Ashworth, S. & Tully, R. J. (2017). Autism awareness training for youth offending team staff members. *Advances in Autism*, 3(4), 240–249. doi: 10.1108/AIA-04-2017-0010

Bates, Y., Crocombe, J., & Leech, N. (2014). An Evaluation of an Autistic Spectrum Disorder Screening Assessment Constructed for Use in a Prison Setting. (Unpublished manuscript).

Brugha, T., Crocombe, J., Cullen, C., Howlin, P., Mills, R., & Wing, L. (2007). *A screening instrument for ASD in prison*. London: Research Autism.

Cashin, A. & Newman, C. (2009). Autism in the criminal justice detention system: A review of the literature. *Journal of Forensic Nursing*, 5(2), 70–75. doi: 10.1111/j.1939-3938.2009.01037.x

Chaplin, E., McCarthy, J., & Underwood, L. (2013). Autistic spectrum conditions and offending: An introduction to the special edition. *Journal of Intellectual Disabilities and Offending Behaviour*, 4(1/2), 5–8. doi: 10.1108/JIDOB-05-2013-0012

Cox, C., Bulluss, E., Chapman, F., Cookson, A., Flood, A., & Sharp, A. (2019). The Coventry Grid for adults: A tool to guide clinicians in differentiating complex trauma and autism. *Good Autism Practice*, 20(1), 76–87.

Crasta, J., Davies., P., & Gavin, W. (2019). Sensory processing predicts social responsiveness in adults with autism. *The American Journal of Occupational Therapy*, 73(4). doi: 10.5014/ajot.2019.73S1-RP103A

de la Cuesta, G. (2010). A selective review of offending behaviour in individuals with autism spectrum disorders. *Journal of Learning Disabilities and Offending Behaviour*, 1(2), 47–58. doi: 10.5042/jldob.2010.0419

Department of Health. (2009). *The Bradley Report. Lord Bradley's review of people with mental health problems or learning disabilities in the Criminal Justice System*. London: DH Publications. Retrieved from: www.rcpsych.ac.uk/pdf/Bradley%20Report11.pdf on 22.07.2020.

Gillberg, C., Gillberg, C., Rastam, M., & Wentz, E. (2001). The Asperger syndrome (and high functioning autism) diagnostic interview (ASDI): A preliminary study of a new structured clinical interview. *Autism*, 5(1), 57–66. doi: 10.1177/1362361301005001006

Helverschou, S. B., Steindal., K., Nøttestad, J. A., & Howlin, P. (2017). Personal experiences of the criminal justice system by individuals with autism spectrum disorders. *Autism*, 22(4), 460–468. doi: 10.1177/1362361316685554

Higgs, T. & Carter, A. J. (2015). Autism spectrum disorder and sexual offending: Responsivity in forensic interventions. *Aggression and Violent Behaviour*, 22, 112–119. doi: 10.1016/j.avb.2015.04.003

Jordan, R. (1999). Evaluating practice: Problems and possibilities. *Autism*, 3(4), 411–434. doi: 10.1177/1362361399003004008

Le Couteur, A., Lord, C., & Rutter, M. (2003). *Autism diagnostic interview-revised*. Torrance, CA: Istern Psychological Services.

Lewis, A., Pritchett, R., Hughes, C., & Turner, K. (2015). Development and implementation of autism standards for prisons. *Journal of Intellectual Disabilities and Offending Behaviour*, 6(2), 68–80. doi: 10.1108/JIDOB-05-2015-0013

McAdam, P. (2012). Knowledge and understanding of the autism spectrum among prison staff. *Prison Service Journal*, 202, 26–30.

McCarthy, J., Chaplin, E., Underwood, L., Forrester, A., Hayward, H., Sabet, J., Young, S., Asherson, P. P., Mills, R. H., & Murphy, D. (2015). Screening and diagnostic assessment of neurodevelopmental disorders in a male prison. *Journal of Intellectual Disabilities and Offending Behaviour*, 6(2), 102–111. doi: 10.1108/JIDOB-08-2015-0018

Michna, I. & Trestman, R. (2016). Correctional management and treatment of autism spectrum disorder. *Journal of American Academy of Psychiatry and the Law*, 44, 253–258.

Myers, F. (2004). *On the borderline? People with learning disabilities and/or autistic spectrum disorders in secure, forensic and other specialist settings.* Edinburgh: The Stationery Office.

National Autistic Society. (2019). Retrieved from: www.autism.org.uk/professionals/ accreditation.aspx on 27.07.2010.

National Autistic Society. (n.d). *Autism Accreditation: Prison standards.* London: Author.

National Institute for Health and Clinical Excellence (NICE). (2012). *Autism: Recognition, referral, diagnosis and management of adults on the autism spectrum.* London: National Institute for Health and Clinical Excellence.

Robinson, L., Spencer, M. D., Thomson, L. D. G., Stanfield, A. C., Owens, D. G. C., Hall, J., & Johnstone, E. C. (2012). Evaluation of a screening instrument for Autistic Spectrum Disorders in prisoners. *PLoS ONE*, 7(5), 1–8. doi: 10.1371/journal.pone.0036078.

Talbot, J. (2008). *Prisoner's voices: Experiences of the criminal justice system by prisoners with learning disabilities and difficulties.* London: Prison Reform Trust. Retrieved from www. prisonreformtrust.org.uk/Portals/0/Documents/No%20One%20Knows%20report-2.pdf

Underwood, L., Forrester, A., Chaplin, E., & McCarthy, J. (2013). Prisoners with neurodevelopmental disorders. *Journal of Intellectual Disabilities and Offending Behaviour*, 4 (1/2), 17–23. doi: 10.1108/JIDOB-05-2013-0011

Vinter, L. P., Dillon, G., & Winder, B. (2020). 'People don't like you when you're different': Exploring the prison experiences of autistic individuals. *Psychology, Crime and Law.* Published online first 19 June 2020. doi: 10.1080/1068316X.2020

Wing, L. (2006). *Diagnostic interview for social and communication disorders 11th Edition.* Bromley, UK: Centre for Social and Communication Disorders.

Supporting autistic people in secure hospitals and beyond

7

Magali-Fleur Barnoux and Peter E. Langdon

Introduction

The Winterbourne View abuse scandal in 2011 and the negative media reports which ensued (Ford, 2018; Kelso, 2018) were pivotal in triggering a series of policy changes aimed at improving care and support for autistic people and/or those with learning disabilities in the United Kingdom. The NHS Transforming Care agenda (Department of Health, 2012) pledged to reduce the numbers of inpatient beds for autistic people and/or those with learning disabilities by implementing a national framework, *Building the Right Support* (NHS England, 2015), which sought to increase community provision for those who display behaviours that challenge, have mental health problems, or present with a risk of engaging in offending or offending-like behaviours.

There are currently 1,115 individuals residing in specialist learning disability forensic services in England and Wales, of which around 50% are thought to be autistic (NHS Digital, 2020). Unfortunately, the number of autistic people in inpatient settings has not greatly changed since 2015 and the Transforming Care agenda has been heavily criticised. One of the reasons why *Building the Right Support* has not achieved its aims is because there is a small, but significant, group of people who require care in a hospital environment under the *Mental Health Act* (1983, as amended 2007) due to mental health problems and associated offending or offending-like behaviours, which cannot be safely managed in the community. Whilst autistic people are no more likely to break the law compared to non-autistic people (King & Murphy, 2014), for many who do commit crimes, contact with the criminal justice system will ensue. Detention in hospital under the *Mental Health Act* 1983 (as amended 2007) for a period of assessment and/or treatment can occur prior to or during a criminal trial, or prior to sentencing. At the disposal stage, where there is a guilty verdict, individuals could receive a fine, community sentence, prison sentence, or detention in a secure hospital.

Across all secure inpatient services in England and Wales, there are secure hospitals commissioned to provide specialist care and treatment for autistic people and those with learning disabilities who have a history of criminal offending

DOI: 10.4324/9781003036722-9

or seriously harmful behaviour (NHS England, 2018). Care and treatment in these specialist inpatient forensic services is tailored to the additional needs of the service users and provided by a specialised workforce including psychiatrists, psychologists, nurses, allied health professionals (e.g., speech and language therapists, occupational therapists), social workers, and support workers. This chapter aims to provide an overview of the characteristics and key factors for consideration in supporting autistic people in a secure hospital environment.

Characteristics of autistic people in secure forensic hospitals in the UK

Circumstances of admission

Autistic individuals are likely to be admitted to secure inpatient hospitals from (i) the community (home address or supported accommodation); (ii) criminal justice agencies (i.e., courts or prisons); or (iii) transferred from another inpatient setting (Wong et al., 2015), with primary reasons for admission attributed to the commission of a criminal offence, a deterioration in mental health, and/ or challenging behaviour which is serious and harmful in nature (Cowley et al., 2005; Lai & Weiss, 2017; Oxley et al., 2013; Wong et al., 2015). However, these are rarely mutually exclusive and often point to the complex overlap between mental health problems, offending behaviour, and challenging behaviour for those who are autistic and/or have a learning disability (Alexander et al., 2016).

For those with criminal convictions, admission to a secure hospital is likely associated with legal requirements around public safety and the need for specialist support related to the characteristics and features of autism and/or comorbid mental health diagnoses which mean they would be extremely vulnerable in a prison environment and necessitate hospital treatment. Conversely, those without a history of criminal offending may be detained in secure hospitals as a result of previous placement breakdowns (e.g., community settings, other inpatient settings) resulting from a deterioration in their mental health and/or challenging behaviour which is offending-like in nature and cannot be managed safely in other settings. These individuals are likely to show behaviours which present a risk of harm to themselves or others, which, if unaddressed, can lead to future involvement with the criminal justice system (CJS).

Mental Health Act *(1983, as amended 2007)*

Autistic individuals residing in forensic inpatient settings in England and Wales may be detained under Part II or Part III of the *Mental Health Act* 1983 (as amended 2007). Part III of the *Mental Health Act* 1983 (as amended 2007) is concerned with patients who have been involved in criminal proceedings and require assessment and/or treatment for a serious mental health problem in a secure hospital environment (sections 35, 36, 37, 38, 47, 48). Some of these sections (37, 47, or 48) can be issued with a Ministry of Justice (MoJ) Restriction Order (Section 41, applied to s37; Section 49, applied to s47 or s48) when there are concerns about public safety. With Restriction Orders, applications must be made by the patient's Responsible Clinician (RC) to the MoJ to grant leave (Section 17), or to authorise a return to prison following treatment. Discharge (usually Conditional Discharge) is obtained by appeal to the First Tier Tribunal (Mental Health) or directly by the RC to the MoJ.

It is thought that around half of autistic individuals in secure inpatient hospitals are detained under Part III of the *Mental Health Act* 1983 (as amended 2007) and have a *current* conviction, caution, or reprimand (NHS Digital, 2020). However, a proportion of this group may instead be detained under Part II of the *Mental Health Act* (2007), where service users may have no *current* criminal proceedings against them but require admission for assessment or treatment of a mental disorder due to the nature and degree of the associated risk (sections 2, 4, 5, 3, 136). Under these, temporary leave (Section 17) and discharge from hospital are decided by the patient's Responsible Clinician. In addition to a serious mental health problem, those under civil sections of the *Mental Health Act* 1983 (as amended 2007) may require care in a secure setting due to a history of contact with the CJS (i.e., previous spent criminal convictions, cautions, or reprimands) and/or a history of behaviour which is offending-like in nature and cannot be safely managed in other settings.

Stay in hospital

The complex overlap of mental health problems, offending behaviour, and challenging behaviour often results in poorer outcomes for autistic people, following admission to secure services (Alexander et al., 2016). If they are admitted, they may have higher levels of restraint, seclusion, enhanced observations, and medication (as required), as well as lengthy stays and delayed discharges from hospital settings, compared to those without developmental disabilities (Esan et al., 2015; Washington et al., 2019).

Underpinning these poor outcomes are the lack of well-defined care pathways within the National Institute for Health and Care Excellence (NICE) guidelines, further complicated by legal restrictions imposed by the MoJ, and the limited capacity and capability of health and social care providers in the community (Barnoux, 2019; Washington et al., 2019). However, there is agreement that a diagnosis of autism alone does not predict treatment outcome (Esan et al., 2015) but rather a range of other factors which require careful consideration in the assessment of risk, interventions, and opportunities for leave and/or discharge from hospital.

Factors to consider in the care and treatment of autistic individuals in secure hospitals

Barnoux et al. (2020) recently undertook a qualitative evaluation of Alexander et al.'s (2016) typology of autistic people detained in hospital under the *Mental Health Act* (1983, as amended 2007) and reported that the subtypes possessed face validity and good inter-rater reliability. In the following subsections, the factors contributing to the typology are outlined, along with implications for how these may inform care pathways (for a detailed overview of the typology see Alexander et al., 2016; Barnoux et al., 2020).

Forensic risk

Historically, a number of high profile publicised cases, alongside research studies based on cases studies and small biased samples, contributed to the misconception that some of the core features of autism play a direct role in certain crime types such as firesetting, violence, and sexual offending (Allen et al., 2008; Siponmaa et al., 2001). Specifically, these studies suggested that deficits in social communication, empathy, cognitive perspective taking, and circumscribed interests were linked to individuals' abilities to predict and understand the consequences of their actions; leaving them at increased vulnerability to criminal offending (Barry-Walsh & Mullen, 2004; Dein & Woodbury-Smith, 2010; Woodbury-Smith & Dein, 2014). Whilst these factors may feature independently in existing theoretical approaches to offending, higher quality research studies suggest the role of autism in the aetiology of offending is relatively small. Autistic people have been reported to commit the full range of criminal offences (Faccini & Allely, 2017; Melvin et al., 2017) and evidence suggests that the range of static and dynamic risk factors documented in the wider offending population do not differ substantially for autistic individuals at risk of offending (Lofthouse et al., 2018; Nicholas et al., 2018).

As in any forensic hospital, the development of care and treatment plans needs to be based upon a well-developed formulation of forensic risk incorporating security measures (e.g., observations, leave, ward activities), psycho-social interventions, and behavioural support. There are a number of actuarial and structured risk assessment tools which are suitable for use with this population and shown to have reasonable predictive validity. For a more detailed discussion on risk assessment, see Chapter 9.

Personality disorder and psychopathy

Personality disorder and psychopathy are well-established factors relevant to the assessment of risk and treatment responsivity. Specific traits seen in these disorders, particularly around empathy, emotional recognition, and regulation, play an integral role in the aetiology of offending. However, the interplay between the clinical features of autism, personality disorder, and/or psychopathic traits requires a nuanced understanding and careful consideration in the assessment of risk and rehabilitation. Where autistic adults present with psychopathy, individuals experience what has been referred to as a cognitive 'double-hit', where an impaired empathic response to others' distress (i.e., *affective empathy*) may co-occur with, but is separate from, the cognitive differences in perspective taking sometimes associated with autism (i.e., *cognitive empathy*; Rogers et al., 2006). Consequently, callous and unemotional traits should not be dismissed as part of the clinical features of autism, but rather should be considered independently in risk assessments, interventions, and opportunities for leave and/or discharge from hospital (Rogers et al., 2006).

Severe and enduring mental health problems

Comorbid mental health problems in autistic people with a history of criminal offending are discussed in detail in Chapter 2. However, for individuals with severe and enduring symptoms (e.g., hallucinations, delusions), treatment readiness for interventions addressing criminogenic needs is likely to be hindered and pharmacological interventions (e.g., anti-psychotics) may be necessary in order to allow for subsequent therapy and rehabilitation. The valued role these treatments have in helping recovery from severe and enduring mental illness should not be underestimated, and while (rightly) there is an increasing drive to prevent and reduce psychotropic prescribing for people with developmental disabilities, it is important that this helpful and necessary policy does not result in the denial of treatment to those who genuinely need it.

Challenging behaviour

Autistic people in secure inpatient services with a history of criminal convictions may present with behaviours which have been labelled as 'challenging', for which specialist support is required alongside support and intervention for mental health issues and/or offending behaviour (Wardale et al., 2014). Professionals should remember to consider that some behaviours may be related to sensory needs. In the ward environment, behaviours described as challenging may include self-injury (e.g., head banging), aggression (e.g., punching, spitting, biting), inappropriate sexual behaviour (e.g., groping), and property damage (e.g., setting fires) which can adversely impact the individual themselves, service users, and staff.

However, within this complex group of people, the conceptualisation of challenging behaviour needs to be nuanced. There are similarities between behaviours that are labelled criminal and those that are seen as challenging, as the underlying reason that drives the behaviour may be similar, but the behavioural manifestation may be different (Barnoux & Langdon, in press). Further, there are instances where some behaviours which would be labelled as 'criminal' would not be seen as such when exhibited by some people with learning disabilities and/or autism due to the requirement for *mens rea* ('guilty state of mind') to be present for a person to be judged to have committed a crime in England and Wales (Barnoux & Langdon, in press). Where behaviour labelled as challenging is 'offending-like', specialist support and intervention in the hospital environment plays an integral part in the reduction of risk, promotion of rehabilitation, and facilitating opportunities for discharge.

Interventions and psychological therapies for autistic people in secure forensic hospitals

Treatment approaches for autistic individuals with a history of offending behaviour

Secure hospitals do not have a package of standardised interventions developed specifically for autistic service users. Rather, interventions and psychological therapies offered in these settings vary greatly and are often contingent on the knowledge and specific expertise of the staff. Underpinning this variability in professional practice is an evidence base still very much in its infancy. In their systematic review on treatment effectiveness for offending behaviour in autistic individuals, Melvin et al. (2017) reported treatment approaches and effectiveness in reducing re-offending varied substantially across studies, highlighting the need for more controlled trials. For a detailed overview, see Chapter 8.

The impact of the clinical features of autism on treatment outcome (i.e., *treatment responsivity*) has garnered increasing attention. In particular, there are a number of structural (e.g., mode of delivery) and psycho-social factors (e.g., empathy, emotion recognition and regulation, cognitive differences, information processing, communication preferences, social vulnerability) which merit careful consideration when adapting and delivering a treatment programme for behaviours labelled as criminal in autistic people (Melvin et al., 2020a, 2020b). There is a body of literature describing adaptations to psychological therapies for use with autistic individuals more generally (e.g., Kerns et al., 2016), and similar adaptations would be required when providing psychological interventions aimed at mitigating forensic risk. For a detailed discussion, see Chapter 8.

Positive behaviour support

Current UK policy advocates the use of behavioural support plans as part of a model of care based on proactive and preventative strategies for managing behaviours that challenge for vulnerable people within various settings (National Offenders Management Services (NOMS), 2013; NICE, 2015a, 2015b; Social Care, Local Government and Care Partnership Directorate, 2014). Positive behavioural support (PBS) is a framework for developing and delivering interventions based on a set of overarching values which promote inclusion, choice, participation, and equality of opportunity (Gore et al., 2013). PBS combines person-centred approaches and evidence-based behavioural science to understand the reason underlying behaviours labelled as challenging and subsequently inform decision-making with the overall aim of improving the quality of a person's life and that of the people around them in the least restrictive way possible (Social Care, Local Government and Care Partnership Directorate, 2014).

In forensic and community settings, PBS can be implemented by a single practitioner, a team of professionals, or at an organisational level (Gore et al., 2013). The implementation of PBS should be person-centred and values-based and include: (i) a *functional assessment* to understand the underlying reasons for challenging behaviour, or in this case, offending or offending-like behaviour; and (ii) the development of a detailed *behaviour support plan* which includes a tiered system of preventative and reactive strategies by which the needs of the person can be met to enhance quality of life. Behaviour support plans should always be co-produced with the individual, their carers, relatives, and/or advocates (*service user involvement*). There may be tensions that arise when co-producing a PBS plan for someone who has a history of criminal offending. Individuals may want to include activities and interests which increase risk, or are offence paralleling behaviours, and these need to be managed carefully. For example, someone who has a sexual interest in children may wish to spend time watching children's television or visiting areas that are frequented by children. Some team members may see this as unproblematic and infantilise the person or attempt to construe such as an unproblematic circumscribed interest. However, such activities and interests would need to be managed carefully for someone where there is a genuine risk of harm.

In a systematic review evaluating the use of, and effectiveness of, PBS in forensic settings, Collins et al. (2021) identified 11 studies focusing on PBS interventions in forensic settings, of which only 5 included service users as participants (as opposed to staff). Findings suggest PBS training (i) improves staff knowledge in the antecedents and causes of challenging behaviour, (ii) increases staff confidence in the management of challenging behaviour, and (iii) is likely to have a positive impact on the care and treatment of service users within forensic settings. However, only 3 of the included studies conducted with service users measured challenging behaviour as an outcome variable. Whilst these studies reported sustained reductions in aggression and challenging behaviour and increased quality of life as a result of implementing PBS (Davies et al., 2019; Dodds et al., 2015; Langdon et al., 2017), none included participants with a diagnosis of autism. Collins et al. (2021) further highlight that the existing evidence base is limited and generally of poor methodological quality, limiting our ability to ascertain the effectiveness of PBS in forensic settings. Improvements are needed in terms of measuring outcomes related to reductions in the frequency and intensity of challenging behaviour and the use of restrictive practices, length of stay, improvements in quality of life, and the longer-term impact of PBS. While more rigorous research is needed, PBS remains a recommended intervention for challenging behaviour and implementation across forensic service lines is likely to contribute positively towards reduction of risk, rehabilitation, discharge from hospital, and support within the community.

Planning for discharge and community care

Discharge planning for autistic people who are in hospital is associated with some specific challenges, many of which are not markedly dissimilar from those faced by people without autism, including those with intellectual disabilities. For some, the potential loss of the structure and routines of an inpatient environment, while adapting to new routines in the community, is challenging. Well-coordinated plans where individuals are afforded time to learn about and experience changes are helpful in promoting successful discharge. This could include ensuring the provision of good information about future accommodation and support coupled with an opportunity to form relationships with new support staff early within the discharge process. The sharing of good information with future providers, coupled with specific training to help mitigate risk (e.g., extensive training in PBS and risk management plans), is also vital. Across much of England, there is a lack of specialist forensic mental health teams focused specifically on autism. While there are teams in some areas for those with intellectual disabilities and there is a national service specification (NHS England, 2017), some of these teams may be experienced in working with autistic people, but they may not be directly commissioned to work with this group.

At times, there may be conflict between different community-based services as to whether they are best placed to provide support to autistic people upon discharge from hospital, especially when they do not also have an intellectual disability.

Conclusion

- There is a small but significant group of autistic people who require specialist care in a hospital environment under the *Mental Health Act* (1983, as amended 2007) due to a serious mental health problem and offending or offending-like behaviours which cannot be safely managed in a community setting.
- Autistic individuals are likely to be admitted to these hospitals from a range of community, criminal justice, or health settings. For some of these individuals, the predominant issue will be one of challenging behaviour, where issues associated with autism, sensory needs, and communication are paramount for their recovery. For others, they are likely to require specialist treatment for enduring mental health problems, while for some, there may be comorbid psychopathy which increases risk for whom longer stays and physical and relational security will be important to help mitigate risk into the future.
- It is thought that around half of autistic individuals in secure inpatient hospitals are detained under criminal sections of the *Mental Health Act* 1983 (as amended 2007) and are likely to have been charged or convicted of a criminal offence or have a current police caution or reprimand. Those that are detained under civil sections are likely to have a history of contact with the criminal justice system and/or a history of behaviour which is offending-like in nature.
- Outcomes for this group are related to factors which point to the complex overlap of mental health problems, offending behaviour, challenging behaviour, and clinical features associated with autism.
- Practising professionals should give careful consideration to forensic risk, personality disorder and psychopathy, severe and enduring mental health problems, and challenging behaviour in the development of individualised care and treatment plans.
- Treatment approaches and effectiveness are varied for this group and more controlled trials are needed. However, treatment responsivity can be improved by adapting and tailoring programmes to meet individuals' needs.
- The use of PBS as part of a model of care has shown to contribute positively towards the reduction of risk, rehabilitation, and opportunities for discharge, though more research is needed.

References

Alexander, R., Langdon, P. E., Chester, V., Barnoux, M., Gunaratna, I., & Hoare, S. (2016). Heterogeneity within autism spectrum disorder in forensic mental health: The introduction of typologies. *Advances in Autism*, 4, 201–209. doi: 10.1108/AIA-08-2016-0021

Allen, D., Evans, C., Hider, A., Hawkins, S., Peckett, H., & Morgan, H. (2008). Offending behaviour in adults with Asperger syndrome. *Journal of Autism and Developmental Disorders*, 38(4), 748–758. doi: 10.1007/s10803-007-0442-9

Barnoux, M. (2019). Community services and transforming care: Reflections and considerations. *Tizard Learning Disability Review*, 24(1), 33–37. https://doi.org/10.1108/TLDR-12-2018-0034

Barnoux, M., Alexander, R., Bhaumik, S., Devapriam, J., Duggan, C., Shepstone, L., ... & Langdon, P. E. (2020). The face validity of an initial sub-typology of people with autism spectrum disorders detained within psychiatric hospitals. *Autism*, 24(7), 1885–1897. doi: 10.1177/1362361320929457

Barnoux, M., & Langdon, P. E. (in press) Positive Behaviour Support. In P. E. Langdon and G. H. Murphy (Eds) *Working within community settings with people with learning disabilities and/or autism who are at risk of coming into contact with criminal justice: A compendium for health and social care staff*. Health Education England.

Barry-Walsh, J. B., & Mullen, P. E. (2004). Forensic aspects of Asperger's Syndrome. *Journal of Forensic Psychiatry & Psychology*, 15(1), 96–107. https://doi.org/10.1080/1478994031000 1638628

Collins, J., Barnoux, M., & Baker, P. (2021). Managing challenging behaviour using applied behaviour analysis and positive behaviour support in forensic settings: A systematic review. *International Journal of Positive Behavioural Support*, 11(1), 15–41.

Cowley, A., Newton, J., Sturmey, P., Bouras, N., & Holt, G. (2005). Psychiatric inpatient admissions of adults with intellectual disabilities: Predictive factors. *American Journal on Mental Retardation*, 110(3), 216–225. doi: 10.1352/0895-8017(2005)110<216:PIAOAW>2.0.CO;2

Davies, B. E., Lowe, K., Morgan, S., John-Evans, H., & Fitoussi, J. (2019). An evaluation of the effectiveness of positive behavioural support within a medium secure mental health forensic service. *Journal of Forensic Psychiatry & Psychology*, 30(1), 38–52. doi:10.1080/14789949. 2018.1459785

Dein, K., & Woodbury-Smith, M. (2010). Asperger syndrome and criminal behaviour. *Advances in Psychiatric Treatment*, 16(1), 37–43. doi: 10.1192/apt.bp.107.005082

Department of Health (2012). *Transforming care: A national response to Winterbourne View Hospital*. London: Department of Health. Retrieved from: https://assets.publishing.service. gov.uk/government/uploads/system/uploads/attachment_data/file/213215/final-report.pdf

Dodds, N., Legg, G., Sinfield, P., Armstrong, D., & Cheng, W. (2015). The application of a positive behavioural support framework in a low secure adolescent inpatient unit. *International Journal of Positive Behavioural Support*, 5(2), 33–42.

Esan, F., Chester, V., Gunaratna, I. J., Hoare, S., & Alexander, R. T. (2015). The clinical, forensic and treatment outcome factors of patients with autism spectrum disorder treated in a forensic intellectual disability service. *Journal of Applied Research in Intellectual Disabilities: JARID*, 28(3), 193–200. doi:10.1111/jar.12121

Faccini, L., & Allely, C. S. (2017). Rare instances of individuals with autism supporting or engaging in terrorism. *Journal of Intellectual Disabilities and Offending Behaviour*, 8(2), 70–82. https://doi.org/10.1108/JIDOB-11-2016-0022.

Ford, R. (2018). Autistic teenagers 'locked in padded cells and abused'. Retrieved 02 December 2018, from *The Sunday Times*: www.thetimes.co.uk/article/autisticteenagers-locked-in-padded-cells-and-abused-b9pbchtkz.

Gore, N. J., McGill, P., Toogood, S., Allen, D., Hughes, J. C., Baker, P., . . . & Denne, L. D. (2013). Definition and scope for positive behavioural support. *International Journal of Positive Behavioural Support*, 3(2), 14–23.

Kelso, P. (2018). Deaths in secure hospitals reviewed by government after Sky investigation. Retrieved 02 December 2018 from: https://news.sky.com/story/deaths-in-securehospitals-reviewed-by-government-after-sky-investigation-11546371

Kerns, C. M., Roux, A. M., Connell, J. E., & Shattuck, P. T. (2016). Adapting cognitive behavioral techniques to address anxiety and depression in cognitively able emerging adults on the autism spectrum. *Cognitive and Behavioral Practice*, 23(3), 329–340. https://doi.org/10.1016/j.cbpra.2016.06.002

King, C., & Murphy, G. H. (2014). A systematic review of people with autism spectrum disorder and the criminal justice system. *Journal of Autism and Developmental Disorders*, 44(11), 2717–2733. doi: 10.1007/s10803-014-2046-5

Lai, J. K., & Weiss, J. A. (2017). Priority service needs and receipt across the lifespan for individuals with autism spectrum disorder. *Autism Research*, 10(8), 1436–1447. https://doi.org/10.1002/aur.1786

Langdon, P. E., Dalton, D., Brolly, K., Temple, P., Thomas, C., & Webster, T. (2017). Using positive behavioural support as a treatment for trauma symptoms with a man with intellectual disabilities. *International Journal of Positive Behavioural Support*, 7(1), 31–37.

Lofthouse, R., Totsika, V., Hastings, R. P., & Lindsay, W. R. (2018). Offenders with Intellectual and Developmental Disabilities: Future Directions for Research and Practice. In W. R. Lindsay & J. L. Taylor (Eds) *The Wiley handbook on offenders with intellectual and developmental disabilities: Research, training, and practice* (pp. 453–471). Hoboken, NJ: Wiley.

Melvin, C. L., Langdon, P. E., & Murphy, G. H. (2017). Treatment effectiveness for offenders with autism spectrum conditions: A systematic review. *Psychology, Crime & Law*, 23(8), 1–29. https://doi.org/10.1080/1068316X.2017.1324027

Melvin, C. L., Langdon, P. E., & Murphy, G. H. (2020a). "I feel that if I didn't come to it anymore, maybe I would go back to my old ways and I don't want that to happen": Adapted sex offender treatment programmes: Views of service users with autism spectrum disorders. *Journal of Applied Research in Intellectual Disabilities*, 33, 739–756. doi: 10.1111/jar.12641

Melvin, C. L., Langdon, P. E., & Murphy, G. H. (2020b). "They're the hardest group to treat, that changes the least". Adapted sex offender treatment programmes for individuals with Autism Spectrum Disorders: Clinician views and experiences. *Research in Developmental Disabilities*, 105, 103721. https://doi.org/10.1016/j.ridd.2020.103721

National Institute for Health and Care Excellence (NICE). (2015a). Challenging behaviour and learning disabilities: Prevention and interventions for people with learning disabilities whose behaviour challenges. (No. Ng11). National Institute for Health Care Excellence. Retrieved from: www.nice.org.uk/guidance/ng11/resources/challenging-behaviour-and-learning-disabilities-prevention-and-interventions-for-people-with-learning-disabilities-whose-behaviour-challenges-pdf-1837266392005

National Institute for Health and Care Excellence (NICE). (2015b). Violence and aggression: Short-term management in mental health, health and community settings. (No. Ng10). London: National Institute for Health Care Excellence. Retrieved from: www.nice.org.uk/guidance/ng10/resources/violence-and-aggression-shortterm-management-in-mental-health-health-and-community-settings-pdf-1837264712389

National Offenders Management Services (NOMS). (2013). *Minimising and managing physical restraint: Safeguarding processes, governance arrangements, and roles and responsibilities.* Retrieved from: https://assets.publishing.service.gov.uk/government/uploads/system/uploads/attachment_data/file/456672/minimising-managing-physical-restraint.pdf

NHS Digital. (2020). *Learning disability services monthly statistics.* Retrieved from: http://digital.nhs.uk/pubs/ldsmAug20

NHS England. (2018). *Service specification medium secure mental health services (adult).* Retrieved from: www.england.nhs.uk/wp-content/uploads/2018/03/adult-medium-secure-service-specification-dec-20.pdf

NHS England. (2017). *Transforming Care – Model Service Specifications: Supporting implementation of the service model.* London: NHS England. Retrieved from: www.england.nhs.uk/wp-content/uploads/2017/02/model-service-spec-2017.pdf

NHS England. (2015). *Building the right support: A national plan to develop community services and close inpatient facilities for people with a learning disability and/or autism who display behaviour that challenges, including those with a mental health condition.* Department of Health. Retrieved from: www.england.nhs.uk/wp-content/uploads/2015/10/ld-nat-imp-plan-oct15.pdf

Nicholas, S., Gray, N. S., & Snowden, R. J. (2018). Static Risk Assessment in Offenders with Intellectual and Developmental Disabilities. In *The Wiley Handbook on Offenders with Intellectual and Developmental Disabilities: Research, Training, and Practice* (pp. 123–140). Hoboken, NJ: Wiley.

Oxley, C., Sathanandan, S., Gazizova, D., Fitzgerald, B., & Puri, B. K. (2013). A comparative review of admissions to an Intellectual Disability Inpatient Service over a 10-year period. *British Journal of Medical Practitioners,* 6(2), 36–40.

Rogers, J., Viding, E., Blair, R. J., Frith, U., & Happé, F. (2006). Autism spectrum disorder and psychopathy: Shared cognitive underpinnings or double hit? *Psychological Medicine,* 36(12), 1789–1798. doi: 10.1017/S0033291706008853

Siponmaa, L., Kristiansson, M., Jonson, C., Nyden, A., & Gillberg, C. (2001). Juvenile and young adult mentally disordered offenders: The role of child neuropsychiatric disorders. *Journal of the American Academy of Psychiatry and the Law,* 29(4), 420–426. PMID: 11785613

Social Care, Local Government and Care Partnership Directorate. (2014). Positive and proactive care: Reducing the need for restrictive interventions. London: Department of Health. Retrieved from: https://assets.publishing.service.gov.uk/government/uploads/system/uploads/attachment_data/file/300293/JRA_DoH_Guidance_on_RP_web_accessible.pdf

Wardale, S., Davis, F., & Dalton, C. (2014). Positive behavioural support training in a secure forensic setting: The impact on staff knowledge and positive behavioural support plan quality. *International Journal of Positive Behavioural Support,* 4(2), 9–13.

Washington, F., Bull, S., & Woodrow, C. (2019). The transforming care agenda: Admissions and discharges in two English learning disability assessment and treatment units. *Tizard Learning Disability Review,* 24(1), 24–32. https://doi.org/10.1108/TLDR-04-2018-0012

Wong, Y. L., Bhutia, R., Tayar, K., & Roy, A. (2015). A five decade retrospective review of admission trends in a NHS intellectual disability hospital. *Advances in Mental Health and Intellectual Disabilities,* 9(3), 108–115. https://doi.org/10.1108/AMHID-07-2014-0030

Woodbury-Smith, M., & Dein, K. (2014). Autism spectrum disorder (ASD) and unlawful behaviour: where do we go from here? *Journal of Autism and Developmental Disorders,* 44(11), 2734–2741. doi: 10.1007/s10803-014-2216-5

Offence focused interventions for autistic people

8

Clare Melvin and
Glynis H. Murphy

Introduction

Individuals with autism can commit illegal behaviours, just like anyone else, and so they may also require interventions for offending behaviour. The human rights and advocacy movements, including social role valorisation, have given individuals with intellectual and developmental disabilities a voice, but those who break the law are subject to the same due process of the Criminal Justice System as others without disabilities. However, a general shift away from punishment only (i.e. prison), and simple 'removal' from society (i.e., institutionalisation), has resulted in many countries responding to crimes by people with disabilities with therapeutic treatment, or interventions for offending behaviour, instead of or alongside incarceration (Ward & Maruna, 2007).

Interventions for offending behaviours

Interventions for offending behaviours have a relatively short history, beginning mainly in the 1970s. The first models for treating sexual offending applied behavioural techniques, with these methods dominating until the 1980s. The principles of social learning theory (Bandura 1977) and adaptations of work by Pavlov (1927) and Skinner (1953) were used to administer both overt and covert conditioning techniques (e.g., electrical aversion therapy and orgasmic reconditioning) for sexual offending.

A cultural shift in the West during the 1980s reoriented justice systems towards 'treatment' over punishment, with cognitive psychology beginning to inform rehabilitation methods. As a result, treatment programmes broadened beyond reconditioning and extinction, to include increasing victim empathy, reducing cognitive distortions and developing pro-social skills. The recognition of these wider issues led to a paradigm shift, resulting in the development of the first cognitive behavioural therapy (CBT) programmes for the treatment

DOI: 10.4324/9781003036722-10

of sexual offending (Marshall & Williams, 1975; Abel et al., 1978, Laws & Marshall, 2003, Marshall & Laws, 2003).

Rehabilitation concepts of *Risk*, *Need* and *Responsivity* feature heavily in traditional offending treatment programmes (Bonta & Andrews, 1988; Andrews & Bonta, 2010). The Risk-Need-Responsivity model (RNR) incorporates assessment of: (i) potential harm an individual poses to society through re-offending (*risk*), (ii) dynamic risk factors or criminogenic needs (*need*) and (iii) engagement or accessibility to treatment (*responsivity*). So, for example, an individual with an increased risk of re-offending would be recommended a higher intensity treatment than someone perceived to be low risk, tailored to (as far as is possible) their specific criminogenic needs. Responsivity concerns the individual in addition to therapist delivery and programme components (i.e., internal and external responsivity (Serin & Kennedy, 1997)). There is a great deal of empirical support for the principles within the RNR model, however, criticisms include: preoccupation with 'risk profiles' and disregarding social or contextual factors, as well as a passive approach to therapy and the use of avoidance goals to prevent offending (Ward & Maruna, 2007; Duwe & Kim, 2018).

Alternative approaches to the RNR model propose a strength-based treatment paradigm, incorporating personal growth and social development as well as risk management, e.g., the Good Lives Model (GLM) (Ward, 2002; Ward & Marshall, 2004). Such approaches suggest treatment should aim to improve quality of life and/or ability to lead a more fulfilling life – 'the good life', in addition to managing risk. The GLM incorporates positive psychology (Aspinwall & Staudinger, 2003; Csikszentmihalyi & Larson, 2014) and has shown promising results (Lindsay et al., 2007), with adaptations for offenders with intellectual or developmental disabilities, and children and young people (Ayland & West, 2006; Malovic et al., 2018).

Early on, there was considerable enthusiasm for CBT programmes for offenders without disabilities, such as the UK prison Sex Offender Treatment Programme (SOTP). Research suggested such programmes were effective (Hanson et al., 2002). More recent reviews and analyses, including carefully controlled research, has suggested that early studies may have over-estimated treatment effects. However, a very recent systematic review has shown that specialist psychological treatment still shows some effectiveness in reducing re-offending (Gannon et al., 2019).

Treatment was initially unavailable for individuals with intellectual disabilities and/or autism, and those deemed cognitively less able were also excluded from therapies. This was particularly true for prison programmes involving CBT, due to the level of cognitive functioning believed to be required to understand the cognitive model (Kroese et al., 1997; Vereenooghe & Langdon, 2013; Beail, 2017). Consequently, for many years, in the UK and USA, those with an IQ below 80 were excluded from prison intervention programmes (Marques et al., 1994; O'Connor, 1996). However, despite these early concerns, adapted programmes have successfully used CBT with offenders with mild to moderate intellectual disabilities since the 1990s for a range of offending behaviours (Clare et al., 1992; Taylor, 2002; Langdon et al., 2013; Taylor et al., 2016); with an adapted prison sex offender programme also developed for those with cognitive challenges (Williams et al., 2007, Williams & Mann, 2010), following the establishment of the Core Programme (Mann & Thornton, 1998).

It may be that the recognition of the need for interventions for those with disabilities, in prisons, and in mental health and community-based services, only became obvious after the closure of institutions. As such, legislation and social policy, in predominantly Western cultures, has evolved to recognise the presence and rehabilitation/treatment needs of offenders with intellectual disabilities. For example, New Zealand's Criminal Procedure (Mentally Impaired Persons) Act 2003, and Intellectual Disability (Compulsory Care and Rehabilitation) Act 2003; Western Australia's recently reviewed Criminal Law (Mentally Impaired Accused) Act 1996, and New South Wales' Diversionary Pathway in The Mental Health (Forensic Provisions) Act 1990. The development of Liaison and Diversion Services in the UK criminal justice system (following the Bradley report; Bradley, 2009), along with social policy and related legislation, such as The Care Act (2014), the NHSE's Building the Right Support (2015) and The Adult Autism Strategy (2010, 2018), has led to a widening of support individuals who offend with intellectual and developmental disabilities in the UK, to include the specific recognition of those with forensic needs, and highlighting those with a diagnosis of autism.

In addressing the demand for those with autism for offending behaviour programmes, there is of course a need to understand the incidence and prevalence rates of criminal behaviours in autism. Figures so far are variable; some literature suggests low occurrences, often lower than in the general population (Howlin, 2004), whilst others report increased rates particularly in specific populations, such as in forensic or mental health settings. See Chapter 4 for an overview of the literature on the prevalence rates of criminal behaviour in autistic people.

Not all individuals with autism who break the law are detained, of course (Lindsay et al., 2014). As such, offending behaviour programmes need to be provided across a variety of organisations and situations, including in the community, under probation services or through community mental health and/or forensic organisations, as well as within prison or inpatient settings (Lindsay & Smith 1998; Murphy, 2010a: Murphy et al., 2010; Langdon et al., 2013; Melvin et al., 2020). Changes to social policy and statutory guidance regarding individuals with autism in the mental health and criminal justice systems illustrate the widening recognition of this niche group of offenders and current attempts to meet their needs.

Current research on the treatment of offenders with autism

The evidence-base regarding best practice for the psychological treatment of individuals on the autistic spectrum with forensic and mental health needs is only just developing (Anderson & Morris, 2006; McConachie et al., 2014; Melvin et al., 2017; Melvin et al., 2019; Huntjens et al., 2020). Questions of efficacy and appropriateness have been raised specifically in relation to offence-focused treatment for those with autism, due to the nature of therapeutic objectives, and the cognitive and behavioural profile associated with the diagnosis. (Murphy, 2010a; Murphy, 2010b; Woodbury-Smith & Dein, 2014; Higgs & Carter, 2015). These include social naivety, cognitive rigidity, difficulties with empathy and communication difficulties (see Figure 8.1).

A handful of case studies constituted the early research on treatment for autistic people who have offended. Many of these focused on the influence of the clinical features or symptoms of autism on the offence committed, with few details regarding treatment. For example, Baron-Cohen (1988) and Mawson et al. (1985) each detailed a case study of violence in autistic young men. In addition to violence, other studies listed sexual offences and arson as prominent in autistic offenders (Siponmaa et al., 2001; Milton et al., 2002; Allen et al., 2008). However, these were individual case reports with no comparative data for non-autistic offenders or autistic non-offenders. Furthermore, since these initial case studies, autistic offenders have been shown to commit a wide variety of offence types, including impersonal threats ('bomb scares') (Faccini & Allely, 2016), theft (Kohn et al., 1998) and firearms offences (Langdon et al., 2013), with little rigorous evidence supporting an especial proclivity for sexual offending or firesetting (King & Murphy, 2014). As such, offending behaviour treatment for autistic individuals needs to cover the whole range of crimes.

Commonly, offending behaviour programmes utilise a cognitive behavioural approach – both for standard programmes and those adapted for individuals with intellectual disabilities. The appropriateness of CBT for individuals with autism has been debated, due to challenges with emotion recognition and expression, including alexithymia, reduced central coherence, difficulties with theory of mind and perspective taking, and within the field of offending, issues with empathy and inflexible thinking styles around offending behaviours (Murphy, 2010b; Woodbury-Smith, 2014; Melvin et al., 2020). Such challenges can manifest as the influence and impact of autism on offending and treatment as depicted in Figure 8.1.

The efficacy of CBT for individuals with autism has been explored within non-forensic populations to positive effect (Attwood, 2004; McConachie et al., 2014, Kilburn et al., 2020). For example, self-reported positive outcomes were

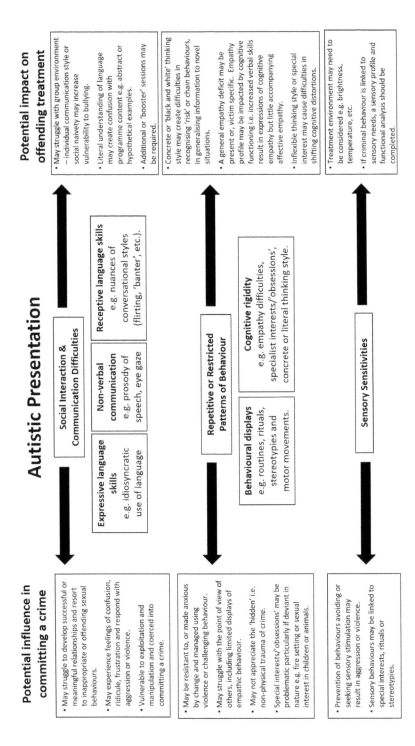

Figure 8.1 Overview of autistic presentation and potential influences on offending and treatment

found in social anxiety following group CBT for autistic individuals (Spain et al., 2017). Further work by Spain and Happé (2019) identified that individuals with autism can benefit from CBT for the treatment of mental health conditions, however, adaptations and flexibility in approach and delivery are essential for autistic individuals.

There do appear to be some difficulties or 'barriers' to achieving positive treatment outcomes, related to the autism diagnosis for offending populations (Figure 8.1), with a number of authors suggesting the need for adaptations such as individual delivery of therapy, psychoeducation, the provision of supplementary or 'booster' sessions and stronger reliance on external management strategies (Higgs & Carter, 2015).

Murphy (2010b) highlighted the treatment challenges faced by a young autistic man and his care team in a high-secure inpatient unit, and Melvin et al. (2020) gathered clinician views regarding the extra challenges encountered in the use of adapted treatment programmes for sexual offending for individuals with autism. Both researchers reported challenges in addressing cognitive distortions and reported that despite extensive psychological input (either in terms of hours or multiple therapists), minimal shift in attitudes relating to offending behaviours was noted. While cognitive aspects of victim empathy, i.e., 'putting themselves in someone else's shoes', were displayed by men with intellectual and developmental disabilities in the Murphy and Melvin papers, the emotional resonance associated with affective empathy tended to be absent in the autistic offenders receiving treatment. Some of the clinicians interviewed in Melvin et al. (2020) suggested fewer displays of emotionally empathic behaviour in those with autism than in sexual offenders with intellectual disabilities alone. However, they did note different aspects of empathy displayed by offenders with autism, i.e., victim and general empathy, and cognitive and affective empathy. For example, there were reports of some empathy displayed towards individuals other than the victims, e.g., sex offenders such as Rolf Harris. These 'empathic abilities' or displays perhaps suggest cognitive distortions around their behaviour towards the victim rather than necessarily a global or pure empathy deficit, and this can also be seen in non-autistic offenders (Marshall et al., 2001; Ward et al., 2006).

The role of empathy (or its absence) in sexual offending is complex. For instance, debates surrounding victim empathy deficits being a form of cognitive distortion, and whether cognitive and affective empathy are separate constructs, are not fully resolved (Marshall et al., 2001; Shalev & Uzefovsky, 2020); nor is the question of empathy itself a protective factor against re-offending (Mann & Barnett, 2013). For sexual offenders with autism, the situation is further complicated by whether any apparent lack of regard or concern for others is due to anti-social tendencies, autistic difficulties, or an interaction of the two.

Despite the concerns of some researchers that autistic people would be unresponsive to offence-focused treatment, a recent systematic review of offender treatment for autistic individuals found variable results regarding responsivity to treatment in autistic offenders (Melvin et al., 2017). Studies identified in the review included a range of treatment approaches for adults and adolescents (predominantly CBT, but also cognitive analytical therapy (CAT), family therapy, and psychopharmacology), for a variety of offences from theft and aggression to sexual offences, firearms offences and manslaughter (Murphy, 2010a; Murphy et al., 2010; Kelbrick & Radley, 2013; Melvin et al., 2020; Murphy & Melvin, 2020). The level of detail regarding treatment approach and responsivity varied within the studies and, for the most part, they were delivered alongside other treatment approaches, and many had undergone multiple 'rounds' of therapy and utilised more than one technique, e.g., CBT and CAT (Kelbrick & Radley, 2013). There was also variability within the findings, with some reporting positive outcomes from a treatment approach, whilst others did not. For example, some case studies refer to the use of medication for offending behaviours (as opposed to for mental health issues, e.g., psychosis or anxiety) to supplement behavioural or psychological treatments, with Kohn et al. (1998) demonstrating a reduction in offending behaviours, and Milton et al. (2002) not. Additionally, Murphy (2010b) utilised CBT, reporting 'minimal effect', whereas CBT was included where treatment had been deemed 'successful' (Kelbrick & Radley, 2013). However, all case studies within the review identified the need for changes or adaptations to therapy for offenders with autism. A later systematic review, this time on adolescent sex offenders with autism, echoed similar findings to Melvin et al.'s (2017) review (Schnitzer et al., 2020). Schnitzer et al. (2020) included three new papers and three studies from the Melvin et al. systematic review, reporting similar inconsistency in positive treatment outcomes for the nine adolescents with autism identified who displayed harmful sexual behaviours. A lack of robust methodology and controlled studies limits the generalisability of treatment outcomes regarding offenders with autism in the published literature.

Despite the lack of robust research, a number of suggestions have been made with regards to working with offenders with autism. These include adaptations that are also beneficial to those with intellectual disabilities, such as shorter sessions, less information per session, use of visual aids and increased repetition of material, in addition to those specific for individuals with autism (Figure 8.1). Autism specific suggestions have included use of concrete examples rather than abstract scenarios, i.e.,

- focusing on legal and illegal behaviours; the nuances of 'risky' or grey areas may be too complex;
- focusing on consequences for 'self' of offending/re-offending rather than consequences for others;

- establishing common language, i.e. awareness of any idiosyncratic communication style or pronoun use;
- continued use of relapse prevention strategies and reminding of the importance of 'staying within the law' ('maintenance' groups can be beneficial here), in addition to external management or support, e.g. enhanced observations, escorts in the community;
- awareness of any sensory needs or sensitivities – both in relation to treatment responsivity and the offending behaviour itself.

(Higgs & Carter, 2015; Melvin et al., 2019; Melvin et al., 2020; Murphy & Melvin, 2020)

Interestingly, few researchers have asked autistic offenders themselves about their views of offending and treatment (e.g., Melvin et al., 2019; Payne et al., 2020). Melvin et al. (2019) interviewed autistic men who had undergone CBT sex offender treatment groups (mainly in health settings) about what they thought they had gained, if anything, from the treatment. Their responses illustrated how important it is to ask service users their views. The men saw the groups as helpful, on the whole, but largely in terms of their achievement of 'social goods', in line with the Good Lives model (Ward, 2002; Ward & Marshall, 2004). They made little or no mention of possible gains in empathy or cognitive distortions, unlike their clinicians (Melvin et al., 2020).

What research does not yet address is whether CBT, or any other form of treatment, makes a real difference to autistic people who have engaged in criminal behaviour, over and above 'treatment as usual'. There are no controlled trials, nor are there any randomised controlled trials as yet in this field. There is a definite need for such 'gold standard' research to be conducted.

Conclusion

Despite a lack of clarity in the evidence-base, adapted and individualised programmes for offenders with autism appear to offer some benefits for autistic individuals. However, whether these programmes are more appropriate than standard (non-adapted) programmes or the alternative of no treatment at all cannot be said to be proven. There is a real need for more rigorous research, comparing adapted programmes to 'treatment as usual', using randomised controlled trials.

References

Abel, G. G., Blanchard, E. B., & Becker, J. V. (1978). An integrated treatment program for rapists. In R. Rada (Ed.), *Clinical aspects of the rapist* (pp.161–214). New York: Grune & Stratton.

Allen, D., Evans, C., Hider, A., Hawkins, S., Peckett, H., & Morgan, H. (2008). Offending behaviour in adults with Asperger syndrome. *Journal of Autism and Developmental Disorders, 38*, 748–758. doi: 10.1007/s10803-007-0442-9

Anderson, S., & Morris, J. (2006). Cognitive behaviour therapy for people with Asperger syndrome. *Behavioural and Cognitive Psychotherapy, 34*(3), 293–303. doi: 10.1017/S1352465805002651

Andrews, D. A., & Bonta, J. (2010). *The psychology of criminal conduct.* Albany, NY: Lexis Nexis/Anderson Pub.

Aspinwall, L. G., & Staudinger, U. M. (2003). *A psychology of human strengths: Fundamental questions and future directions for a positive psychology.* American Psychological Association.

Attwood, T. (2004). Cognitive behaviour therapy for children and adults with Asperger's syndrome. *Behaviour Change, 21*(3), 147–161. doi: 10.1375/bech.21.3.147.55995

Ayland, L., & West, B. (2006). The Good Way model: A strengths-based approach for working with young people, especially those with intellectual difficulties, who have sexually abusive behaviour. *Journal of Sexual Aggression, 12*(2), 189–201. doi: 10.1080/13552600600841680

Bandura, A. (1977). Self-efficacy: Toward a unifying theory of behavioral change. *Psychological Review, 84*(2), 191–215. doi: 10.1037/0033-295X.84.2.191

Baron-Cohen, S. (1988). An assessment of violence in a young man with Asperger's syndrome. *Journal of Child Psychology and Psychiatry, 29*(3), 351–360. doi: 10.1111/j.1469-7610.1988.tb00723.x.

Beail, N. (2017). Psychological therapies and people who have ID: A report from the Royal College of Psychiatrists and British Psychological Society. *Advances in Mental Health and Intellectual Disabilities, 11*(1), 24–26. doi: 10.1108/AMHID-09-2016-0021

Bonta, J., & Andrews, D. A. (1988). *The psychology of criminal conduct.* Routledge.

Bradley, K. J. C. B. (2009). *The Bradley Report: Lord Bradley's review of people with mental health problems or learning disabilities in the criminal justice system*, Department of Health London. Retrieved from: https://webarchive.nationalarchives.gov.uk/ukgwa/20130123195930/http://www.dh.gov.uk/en/Publicationsandstatistics/Publications/PublicationsPolicyAndGuidance/DH_098694

Clare, I. C., Murphy, G. H., Cox, D., & Chaplin, E. (1992). Assessment and treatment of fire-setting: A single-case investigation using a cognitive-behavioural model. *Criminal Behaviour and Mental Health, 2*(3), 253–268. doi: 10.1002/cbm.1992.2.3.253

Csikszentmihalyi, M., & Larson, R. (2014). *Flow and the foundations of positive psychology. Toward a psychology of optimal experience* (pp.209–226). New York, London: Springer.

Dein, K., & Woodbury-Smith, M. (2010). Asperger syndrome and criminal behaviour. *Advances in Psychiatric Treatment, 16*(1), 37–43. doi:10.1192/apt.bp.107.005082

Duwe, G., & Kim, K. (2018). The neglected "R" in the Risk-Needs-Responsivity Model: A new approach for assessing responsivity to correctional interventions. *Justice Evaluation Journal, 1*(2), 130–150. doi: 10.1080/24751979.2018.1502622

Faccini, L., & Allely, C. S. (2016). Mass violence in individuals with Autism Spectrum Disorder and Narcissistic Personality Disorder: A case analysis of Anders Breivik using the "Path to Intended and Terroristic Violence" model. *Aggression & Violent Behavior, 31*, 229–236. doi: 10.1016/j.avb.2016.10.002

Gannon, T. A., Olver, M. E., Mallion, J. S., & James, M. (2019). Does specialized psychological treatment for offending reduce recidivism? A meta-analysis examining staff and program variables as predictors of treatment effectiveness. *Clinical Psychology Review, 73*, 101752. doi: 10.1016/j.cpr.2019.101752

Hanson, R. K., Gordon, A., Harris, A. J., Marques, J. K., Murphy, W., Quinsey, V. L., & Seto, M. C. (2002). First report of the collaborative outcome data project on the effectiveness of psychological treatment for sex offenders. *Sexual Abuse: A Journal of Research and Treatment*, 14(2), 169–194. doi: 10.1177/107906320201400207

Higgs, T., & Carter, A. J. (2015). Autism spectrum disorder and sexual offending: Responsivity in forensic interventions. *Aggression and Violent Behavior*, 22, 112–119. doi: 10.1016/j. avb.2015.04.003

Howlin, P. (2004). *Autism and Asperger syndrome: Preparing for adulthood*. Abingdon, Oxon: Routledge.

Huntjens, A., van den Bosch, L. M. C. W., Sizoo, B., Kerkhof, A., Huibers, M. J. H., & van der Gaag, M. (2020). The effect of dialectical behaviour therapy in autism spectrum patients with suicidality and/or self-destructive behaviour (DIASS): Study protocol for a multicentre randomised controlled trial. *BMC Psychiatry*, 20(1), 127. doi: 10.1186/s12888-020-02531-1

Kelbrick, M., & Radley, J. (2013). Forensic rehabilitation in Asperger syndrome: A case report. *Journal of Intellectual Disability and Offending Behaviour*, 4(1), 60–64. doi: 10.1108/JIDOB-03-2013-0007

Kilburn, T. R., Sørensen, M. J., Thastum, M., Rapee, R. M., Rask, C. U., Arendt, K. B., Carlsen, A. H., & Thomsen, P. H. (2020). Group based cognitive behavioural therapy for anxiety in children with autism spectrum disorder: A randomised controlled trial in a general child psychiatric hospital setting. *Journal of Autism and Developmental Disorders*, 1–14. doi: 10.1007/s10803-020-04471-x

King, C., & Murphy, G. H. (2014). A systematic review of people with autism spectrum disorder and the criminal justice system. *Journal of Autism and Developmental Disorders*, 44(11), 2717–2733. DOI 10.1007/s10803-014-2046-5

Kohn, Y., Fahum, T., Ratzoni, G., & Apter, A. (1998). Aggression and sexual offense in Asperger's syndrome. *Israel Journal of Psychiatry and Related Sciences*, 35(4), 293–299. PMID: 9988987

Kroese, B. S., Dagnan, D., & Loumidis, K. (1997). *Cognitive-behaviour therapy for people with learning disabilities*. London: Routledge.

Langdon, P. E., Murphy, G. H., Clare, I. C. H., Palmer, E. J., & Rees, J. (2013). An evaluation of the EQUIP treatment programme with men who have intellectual or other developmental disabilities. *Journal of Applied Research in Intellectual Disabilities*, 26(2), 167–180. doi: 10.1111/jar.12004.

Laws, D. R., & Marshall, W. L. (2003). A brief history of behavioral and cognitive behavioral approaches to sexual offenders: Part 1. Early developments. *Sexual Abuse: A Journal of Research and Treatment*, 15(2), 75–92. doi: 10.1177/107906320301500201

Lindsay, W. R., & Smith, A. H. W. (1998). Responses to treatment for sex offenders with intellectual disability: A comparison of men with 1- and 2-year probation sentences. *Journal of Intellectual Disability Research*, 42(5), 346–353. doi: 10.1046/j.1365-2788.1998.00147.x

Lindsay, W. R., Carson, D., O'Brien, G., Holland, A. J., Taylor, J. L., Wheeler, J. R., & Steptoe, L. (2014). A comparison of referrals with and without autism spectrum disorder to forensic intellectual disability services. *Psychiatry, Psychology & Law*, 21(6), 947–954. doi: 10.1080/13218719.2014.918081

Lindsay, W. R., Ward, T., Morgan, T., & Wilson, I. (2007). Self-regulation of sex offending, future pathways and the Good Lives Model: Applications and problems. *Journal of Sexual Aggression*, 13(1), 37–50. doi: 10.1080/13552600701365613

Malovic, A., Rossiter, R., & Murphy, G. H. (2018). Keep safe: The development of a manualised group CBT intervention for adolescents with ID who display harmful sexual behaviours. *Journal of Intellectual Disabilities and Offending Behaviour*, 9(1), 49–58. doi: 10.1108/JIDOB-10-2017-0023

Mann, R. E., & Barnett, G. D. (2013). Victim empathy intervention with sexual offenders: Rehabilitation, punishment, or correctional quackery? *Sexual Abuse: Journal of Research and Treatment*, 25(3), 282–301. doi: 10.1177/1079063212455669.

Mann, R. E., & Thornton, D. (1998). The evolution of a multisite sexual offender treatment program. In W. L. Marshall, Y. M. Fernandez, S. M. Hudson, & T. Ward (Eds.), *Sourcebook of treatment programs for sexual offenders* (pp.47–57). New York and London: Plenum Press.

Marques, J. K., Day, D. M., Nelson, C., & West, M. A. (1994). Effects of cognitive-behavioral treatment on sex offender recidivism: Preliminary results of a longitudinal study. *Criminal Justice and Behavior*, 21(1), 28–54. doi: 10.1177/0093854894021001004

Marshall, W. L., & Laws, D. R. (2003). A brief history of behavioral and cognitive behavioral approaches to sexual offender treatment: Part 2. The modern era. *Sexual Abuse: A Journal of Research and Treatment*, 15(2), 93–120. doi: 10.1177/107906320301500202

Marshall, W., & Williams, S. (1975). A behavioral approach to the modification of rape. *Behavioural and Cognitive Psychotherapy*, 3(4), 78–78. doi: 10.1017/S2041348300004663

Marshall, W. L., Hamilton, K., & Fernandez, Y. (2001). Empathy deficits and cognitive distortions in child molesters. *Sexual Abuse: A Journal of Research and Treatment*, 13(2), 123–130. doi: 10.1177/107906320101300205.

Mawson, D. C., Grounds, A., & Tantam, D. (1985). Violence and Asperger's syndrome: A case study. *The British Journal of Psychiatry*, 147(5), 566–569. doi: 10.1192/bjp.147.5.566

McConachie, H., McLaughlin, E., Grahame, V., Taylor, H., Honey, E., Tavernor, L., Rodgers, J., Freeston, M., Hemm, C., Steen, N., & Le Couteur, A. (2014). Group therapy for anxiety in children with autism spectrum disorder. *Autism*, 18(6), 723–732. doi: 10.1177/1362361313488839.

Melvin, C. L., Langdon, P. E., & Murphy, G. H. (2017). Treatment effectiveness for offenders with autism spectrum conditions: A systematic review. *Psychology, Crime & Law*, 23(8), 748–776. doi: 10.1080/1068316X.2017.1324027

Melvin, C. L., Langdon, P. E., & Murphy, G. H. (2019). "I feel that if I didn't come to it anymore, maybe I would go back to my old ways and I don't want that to happen": Adapted sex offender treatment programmes: Views of service users with autism spectrum disorders. *Journal of Applied Research in Intellectual Disabilities*, 33(4), 739–756. doi: 10.1111/jar.12641

Melvin, C. L., Langdon, P. E., & Murphy, G. H. (2020). "They're the hardest group to treat, that changes the least". Adapted sex offender treatment programmes for individuals with Autism Spectrum Disorders: Clinician views and experiences. *Research in developmental disabilities*, 105, 103721. doi: 10.1016/j.ridd.2020.103721

Milton, J., Duggan, C., Latham, A., Egan, V., & Tantam, D. (2002). Case history of co-morbid Asperger's syndrome and paraphilic behaviour. *Medicine Science and the Law*, 42(3), 237–244. doi: 10.1177/002580240204200308

Murphy, D. (2010a). Extreme violence in a man with an autistic spectrum disorder: Assessment and treatment within high-security psychiatric care. *Journal of Forensic Psychiatry & Psychology*, 21(3), 462–477. doi: 10.1080/14789940903426885

Murphy, D. (2010b). Understanding offenders with autism-spectrum disorders: What can forensic services do? *Advances in Psychiatric Treatment*, 16(1), 44–46. doi: 10.1192/apt.bp.109.006775

Murphy, G., & Melvin, C. (2020). Cognitive behavioural therapy for sexual offenders with autism spectrum disorders: A case study. In G. Murphy & C. Melving, *Cases on teaching sexuality education to individuals with autism* (pp.164–182). Hershey, PA: IGI Global.

Murphy, G. H., Sinclair, N., Hays, S.-J., Heaton, K., Powell, S., Langdon, P., S … & Craig, L. (2010). Effectiveness of group cognitive-behavioural treatment for men with intellectual disabilities at risk of sexual offending. *Journal of Applied Research in Intellectual Disabilities*, 23(6), 537–551. doi: 10.1111/j.1468-3148.2010.00560.x

O'Connor, W. (1996). A problem-solving intervention for sex offenders with an intellectual disability. *Journal of Intellectual and Developmental Disability*, 21(3), 219–235. doi: 10.1080/13668259600033151

Pavlov, I. P. (1927). *Conditioned reflexes: An investigation of the physiological activity of the cerebral cortex.* Oxford University Press.

Payne, K-L., Maras, K., Russell, A. J., & Brosnan, M. J. (2020). Self-reported motivations for offending by autistic sexual offenders. *Autism*, 24(2), 307–320. doi: 10.1177/1362361319858860

Schnitzer, G., Terry, R., & Joscelyne, T. (2020). Adolescent sex offenders with autism spectrum conditions: Currently used treatment approaches and their impact. *The Journal of Forensic Psychiatry & Psychology*, 31(1), 17–40. doi: 10.1080/14789949.2019.1659388

Serin, R. C., & Kennedy, S. (1997). *Treatment readiness and responsivity: Contributing to effective correctional programming.* Correctional Service Canada, Corporate Development, Research Branch.

Shalev, I., & Uzefovsky, F. (2020). Empathic disequilibrium in two different measures of empathy predicts autism traits in neurotypical population. *Molecular Autism*, 11(1), 1–13. doi: 10.1186/s13229-020-00362-1

Siponmaa, L., Kristiansson, M., Jonson, C., Nyden, A., & Gillberg, C. (2001). Juvenile and young adult mentally disordered offenders: The role of child neuropsychiatric disorders. *Journal of the American Academy of Psychiatry and the Law*, 29(4), 420–426. PMID: 11785613

Skinner, B. F. (1953). Some contributions of an experimental analysis of behavior to psychology as a whole. *American Psychologist*, 8(2), 69. doi: 10.1037/h0054118

Spain, D., Sin, J., Harwood, L., Mendez, M. A., & Happé, F. (2017). Cognitive behaviour therapy for social anxiety in autism spectrum disorder: A systematic review. *Advances in Autism*, 3(1), 34–46. doi: 10.1108/AIA-07-2016-0020

Spain, D., & Happé, F. (2019). How to optimise cognitive behaviour therapy (CBT) for people with autism spectrum disorders (ASD): A Delphi study. *Journal of Rational-Emotive & Cognitive-Behavior Therapy*, 38, 184–208. doi: 10.1007/s10942-019-00335-1

Taylor, J. L. (2002). A review of the assessment and treatment of anger and aggression in offenders with intellectual disability. *Journal of Intellectual Disability Research*, 46, 57–73. doi: 10.1046/j.1365-2788.2002.00005.x.

Taylor, J. L., Novaco, R. W., & Brown, T. (2016). Reductions in aggression and violence following cognitive behavioural anger treatment for detained patients with intellectual disabilities. *Journal of Intellectual Disability Research*, 60(2), 126–133. doi: 10.1111/jir.12220.

Vereenooghe, L., & Langdon, P. E. (2013). Psychological therapies for people with intellectual disabilities: A systematic review and meta-analysis. *Research in Developmental Disabilities*, 34(11), 4085–4102. doi: 10.1016/j.ridd.2013.08.030.

Ward, T. (2002). The management of risk and the design of good lives. *Australian Psychologist*, 37(3), 172–179. doi: 10.1080/00050060210001706846

Ward, T., & Marshall, W. L. (2004). Good lives, aetiology and the rehabilitation of sex offenders: A bridging theory. *Journal of Sexual Aggression*, 10(2), 153–169. doi: 10.1080/13552600412331290102

Ward, T., & Maruna, S. (2007). *Rehabilitation: Beyond the risk paradigm.* Abingdon, Oxon: Routledge.

Ward, T., Polaschek, D. L. L., & Beech, A. R. (2006). *Theories of sexual offending.* Wiley & Sons.

Williams, F., & Mann, R. E. (2010). The treatment of intellectually disabled sexual offenders in the National Offender Management Service: The Adapted Sex Offender Treatment Programmes. In L. A. Craig, W. R. Lindsay, & K. D. Browne (Eds.), *Assessment and treatment of sexual offenders with intellectual disabilities: A handbook* (pp.293–315). Wiley-Blackwell.

Williams, F., Wakeling, H., & Webster, S. (2007). A psychometric study of six self-report measures for use with sexual offenders with cognitive and social functioning deficits. *Psychology, Crime & Law*, 13(5), 505–522. doi: 10.1080/10683160601060739

Woodbury-Smith, M. (2014). Editorial: ASD and illegal behaviors. *Journal of Autism and Developmental Disorders*, 44(11), 2679–2681. doi: 10.1007/s10803-014-2237-0

Woodbury-Smith, M., & Dein, K (2014). Autism Spectrum Disorder (ASD) and unlawful behaviour: Where do we go from here? *Journal of Autism and Developmental Disorders*, 44(11), 2734–2741. doi: 10.1007/s10803-014-2216-5

Risk assessment with autistic people

9

David Murphy

What is a risk assessment?

Whilst individuals with autism represent a diverse and relatively small proportion of the offender population, they present with difficulties and needs different from other offender groups (Murphy, 2010a; Woodbury-Smith & Dein, 2014; Higgs & Carter, 2015). A fundamental part of the care of individuals with autism who have or are at risk of offending is the assessment, formulation and management of problematic behaviour; whether that be inappropriate sexual conduct, harassment, fire setting, acting on extremist beliefs or interpersonal violence. Risk refers to a hazard that is incompletely understood and whose occurrence can only be forecast with uncertainty. Risk is also multi-faceted; including the specific behaviour, frequency and seriousness, as well as the specific circumstances of an individual, their motivation and previous experiences. Whilst actual behaviours are important, the emphasis of risk assessments should be on developing a formulation of why an individual chose to engage in harmful behaviour, and identifying all factors that may have influenced that decision (Hart, 2001). A risk assessment should therefore make evidence based, informed, and transparent decisions to guide an individual's risk management.

Within the United Kingdom, best practice for managing risk is outlined in guidelines by the Department of Health (2007), as well as more broadly in the risk need responsivity (RNR) model of offender rehabilitation (Bonta & Andrews, 2017). Among the points highlighted, best practice involves making decisions based on knowledge of the research evidence, the individual service user and their social context, and the assessor's clinical judgement. Risk assessments following the Structured Clinical Judgement approach (SCJ) are also recommended. The SCJ approach integrates empirical evidence on risk factors for offending, and the use of specific risk assessment tools or guides to clinical judgement. The importance of identifying protective factors for reducing risk of re-offending has also been recognised (Serin et al., 2016). Whilst structured risk assessments are considered to result in better decision

DOI: 10.4324/9781003036722-11

making, there is a need to validate such tools with specific patient groups, such as individuals with autism (Royal College of Psychiatrists, 2008).

How useful are current structured risk assessment tools?

Although case descriptions of individuals with autism highlight the importance of considering associated difficulties in offence formulations (Murphy, 2010b; Staufenberg, 2007), research examining how formal risk assessment aids apply to such individuals is limited. Among the range of general and offence specific risk assessment tools available in contemporary practice, the HCR-20 (Webster et al., 1997), and updated HCR-20v3 (Douglas et al., 2013), is common across a range of secure and community settings, and widely researched (Singh et al., 2014). The 20 item HCR-20v3 identifies the issues in an individual's history, as well as presence and relevance of current dynamic issues and future risk management requirements, empirically linked to risk for interpersonal violence. The issues associated with the HCR-20v3 are also relevant to many other risk assessment tools and offence behaviours.

In a small study completed in one High Secure Psychiatric Care (HSPC) hospital (Murphy, 2013), the relevance of the HCR-20 items for 20 individuals with autism was examined. Whilst all admissions to HSPC present a 'grave and immediate' risk to others, it was possible to divide the sample into 'high' and 'low' violence groups using the Violence Rating Scale (Robertson et al., 1987). Individuals in the 'high' violence group included those with offences involving murder or severe injury (including rape). In contrast, individuals within the 'low' violence group included those with offences of assault or where there was no direct physical harm to victims. Whilst no group differences were present in the number of HCR-20 items endorsed, nine items were present in 50% or less of the whole sample, and a history of previous violence and vulnerability to future stress was present in all. No significant group differences were observed in full scale IQ or performance within the revised eyes task (a social perceptual theory of mind test) (Baron-Cohen et al., 2001). However, individuals within the 'high' violence group had lower verbal abilities (specifically in word knowledge and abstract verbal reasoning), perhaps highlighting the role of poor verbal communication skills in the aetiology of violence.

Whilst this analysis is useful for examining the relevance of some conventional risk items to individuals with autism, there was considerable case variation. For example, some individuals had histories of alcohol and illicit substance misuse, and/or psychosis. A major limitation of HCR-20 ratings, as well as other formal risk assessment aids, is the absence of an explanation of why someone may have particular difficulties. Thus, the underlying reason for a history of relationship instability will differ between someone with a personality disorder and someone with autism. Anecdotally, for many individuals, their HCR-20 profiles added very little to their offence formulations and case management. Using two other violence risk assessment aids – the HKT-R (similar to the HCR-20) and the Structured Assessment of Protective Factors for violence risk (SAPROF) – Dutch clinicians examining inpatients with autism displaying physical aggression drew similar conclusions (Bosch et al., 2020). Girardi et al. (2019) found that the HCR-20v3 could help predict risk judgements for physical aggression for individuals with autism in medium secure care, but not verbal aggression.

Role of psychopathy

Characterised by a collection of personality features and behaviour including callousness, lack of remorse and empathy deficits, research consistently finds a strong association between the presence of psychopathy and an increased risk of future offending (Hare et al., 2000). Although some authors (Fitzgerald, 2003) highlight similarities between some features of autism and some psychopathic traits (e.g., empathy difficulties), as well as differences (Bjørkly, 2009), research does not suggest that higher scores are more likely for individuals with autism on the Hare Psychopathy Checklist revised (PCL-R; Hare, 2003). Within HSPC a sample of 'high risk' individuals with autism were found to have PCL-R profiles lower than other patient groups although with elevated facet two scores, i.e., affective features including a lack of remorse or guilt, shallow affect, callousness/lack of empathy, and a failure to accept responsibility (Murphy, 2007). Other researchers (e.g., Rogers et al, 2006) have suggested the idea of a 'double hit' of difficulties for those who have both autism and psychopathy.

Clinical experience with individuals who have autism and psychopathic traits suggests that they are typically a difficult group to engage. Whilst the relationship is complex, 'extreme' empathy deficits, egocentricity and deliberate inconsistent answers to questions during interviews, in the context of relatively good verbal communication abilities, appear to be characteristic of these individuals (Murphy, 2018). Whilst an examination of psychopathy is important to consider in a risk assessment it is necessary to follow Hare's (2003) recommendation to 'exercise clinical judgement with the interpretation of psychopathic traits among individuals with unusual presentations'.

Autism issues relevant to risk assessment and management

If many of the risk items within conventional structured risk assessment tools do not add much to our understanding of risk for offending in someone with autism, what should we be assessing? Clinical experience, as well as a growing body of published case studies (Haskins & Silva, 2006; Murrie et al., 2002) and reviews (de la Cuesta, 2010), highlight a number of features associated with autism potentially increasing an individual's vulnerability towards such behaviour. These include difficulties with perspective taking and appreciating rather than necessarily recognising the views of others, central cohesion (difficulties with appreciating the whole context of a situation rather than irrelevant details) and difficulties with different dimensions of executive functioning (notably appreciating the consequences of one's actions and very literal interpretations). Cognitive dysfunction, combined with social naivety, may also be problematic for individuals vulnerable to exploitation and some forms of sexual offending (Payne et al., 2019), as might a failure to deal with sensory hypersensitivity or feelings of being overwhelmed by demands. For others, a combination of cognitive dysfunction with pursuing deviant preoccupations may be particularly problematic (Barry-Walsh & Mullen, 2004: Woodbury-Smith et al., 2010).

In some situations, the lack of internal central cohesion and presence of 'compartmentalising' characteristics may lead to the development of inner preoccupations and maladaptive fantasies (Silva et al., 2004), especially where an isolated individual may spend long periods of time online engaged in activities that reinforce fantasy ideas (Higham et al., 2016). Such factors may also increase an individual's vulnerabilities towards extremism (Von Behr et al., 2013). This was the finding in the case of Nicky Reilly, a young man convicted of attempting to bomb a restaurant (a failed suicide attack), but whose own vulnerabilities to preoccupations, social isolation and naivety were exacerbated by information found online and who was likely groomed by others linked to extremism ideology (BBC News, 2018). Clinical experience suggests that online information can be used to carry out an offence – e.g., identifying potential locations – and can contribute towards many offence types (Mesibov & Sreckovic, 2017). Any long-term risk management plan should therefore consider the means and legal framework by which internet use may be monitored.

Psychiatric co-morbidity and illicit substance misuse have also been identified as risk factors for violence among individuals with autism (Newman & Ghaziuddin, 2008; Långström et al., 2009). It has been suggested that individuals with autism may be particularly vulnerable to acting on delusions and hallucinations (e.g., Wachtel & Shorter, 2013: Frizzell et al., 2019). The presence of developmental disorders of anti-social behaviour has also been highlighted for a small number of offenders with autism (e.g., Woodbury-Smith et al., 2005), as well as past traumas (Im, 2016). Where co-morbid mental illness is suspected, as well as personality disorder, there may be interaction with the cognitive and affective difficulties associated with autism, perhaps further compromising cognitive capacity and decision making.

A less explored area of risk assessment is an individual's vulnerability towards developing dysfunctional coping strategies for dealing with feelings of resentment. Clinical experience suggests some individuals experience a profound alienation from other adults and develop maladaptive coping strategies for dealing with emotional regulation difficulties. Many individuals may also experience intense feelings of being mistreated, becoming hypersensitive to perceived criticism, perhaps leading to rumination and feelings of revenge (e.g., Murphy, 2010b). Such vulnerabilities for grudge bearing and resentment may also be seen in an individual's expression of anger. Murphy (2014) attempted to quantify the anger expression difficulties observed among individuals with autism detained in HSPC by examining their State Trait Anger Expression Inventory 2 (STAXI 2) profiles. The STAXI 2 (Speilberger, 1999) is a self-report measure designed to assess an individual's experience and expression of anger. For all individuals, the 'anger expression in' score (associated with the suppression of angry feelings rather than expressing them verbally or physically) was highest with the 'anger expression out' score the lowest. Additionally, anger expression difficulties presented differently in those with problematic preoccupations. Individuals with offending linked to revenge, or an obsession towards a particular person, appeared to have more problematic STAXI 2 profiles than those with offences that were more reactive and impulsive in nature, such as failures to deal with interpersonal conflict situations, or changes in their immediate environment. Although it remains to be established how typical these STAXI 2 profiles are within other autistic populations, it seems that a 'suppressed' anger style is common among those admitted to HSPC. Such individuals also appear to have more incidents involving interpersonal conflict with staff and other patients (Murphy et al., 2017). These findings also provide further evidence suggesting that, for some, emotional regulation issues (including perhaps a suppressed anger profile) are linked to interpersonal violence but not captured in formal risk measures. It has also been suggested that such anger profiles may relate to the underlying perseverative cognitive style present among many individuals with autism (Mazefsky et al., 2012).

In summary, individuals with autism can present with many associated vulnerability factors that in some situations can increase their risk towards offending. It is unlikely that any single factor is responsible. More likely, risk will be linked to a combination of difficulties within the context of the immediate environment and personal circumstances (see case example, Table 9.1).

Table 9.1 Case example of risk assessment, formulation and management[1]

Background	MB, aged 30 years with a history of early neglect and physical abuse, was admitted to HSPC from medium secure care following threats of violence to staff perceived as abusing his rights. MB's original index offence (the offence resulting in his conviction) involved sending an explosive device to a probation officer who he believed had wrongly portrayed him as a paedophile. No prior history of violence or law breaking present, and no history of alcohol or illicit substance misuse. Prior to admission, MB had never been assessed for autism. Previous diagnoses included anti-social personality disorder and psychosis (based on 'paranoid' ideas about probation services).
Assessment	Detailed exploration of presenting difficulties and history, including comprehensive neuropsychological assessment (focusing on thinking style), autism diagnostic assessment (following observations of intolerance to noise, need for predictability and preoccupations in everyday routines), as well as risk assessment using the HCR-20v3 and STAXI 2. Psychiatric assessment excluded psychosis. No evidence indicating psychopathy.
Formulation	The HCR-20v3 added little to the formulation of presenting difficulties and risk. These were framed in terms of MB's early experience of neglect and physical abuse, combined with thinking style characterised by making literal interpretations, perseverative errors, perspective-taking difficulties and focus on details, need for predictability, social isolation and low self-esteem. All contributed towards MB's core beliefs linked to a mistrust of authority, vulnerability towards making negative interpretations of others, justification for views and grudge bearing. The STAXI 2 highlighted a 'suppressed' anger style. Sensory sensitivities present but not considered relevant to risk.
Management	Psychoeducation exploring MB's experience and acceptance of autism. Adapted CBT to address thinking bias to form negative interpretations of others' actions, as well as suppressed anger style. A collaborative risk management plan encouraged development of protective factors including prosocial interests and opportunities to promote self-esteem through further education and work activities. The nursing team were also encouraged to adopt an autism-informed approach.
Outcome	Although reluctant to accept the autism diagnosis, it was possible to encourage MB to acknowledge this, to challenge his negative bias in thinking/grudge bearing and consider alternative perspectives. More adaptive ways of challenging perceived negative comments by others were developed including collaborative formulation of understanding risks for interpreting and acting on perceived wrongdoing, as well as developing protective factors including improved self-esteem through education, positive relationships, social inclusion and valued work activities. In combination, these interventions eventually led MB to move back to medium secure care and transfer to the community. Of particular significance was the shift in the multi-disciplinary team (MDT) formulation of MB's difficulties from a personality disorder driven view to an autism/trauma informed one.

Future of risk assessment with autism

To date, there are only a limited number of small-scale studies based on male samples from which to draw any guidance. Discussion with experienced clinicians suggests that current risk assessment aids used in isolation fail to capture the specific difficulties associated with autism which can increase an individual's vulnerability towards offending or problem behaviour. This is important as the literature and clinical experience suggests that typically it is a combination of difficulties associated with autism that has a significant influence on everyday functioning, often at key stages of an individual's life or in a particular set of social circumstances (de la Cuesta, 2010). For example, difficulties with egocentricity, social naivety, emotional regulation, pursuing a problem preoccupation and rumination, within the context of specific cognitive characteristics (such as rigidity in problem solving and a failure to think through consequences of actions) and sensory processing (often hypersensitivity towards a particular stimulus) have a profound impact on an individual's decision making and behaviour. Failure to include these difficulties in a risk assessment of an individual with autism is likely to result in an inadequate risk formulation and poor risk management plans. However, formal assessment of many difficulties such as cognitive functioning may be limited outside specialist services. In these situations, a simple checklist (Murphy, 2013; White et al., 2017) capturing relevant difficulties, even if based on an informed judgement, is useful (see Table 9.2). Most clinicians through sensitive questioning should be able to comment on an individual's egocentricity, difficulties with perspective taking and emotional regulation, vulnerability to rumination and grudge bearing, and problematic preoccupations. Where co-morbid psychiatric disorder and psychopathy are suspected, an informed judgement or opinion from an experienced colleague is required.

Future risk assessment research for individuals with autism should explore the application and adaptation of current risk tools. There is a need for greater understanding of the factors influencing the decision-making processes of individuals with autism, as well as 'protective' factors that might reduce vulnerability towards offending. Whilst we may have a good understanding of the difficulties associated with autism, it is likely that a different set of factors reduce an individual's vulnerability towards offending (Murphy, 2010a; Gunasekaran, 2012). Context is crucial and for some individuals, social inclusion helps protect against developing problem behaviours. For many individuals, making their immediate environment 'autism friendly' is important, and 'the crucial elements for appropriate care lie in carefully structuring the environment and the daily programme, and in training staff in the psychological strategies to be used' (Wing, 1997, p. 255).

Table 9.2 Checklist of autism difficulties to assess if potentially linked with an individual's offending

Difficulty	During interview
Communication difficulties	Ability to engage in reciprocal discussion, presence of verbal and non-verbal communication issues.
Sensory sensitivity – hyper or hypo sensitivity (such as to light, noise, touch, proximity of other people, etc.)	Establish any sensory avoidance or sensation seeking behaviours – consider using a questionnaire such as Adolescent and Adult Sensory Profile. Consider an individual's reaction to sensory overloads (meltdowns).
Emotional regulation difficulties	Identify any anger or emotion expression difficulties through interview and consider using self-report questionnaires such as STAXI, etc.
Preoccupations and interests	Identify presence and function of preoccupations and interests (positive, deviant or linked to offending).
Need for predictability and routines	Establish any need for predictability and routine in life, including potential role in offending and capacity to tolerate deviation from routines.
Social/interpersonal naivety	Explore potential for being easily led by others, as well as compliance.
Cognitive style (including theory of mind, perspective taking, literal thinking, central cohesion, etc.).	Assess difficulties with appreciating the perspectives of others, capacity to consider alternative solutions and interpretations of events/consequences. Consider neuropsychological assessment (including social cognition tasks such as revised eyes task, as well as non-social cognition tasks such as proverbs test and flexibility with strategy formation).
Co-occurring conditions	Identify and explore role of any other co-occurring conditions such as other neurodevelopmental conditions, personality dysfunction, psychopathy, mood disorders and psychosis (notably any delusional beliefs and hallucinations). Past traumas.

Early diagnosis and interventions may also reduce the likelihood of problem behaviours developing (Howlin, 2000), as might the appropriate management of co-morbid psychosis (Kelbrick & Radley, 2013). In contrast to the views of some authors (Westphal & Allely, 2019), it seems likely that given the diversity in individual circumstances, presenting difficulties and offending behaviours, no single risk assessment tool will capture all relevant factors. Instead, an individual risk formulation based on information obtained from appropriate structured risk assessment aids, supplemented by a comprehensive assessment of the features associated with autism, and an individual's personal circumstances, would seem the most robust method (Murphy, 2013; Shine & Cooper-Evans, 2016).

Where possible, assessments, formulations and subsequent management should be collaborative with the individual, include family members, be multi-disciplinary, and involve a multi-agency response. With regard to autism characteristics and co-morbidities, much remains to be established in identifying the predictors of positive therapeutic forensic outcomes, as well as the potential role of culture and ethnicity. In terms of the future of risk assessments with individuals who have autism, particularly within secure settings (where it might be difficult to replicate real life settings), and where there is a need to familiarise individuals with new environments or 'triggers' for risk, it is likely that new technologies including computer simulation (Wilk et al., 2009) and virtual reality will enhance the process (Benbouriche et al., 2014).

Note

1 All names and identifying information have been changed.

References

Baron-Cohen, S., Wheelwright, S., Hill, J., Raste, Y. & Plumb, I. (2001). The 'Reading the Mind in the Eyes' Test revised version: A study with normal adults and adults with Asperger's syndrome or high functioning autism. *Journal of Child Psychology and Psychiatry*, 42(2), 241–251.

Barry-Walsh, J. B. & Mullen, P. (2004). Forensic aspects of Asperger's syndrome. *The Journal of Forensic Psychiatry and Psychology*, 15(1), 96–107. https://doi.org/10.1080/147899403100 01638628

BBC News. (2018). Failed Exeter bomber Nicky Reilly was 'easy target for radicalisation'. Retrieved from: www.bbc.co.uk/news/uk-england-devon-46344833

Benbouriche, M., Nolet, K., Trottier, D. & Renaud, P. (2014). *Virtual reality applications in forensic psychiatry.* In Proceedings of the virtual reality international conference. Laval Virtual (VRIC' 14). 9–11 April 2014, Laval, France.

Bjørkly, S. (2009). Risk and dynamics of violence in Asperger's syndrome: A systematic review of the literature. *Aggression and Violent Behavior*, 14, 306–312. https://doi.org/10.1016/j.avb.2009.04.003

Bonta, J. & Andrews, D.A. (2017). The Risk-Need-Responsivity model of offender assessment and treatment. In *The Psychology of Criminal Conduct*. London and New York: Routledge Taylor & Francis Group.

Bosch, R., Chakhssi, F. & Hummelen, K. (2020). Inpatient aggression in forensic psychiatric patients with autism spectrum disorder: The role of risk and protective factors. *Journal of*

Intellectual Disabilities and Offending Behaviour, 11(2), 93–100. https://doi.org/10.1108/JIDOB-05-2019-0008

de la Cuesta, G. (2010). A selective review of offending behaviour in individuals with autism spectrum disorders. *Journal of Learning Disabilities and Offending Behaviour*, 1(2), 47–58. https://doi.org/10.5042/jldob.2010.0419

Department of Health. (2007). Best practise in managing risk: Principles and evidence for best practise in the assessment and management of risk to self and others in mental health services. Document prepared for the National Mental Health Risk Management Programme. Department of Health. Retrieved from: https://assets.publishing.service.gov.uk/government/uploads/system/uploads/attachment_data/file/478595/best-practice-managing-risk-cover-webtagged.pdf

Douglas, K. S., Hart, S. D., Webster, C. D. & Belfrage, H. (2013) *HCR-20^v3*. Mental Health, Law and Policy Institute. Simon Fraser University. Canada.

Fitzgerald, M. (2003). Callous/unemotional traits and Asperger's syndrome? *Journal of the American Academy of Child and Adolescent Psychiatry*, 42(9), 1011. https://doi.org/10.1192/bjp.191.3.265

Frizzell, W., Howard, L., Cameron Norris, H. & Chien, J. (2019). Homicidal ideation and individuals on the autism spectrum. *Journal of Forensic Sciences*, 64(4), 1259–1295. https://doi.org/10.1111/1556-4029.14002

Girardi, A., Hancock-Johnson, E., Thomas, C. & Wallang, P. (2019). Assessing the risk of inpatient violence in autism spectrum disorder. *Journal of American Academy of Psychiatry and Law*, 47(4), 427–436. https://doi.org/10.29158/JAAPL.003864-19

Gunasekaran, S. (2012). Assessment and management of risk in autism. *Advances in Mental Health and Intellectual Disabilities*, 6(6), 314–320. https://doi.org/10.1108/20441281211285964

Hare, R. (2003). *The Psychopathy Checklist revised*. Toronto, Ontario, Canada: Multi Health Systems.

Hare, R., Clark, D., Grann, M. & Thornton, D. (2000). Psychopathy and the predictive validity of the PCL-R: an international perspective. *Behavioural Science and the Law*, 18, 623–645. https://doi.org/10.1002/1099-0798(200010)18:5<623::aid-bsl409>3.0.co;2-w

Hart, S. (2001). Assessing and managing violence risk. In *HCR-20 Violence Risk Management Companion Guide*. Edited by Douglas, K., Webster, C., Hart, S., Eaves, D. & Ogloff, J. Canada: Mental Health Law and Policy Institute. Simon Fraser University.

Haskins, B. & Silva, A. (2006). Asperger's disorder and criminal behaviour: Forensic psychiatric considerations. *Journal of the American Academy of Psychiatry and Law*, 34(3), 374–384. PMID: 17032961

Higgs, T. & Carter, A. (2015). Autism spectrum disorders and sexual offending: Responsivity in forensic interventions. *Aggression & Violent Behavior*, 22, 112–119. https://doi.org/10.1016/j.avb.2015.04.003

Higham, L., Piracha, I. & Crocombe, J. (2016). Asperger syndrome, internet and fantasy versus reality – A forensic case study. *Advances in Mental Health and Intellectual Disabilities*, 10(6), 349–354. https://doi.org/10.1108/AMHID-07-2015-0034

Howlin, P. (2000). Outcome in adult life for more able individuals with autism or Asperger's syndrome. *Autism*, 4(1), 63–83. https://doi.org/10.1177/1362361300004001005

Im, D. (2016). Trauma as a contributor to violence in autism spectrum disorder. *The Journal of the American Academy of Psychiatry and Law*, 44(2), 184–192. PMID: 27236173

Kelbrick, M. & Radley, J. (2013). Forensic rehabilitation in Asperger syndrome: A case report. *Journal of Intellectual Disabilities and Offending Behaviour*, 4(1–2), 60–64. https://doi.org/10.1108/jidob.2013.55404aaa.001

Långström, N., Grann, M., Ruchkin, V., Sjöstedt, G. & Fazel, S. (2009). Risk factors for violent offending in autism spectrum disorder: A national study of hospitalised individuals. *Journal of Interpersonal Violence*, 24, 1358–1370. https://doi.org/10.1177/0886260508322195

Mazefsky, C., Pelphrey, K. & Dahl, R. (2012). The need for a broader approach to emotion regulation research in autism. *Child Development Perspectives*, 6(1), 92–97. https://doi.org/10.1111/j.1750-8606.2011.00229.x

Mesibov, G. & Sreckovic, M. (2017). Child and juvenile pornography and autism spectrum disorder. In *Caught in the Web of the Criminal Justice System: Autism, Developmental Disabilities and Sex Offences*. Edited by Dubin, L. & Horowwitz, E. London and Philadelphia: Jessica Kingsley Publishers.

Murphy, D. (2007). Hare Psychopathy Checklist Revised profiles of male patients with Asperger's syndrome detained in high security psychiatric care. *Journal of Forensic Psychiatry and Psychology*, 18(1), 120–126. https://doi.org/10.1080/14789940601014777

Murphy, D. (2010a). Understanding offenders with autism spectrum disorders: What can forensic services do? *Advances in Psychiatric Treatment*, 16, 44–46. https://doi.org/10.1192/apt.bp.109.006775

Murphy, D. (2010b). Extreme violence in a man with an autistic spectrum disorder: Assessment and treatment within high security psychiatric care. *Journal of Forensic Psychiatry and Psychology*, 21(3), 462–477. https://doi.org/10.1080/14789940903426885

Murphy, D. (2013). Risk assessment of offenders with an autism spectrum disorder. *Journal of Intellectual Disabilities and Offending Behaviour*, 4(2), 33–41. https://doi:org/10.1108/JIDOB-02-2013-0004

Murphy, D. (2014). Self-reported anger among individuals with an autism spectrum disorder detained in high security psychiatric care. *Journal of Forensic Psychiatry and Psychology*, 25(1), 100–112. https://doi.org/10.1080/14789949.2013.862291

Murphy, D. (2018). Interviewing individuals with an autism spectrum disorder in forensic settings. *International Journal of Forensic Mental Health*, 17(4), 310–320. https://doi.org/10.1080/14999013.2018.1518939

Murphy, D., Bush, E. & Puzzo, I. (2017). Incompatibilities and seclusions of patients with an autism spectrum disorder detained in high secure psychiatric care. *Journal of Intellectual Disabilities and Offending Behaviour: Practice, Policy and Research*, 8(4), 188–200. https://doi.org/10.1108/JIDOB-05-2017-0007

Murrie, D., Warren, J., Kristiansson, M. & Dietz, P. (2002). Asperger's syndrome in forensic settings. *International Journal of Forensic Mental Health*, 1(1), 59–70. https://doi.org/10.1080/14999013.2002.10471161

Newman, S. & Ghaziuddin, M. (2008). Violent crime in Asperger's syndrome: The role of psychiatric co-morbidity. *Journal of Autism and Developmental Disorders*, 38, 1848–1852. https://doi.org/10.1007/s10803-008-0580-8

Payne, K., Maras, K., Russell, A., & Brosnan, M. (2019). Self-reported motivations for offending by autistic offenders, *Autism*, 24(2), 307–320. https://doi.org/10.1177/1362361319858860

Robertson, G., Taylor, P. & Gunn, J. (1987). Does violence have cognitive correlates? *British Journal of Psychiatry*, 151, 63–68. https://doi.org/10.1192/bjp.151.1.63

Rogers, J., Viding, E., Blair, J., Frith, U. & Happé, F. (2006). Autism spectrum disorder and psychopathy: Shared cognitive underpinnings or double hit? *Psychological Medicine*, 36, 1789–1798. https://doi.org/10.1017/S0033291706008853

Royal College of Psychiatrists. (2008). *Rethinking risk to others in mental health services*. Final report of a scoping group. College report CR150. Royal College of Psychiatry, London.

Retrieved from: www.rcpsych.ac.uk/docs/default-source/improving-care/better-mh-policy/
college-reports/college-report-cr201.pdf?sfvrsn=2b83d227_2

Serin, R., Chadwick, N. & Lloyd, C. (2016). Dynamic risk and protective factors. *Psychology, Crime & Law*, 22(1–2), 151–170. https://doi.org/10.1080/1068316X.2015.1112013

Shine, J. & Cooper-Evans, S. (2016). Developing an autism specific framework for forensic case formulation. *Journal of Intellectual Disabilities and Offending Behaviour*, 7(3), 127–139. https://doi.org/10.1108/JIDOB-04-2015-0006

Silva, A., Ferrari, M. & Leong, G. (2004). The case of Jeffrey Dahmer: Sexual serial homicide from a neuropsychiatric developmental perspective. *Journal of Forensic Science*, 47, 1347–1359. PMID: 12455663

Singh, J., Fazel, S., Gueorguieva R. & Buchanan, A. (2014). Rates of violence in patients classified as high risk by structured risk assessment instruments. *British Journal of Psychiatry*, 204(3), 180–187. https://doi.org/10.1192/bjp.bp.113.131938

Speilberger, C. (1999). *State Trait Anger Expression Inventory 2*. Odessa, FL. Psychological Assessment Resources.

Staufenberg, E. (2007). Risk appraisal in developmental forensic neuropsychiatry: An introduction and guide to the existing knowledge and clinical practice basis. *Advances in Mental Health and Learning Disabilities*, 1(4), 33–43. https://doi.org/10.1108/17530180200700042.

Von Behr, I., Reding, A., Edwards, C. & Gribbon, L. (2013). *Radicalisation in the digital era: the use of the internet in 15 cases of terrorism and extremism*. RAND EUROPE. www.rand.org/content/dam/rand/pubs/research_reports/RR400/RR453/RAND_RR453.pdf

Wachtel, L. & Shorter, E. (2013). Autism plus psychosis: A 'one-two punch' risk for tragic violence? *Medical Hypotheses*, 81(3), 404–409. https://doi.org/10.1016/j.mehy.2013.05.032

Webster, C., Douglas, K., Eaves, D. & Hart, S. (1997). *HCR-20 version 2: assessing risk for violence*. Mental Health Law and Policy Institute. Simon Fraser University.

Westphal, A. & Allely, C. (2019). The need for a structured approach to violence risk assessment in autism. *Journal of American Academy of Psychiatry and Law*, 47(4), 437–439.

White, S., Meloy, J., Mohandie, K. & Kienlen, K. (2017). Autism spectrum disorder and violence: Threat assessment issues. *Journal of Threat Assessment and Management*, 4(3), 144–163. https://doi.org/10.1037/tam0000089

Wilk, L., Edelbring, S., Svensson, A., Karigren, K., Kristiansson, M. & Fors, U. (2009). A pilot for a computer based simulation system for risk estimation and treatment of mentally disordered offenders. *Information for Health and Social Care*, 34(2), 106–115. https://doi.org/10.1080/17538150903014395

Wing, L. (1997). Asperger's syndrome: management requires diagnosis. *The Journal of Forensic Psychiatry*, 8(2), 253–257. https://doi.org/10.1080/09585189708412008

Woodbury-Smith, M., Clare, I., Holland, A., Kearns, A., Staufenberg, E. & Watson, P. (2005). A case control study of offenders with high functioning autistic spectrum disorders. *The Journal of Forensic Psychiatry and Psychology*, 16(4), 747–763. https://doi.org/10.1080/14789940500302554

Woodbury-Smith, M., Clare, I., Holland, A., Watson, P., Bambrick, M., Kearns, A. & Staufenberg, E. (2010). Circumscribed interests and offenders with autism spectrum disorders: A case control study. *The Journal of Forensic Psychiatry and Psychology*, 21(3), 366–377. https://doi.org/10.1080/14789940903426877

Woodbury-Smith, M. & Dein, K. (2014). Autism Spectrum Disorders (ASD) and unlawful behaviour: Where do we go from here? *Journal of Autism and Developmental Disorders*, 44(11), 2734–2741. https://doi.org/10.1007/s10803-014-2216-5

Part III
Clinical issues

Strategies for supporting autistic people

10

*Sarah Cooper, Andy Inett,
Zoë Eastop and
Kirsty Taylor*

Introduction

Navigating the Criminal Justice System (CJS) and forensic mental health (FMH) settings can be particularly distressing for individuals with autism (Robertson & McGillivray, 2015). The social and physical environment is often incompatible with their needs (Allely, 2018; Murphy, Bush, & Puzzo, 2017), and the specific social communication and sensory difficulties can lead to maladaptive coping and poorer outcomes. These include difficulties with therapeutic engagement (Allely, 2018; Murphy, Bush, & Puzzo, 2017), inter-personal conflict, higher seclusion rates (Allely, 2018; Murphy, Bush, & Puzzo, 2017; Murphy & Allely, 2019) and longer hospital admissions (Haw et al., 2013; Bathgate, 2017). Assessing and understanding the unique challenges and needs for individuals with autism can lead to implementing a number of reasonable adjustments (Allely, 2018). A requirement to do so is set out in the *Autism Act* (2009) which brought about the first ever strategy for improving the lives of individuals with autism in England, with service providers legally obligated to work towards improved standards.

Using the five core principles set out in the SPELL framework (National Autistic Society, 2013b), this chapter highlights best practice approaches by using clinical examples to offer guidance on support strategies for both the person, and those supporting them in the following areas:

- Coping with change/transition;
- Communication;
- Support to engage with interventions;
- Managing anxiety;
- Decision making.

DOI: 10.4324/9781003036722-13

SPELL Principle 1: Structure

Problems with imagination can make unknown and unfamiliar environments particularly challenging. Offering structure, predictability and routine can help improve the experiences of individuals with autism (Murphy & Allely, 2019). Strategies could include:

- Visual prompts, diaries, timetables;
- Defining rules and boundaries, explaining their rationale;
- Avoiding sudden changes where possible;
- Having structured procedures for clinical meetings and daily routines (use tick lists), discuss format, attendees, aims in advance;
- Giving written/pictorial feedback on meeting outcomes;
- Using language used by the individual;
- Structuring breaks and planned endings, minimising waiting times;
- Consistency in support.

Coping with change/transition

Progressing to less restrictive environments represents positive change and progression (Morrissey et al., 2017). However, it can also be a time of significant uncertainty (Mezey et al., 2010) and the loss of a secure base (Mann et al., 2014). Individuals with autism may be more vulnerable to institutionalisation and require specific support to prepare for community reintegration (Moloney & Gulati, 2019). Whilst many aspects of forensic provision can be distressing for individuals with autism, the routine and familiarity can also be seen as a relief (National Autistic Society, 2007; Royal College of Psychiatrists, 2006). Transferring to an unfamiliar or inappropriate environment can cause significant distress and lead to the resurgence of offending behaviours (Wing, 1997).

Box 10.1   Case study 1

David struggled with transitions; previous transfers between secure unit wards led to upsurges in highly risky behaviours and ultimately to failed moves. When David was ready to transfer to a locked rehabilitation unit, a collaborative transition plan was developed to ensure that his treatment gains would not be lost. The plan included a timetabled

---

schedule of increasing time to the ward, with activities and names of supporting staff, and meetings with the wider multidisciplinary team (MDT). David attended a "moving on group" developed by the first author of this chapter. Drawing on principles from the recovery literature (Adshead et al., 2005; Drennan & Alred, 2012; Mann et al., 2014), Good Lives Model (Ward, 2002) and resources from Ingamells and Morrissey's (2014) skills-based intervention training, the programme aimed to facilitate a way to support transition. For David, the content was adapted to apply to his progression from low secure to locked rehab; he was supported to think about the changes he would encounter and to develop internal resources to cope with them. Feelings of loss and uncertainty were labelled and normalised and he was supported to think about what his life might be like in the rehab ward. New rules, reduced restrictions, increased autonomy and development of adaptive skills were considered. Motivated to succeed, David engaged well with the group and produced a moving on plan, helping him anticipate the challenges and what he and others could do to manage them. David managed a safe transition to the unit. A similar approach was used to support his successful transition to a community placement.

SPELL Principle 2: Positive approaches and expectations

Establish and reinforce self-confidence and self-esteem by building on natural strengths, interests and abilities. This may include:

- Assessment of needs, strengths, interests and abilities;
- Comprehensive assessments of communication needs;
- Opportunities for occupation and employment;
- Positive rather than negative instructions ("Try X" rather than "Don't do Y");
- Structured, graded exposure to new experiences;
- Goal setting and reward/incentive programmes;
- Positive Behaviour Support (PBS) plans.

Griffiths and Wilcox (2013) demonstrate positive outcomes of utilising PBS in a medium secure unit. Anecdotally, positive outcomes have been found in our low secure setting (Sarah Cooper and Andy Inett).

Box 10.2   Case study 2

David was extremely skilled in making costumes. This activity provided him immense satisfaction and an identity of which he was proud. David also had a history of violence, including using makeshift weapons. Costume and craft hobbies were a strong protective factor, but required access to contraband items including needles and scissors. A collaborative care plan was drawn up with David, allowing him supervised access to these items. Expectations were clearly stipulated and rules regarding their use were clearly defined. David worked with the care plan and continued to develop craft skills.

Communication

Speech, language and communication needs of people with autism must be identified and supported to enable progress through the CJS/FMH systems with positive outcomes. The Five Good Communication Standards (Royal College of Speech and Language Therapists, 2013) were developed as a resource to promote the use of reasonable adjustments for people with learning disabilities and/or autism in hospital or residential settings. Their application is increasing in a range of settings including CJS/FMH services (see Box 10.3).

Box 10.3   Good Communication Standards adapted from Royal College of Speech and Language Therapists

Standard 1: There will be a detailed description of how best to communicate with the individual.

Standard 2: Services demonstrate how they support individuals with communication needs to be involved with decisions about their care and their services.

Standard 3: Staff value and competently use the best approaches to communication with each individual they support.

Standard 4: Services create opportunities, relationships and environments that make individuals want to communicate.

Standard 5: Individuals are supported to understand and express their needs in relation to their health and wellbeing.

Considering how these apply to an individual's situation, in terms of their environment, opportunities and recovery, enables identification of strategies to enhance an individual's communication skills.

Box 10.4   Case study 3

Keith, with diagnoses of autism and schizophrenia, had difficulties retaining and using information relating to his care and treatment on an FMH ward. An autism profile was completed, using the passport to individual autism support (National Autistic Society, 2013a), enabling him and others to consider the many factors that affected all aspects of his daily living, including his recovery. Key areas of consideration included sensory integration differences and their impact on Keith's ability to engage with activities, as well as social communication and interaction difficulties. The following strategies were developed:

- Given his difficulties with understanding others' perceptions, Keith benefited from support to help structure his narratives to provide relevant and necessary information. A visual tool was developed to identify each key component of a narrative, including how the characters were feeling and the impact and consequences of the actions. It was also anticipated that developing his narrative skills would support his autobiographical memory (Nelson & Fivush, 2020). This enabled Keith to express a more accurate and detailed account of events and staff to better understand his reasoning for decisions and actions. Keith was able to work with the team to identify potential problems for future similar situations, and discuss possible actions to reduce or avoid a more challenging experience.
- Social Stories™ (Gray, 2004) were developed to support Keith to rehearse situations, resulting in better prediction of his level of anxiety.
- Tools from the Social Thinking Methodology (Crooke & Garcia Winner, 2020) were available to explore his reflection on using social communication skills. The team considered the kinds of questions and prompts used in clinical meetings to support Keith's ability to provide relevant and necessary information (Norris et al., 2020).
- Keith was supported to prepare for a Mental Health Tribunal to be held via videoconferencing. Key factors that might be distracting or challenging for Keith (Zolyomi et al., 2019) were listed for him to identify whether, based on his experience, he considered them a problem that would require reasonable adjustments to be made. This allowed consideration of his sen-

sory needs (e.g., brightness of the room and screen), and social communication and interaction needs, such as eye contact and turn taking.

- A written timetable was used to support him plan each day to include activities of daily living, appointments and leisure pursuits (TEACCH; Mesibov et al., 2004).

The Speech and Language Therapist (SaLT) offered informal training to staff to support their understanding of Keith's social communication needs and recommended strategies. Staff were also encouraged to complete "The Box" training (Royal College of Speech and Language Therapists, 2018), complementing their knowledge gained through experience and other autism training. Keith was able to use the recommended strategies with good effect, supporting his communication needs. Staff maintained their enthusiasm to support these needs, enabling increased collaboration to promote Keith's recovery.

Support to engage with interventions

The last decade has also seen specialised and adapted approaches to improve experiences and outcomes for individuals with autism (Murphy & Mullens, 2017; Allely, 2018). In the UK, guidance from the National Institute for Health and Care Excellence (2012) includes recommendations for adapting cognitive and behavioural interventions for individuals with autism. Recent studies offer practical advice on how to adapt Cognitive Behaviour Therapy (CBT)-based interventions (e.g., Kerns et al., 2016; Higgs & Carter, 2015). These principles can be applied to adapted CBT-offence-based interventions.

Some attendees with autism can experience specific difficulties during group work, including high levels of social anxiety and sensitivity to high noise levels within the environment. Social skills deficits can lead to group members perceiving others' behaviour as rude. Some group members may also focus on lengthy discussions of their specific interests, which can lead to frustration from others. Excessive focus on small details can also create difficulties if participants fixate on them and lose sight of the theme of discussion or activity.

Cognitive rigidity and avoidance of change in routine can underlie reluctance to accept relapse prevention strategies suggested by others to safely manage risky behaviour. Gradually building new routines and the use of social stories and new scripts for behavioural routines can help to facilitate change.

> **Box 10.5   Case study 4**
>
> Freddie, an 18-year-old with autism, had perseverative interests in Lego and superheroes, and sensory sensitivities around touch. He fiddled with putty during sexual offending treatment programme (SOTP) group sessions, enjoying the tactile sensation which was self-soothing, helping him to manage his anxiety. The group learnt to accept this. He also displayed high levels of social naivety and very limited knowledge and experience of sexual/intimate relationships. He was at risk of ridicule by other group members who had wider life experience and more neurotypical presentations. With boundary management by facilitators to prevent him from being targeted, the group gradually became more accepting of Freddie's differences. His interest in superheroes was incorporated in his relapse prevention plan, to use as a distraction fantasy for risky sexual thoughts.

Support outside of the intervention itself may be needed to practise and generalise strategies from the group session to everyday life. Support staff, family members or other carers may, with guidance from therapists, focus support in a number of areas:

- Prompting emotional regulation strategies to manage triggering situations, such as conflict with peers;
- Providing support to manage transitions or changes (e.g., last minute changes to plans because of the presence of risk triggers in the environment);
- Agreeing behavioural contracts, "scripts" or social stories for response when faced with risk behaviours or environments – reminding the person of the potential negative impact of their behaviour on others;
- Support with structuring activities and daily schedules.

Vulnerabilities of individuals with autism have been found to be reduced where information about their condition is shared with professionals (Allen et al., 2008). As part of the adapted EQUIP programme designed to address moral reasoning, distorted cognitions and social skills (Langdon et al., 2013), staff receive training on the CBT principles underlying the intervention, and the specific strategies used to help manage difficult situations. For example, EQUIP uses the concept of the "clown in the ring" to understand how more anti-social peers can attempt to involve the participant in conflict and risky behaviour. Individuals with autism may be socially isolated and more vulnerable to anti-social peer influence, seeking a sense of belonging and a peer group. Pictorial material showing a clown puppet attempting to use its strings to draw others into the ring is used, and the participant is encouraged to use imaginary scissors to "cut the strings" should this happen. This was successfully generalised, with staff and participants mimicking the action of cutting with scissors using their fingers on the ward when they noticed participants being the "clown" and attempting to draw others into the ring.

SPELL Principle 3: Empathy

Seeing and understanding the world from the perspective of someone with autism is critical to improving their experiences. Empathy and understanding can be developed through:

- Assessing what motivates or interests;
- Assessing what frightens, preoccupies and distresses;
- The quality of the relationship between the person and supporter;
- Proactive approach, anticipating difficult situations.

Personal attributes are of equal value to knowledge and understanding when supporting individuals with autism (National Institute for Health and Care Excellence, 2012; Peeteers & Jordan, 2010; Worthington, 2016). Studies have shown staff to lack understanding of how best to support individuals with autism (Misra et al., 2013; Murphy & McMorrow, 2015) and in correctional settings this has led to reduced empathy in staff (Shively, 2004). There is a need for autism training (MacDonald et al., 2017; Murphy & Allely, 2019), with emphasis on a values-based approach, creating a non-judgemental culture with understanding, flexibility and empathy (National Institute for Health and Care Excellence, 2012).

In our service (Sarah Cooper and Andy Inett), case vignettes, patient formulations, experiential exercises and reflective discussions were incorporated into an autism training package. An internal evaluation of the training showed improved knowledge and understanding. Staff were able to reflect on how they might apply their knowledge to support patients with autism, indicating an increased capacity for understanding and empathy, particularly when we consider Milton's (2012) conceptualisation of "double empathy". Positive outcomes have been captured in other awareness-based programmes, including those delivered to the police (Murphy, Kelleher & Gulati, 2017).

SPELL Principle 4: Low arousal

Calm, well-ordered environments aid concentration and reduce anxiety. Strategies to help limit arousal include:

- Sensory integration assessments;
- Minimal distractions;

- Additional time for individuals to process information and formulate responses;
- Present information in a sequential and concrete manner;
- Adjustments to ward design such as position of rooms;
- Identify strategies that relax the individual.

Anxiety

Individuals with autism are more vulnerable to developing symptoms of anxiety (Galanopoulos et al., 2014). Biological differences in brain structure and function (Herrington et al., 2017), increased risk of exposure to traumatic and stigmatising events (Weiss & Fardella, 2018), challenges arising from the "triad of impairments" (Wing, 1981), hidden sensory hypersensitivities (Bogdashina, 2003) and emotional regulation issues (Mazefsky et al., 2013) may exacerbate difficulties. Anxiety may be experienced at every step through the CJS/FMH systems. Individuals with autism may have difficulty in communicating these experiences (Davis et al., 2011; Nimmo-Smith et al., 2020); staff require awareness of the needs of individuals with autism to understand support strategies to reduce these difficulties.

Anxiety may manifest in various ways including problem behaviours, social avoidance, difficulties establishing and maintaining peer relationships and disruptions in family functioning (Nadeau et al., 2011), all impacting further on experiences during detention (Shively, 2004). Guidance for police and court personnel has been created by the National Autistic Society (2020), describing how arrest, interviewing and court processes may be experienced by someone with autism and ways to reduce distress levels (see Chapter 5).

Clinical experience and observation readily demonstrate that change and disruption to routine is frequently encountered in inpatient forensic settings. Attending clinical meetings may be a further source of anxiety. A UK high secure hospital study found that such experiences were sources of anxiety for individuals with autism (Murphy & Allely, 2019).

SPELL Principle 5: Links

Establish communication between all invested parties to facilitate an inclusive approach, with the individual with autism held at the centre:

- Engage the individual and wider support system in the therapeutic process;
- Create opportunities for community engagement and integration;
- Build and develop skills;

- Explore interests away from unhelpful/unlawful circumscribed interests;
- Discharge planning.

Decision making

In the UK, underpinned by the *Equality Act* (2010), the Department of Health (2010, 2014) has set out clear expectations that public services, including the NHS and CJS, make reasonable adjustments in meeting the needs of individuals with autism, facilitating increased choice and control over their lives.

Luke et al. (2011) highlight that individuals with autism may be more motivated by fear of failure than reward and emphasise logical consistency at the expense of integrating emotional information. Their study using questionnaires including the General Decision Making Style Inventory (GDMS) found that people with autism ($n = 38$) experienced greater difficulty with decision making – focussed on anxiety, exhaustion and a tendency to avoid decision making – than a matched neuro-typical group ($n = 40$). The social communication differences of those with autism are particularly relevant to assessments of the person's ability to make decisions about their treatment and care, especially when formal assessments of capacity (Department of Health, 2005) are required to provide the appropriate legal frameworks for supervision.

Box 10.6   Case study 5

James had diagnoses of autism and paranoid schizophrenia. James' paranoid beliefs included him feeling harassed, threatened and persecuted by others. These were further complicated by features of his autism, with difficulty reading others' intentions leading to paranoid misinterpretations. James was ready for discharge but felt safe in the hospital environment. Previous transitions between services had caused him significant anxiety, leading to a decline in his mental state and behaviours that sabotaged a move. A supported living placement had been identified. James was supported to visit the placement and had several meetings with the manager, offering him a more tangible way to develop an idea of what it would be like to live there. James was supported by familiar ward staff to reduce his anxiety in these meetings. Another meeting was supported by a parent, allowing James to hear the views and receive reassurances from important family members. At initial assessment of James' capacity to make the decision about where he should live, he was unable to consider or use the information about his support and lifestyle at the placement and therefore lacked capacity to make the decision. At the time of proposed transfer, James' mental state was additionally destabilised by external events beyond the control of James or the team. It was agreed that his capacity should be reassessed following a period of extended leave to the placement, initially with 24-hour support from familiar staff alongside the placement staff. It was anticipated that this would enable James to make a more tangible assessment of his own safety at the placement.

James quickly identified that he felt safe and did not need the planned extended period of intensive additional support; it was gradually withdrawn. At a further capacity assessment, James was able to understand, retain and weigh up the information needed to make the decision; he had regained capacity. This had important implications – e.g., he could hold keys to the front door. James was successfully discharged to the placement and continues to flourish there.

Box 10.7   Case study 6

Gary had been in the prison healthcare unit for months, although he had no mental illness or physical health problems, having been admitted there for assessment. He had settled well after a period of disturbed behaviour, finding support from staff interaction and his role as landing cleaner. Proposed transfer back to the ordinary wing caused Gary anxiety and staff were concerned about risk of serious self-harm. The psychologist worked with Gary, the healthcare team, wing staff and the Safer Custody team to devise a graduated plan of time on the ordinary wing and a social stories format for the plan, which specified sources of support and what would happen at each stage and used Gary's favourite animation characters. Visits to the ordinary wing were supported by named healthcare team members and an identified officer. He was able to make a successful transition and complete his sentence.

Conclusion

Individuals with autism are likely to encounter greater difficulties in navigating through CJS and FMH settings. Using the SPELL framework (National Autistic Society, 2013b) the authors of this chapter shared some clinical cases to offer guidance on adapting approaches to meet the needs of individuals with autism. The National Autistic Society (2021) offers accreditation to services which demonstrate they can meet the values and principles set out in supporting individuals with autism. This has been achieved in some UK prison settings (Lewis et al., 2015). Accreditation has not yet been achieved in inpatient forensic settings, although work is beginning in some services, with an emphasis on co-production. Murphy and Allely (2019) highlight that, in high secure hospital settings, adjustments must be balanced with the clinical demands and risk management needs; this is likely to be the case for other forensic inpatient settings.

References

Adshead, G., Charles, S., & Pyszora, N. (2005). Moving on: A group for patients leaving a high security hospital. *Group Analysis*, 38, 380–394. doi: 10.1177/0533316405055390

Allely, C. S. (2018). A systematic PRISMA review of individuals with autism spectrum disorder in secure psychiatric care: Prevalence, treatment, risk assessment and other clinical considerations. *Journal of Criminal Psychology*, 8(1), 58–79. doi: 10.1108/JCP-06-2017-0028

Allen, D., Evans, C., Hider, A., Hawkins, S., & Peckett, H. (2008). Offending behaviour in adults with Asperger syndrome. *Journal of Autism Developmental Disorder*, 38, 748–758. doi: 10.1007/s10803-007-0442-9

Autism Act (2009). London: HMSO.

Bathgate, D. (2017). ASD and offending: Reflections of practice in from a New Zealand perspective. *Journal of Intellectual Disabilities and Offending Behaviour*, 8(2), 90–98. https://doi.org/10.1108/JIDOB-07-2016-0012

Bogdashina, O. (2003). *Sensory perceptual issues in autism and Asperger syndrome*. London and Philadelphia: Jessica Kingsley Publishers.

Crooke, P., & Garcia Winner, M. (2020) *The Social Thinking Methodology – layers of evidence*. Think Social Publishing, Inc. Retrieved from: www.socialthinking.com/Articles?name=social-thinking-where-is-the-evidence

Davis, T. E., Moree, B. N., Dempsey, T., Reuther, E. T., Fodstad, J. C., & Hess, J. A. (2011). The relationship between autism spectrum disorders and anxiety: The moderating effect of communication. *Research in Autism Spectrum Disorders*, 5(1), 324–329. doi: 10.1016/j.rasd.2010.04.015

Department of Health. (2005). *Mental Capacity Act*. London: HMSO.

Department of Health. (2010). *Implementing "fulfilling and rewarding lives". Statutory guidance for local authorities and NHS organisations to support implementation of the autism strategy*. Crown copyright, UK. Retrieved from: https://assets.publishing.service.gov.uk/government/uploads/system/uploads/attachment_data/file/216129/dh_122908.pdf

Department of Health. (2014). *Positive and proactive care: Reducing the need for restrictive interventions*. Social Care, DOH, UK. Retrieved from: https://assets.publishing.service.gov.uk/government/uploads/system/uploads/attachment_data/file/300293/JRA_DoH_Guidance_on_RP_web_accessible.pdf

Drennan, G., & Alred, D. (2012). *Secure recovery: Approaches to the recovery in forensic mental health services*. Oxon, UK: Routledge.

Equality Act (2010). London: HMSO.

Galanopoulos, A., Robertson, D., Spain, D., & Murphy, C. (2014). Mental health supplement. *Your Autism Magazine*, 8(4).

Gray, C. (2004). Social stories 10.0: The new defining criteria. *Jenison Autism Journal*, 15(4), 1–21.

Griffiths, J., & Wilcox, D. (2013). Positive behaviour support in a medium secure environment. *Mental Health Practices*, 16(10), 24–27. doi: 10.7748/mhp2013.07.16.10.24.e857

Haw, C., Radley, J., & Cooke, L. (2013). Characteristics of male autistic spectrum patients in low security: Are they different from non-autistic low secure patients? *Journal of Intellectual Disabilities and Offending Behaviour*, 4, 24–32. https://doi.org/10.1108/jidob-03-2013-0006

Herrington, J. D., Maddox, B. B., & Kerns, C. M. (2017). Amygdala volume differences in autism spectrum disorder are related to anxiety. *Journal of Autism and Developmental Disorders*, 47, 3682–3691. https://doi.org/10.1007/s10803-017-3206-1

Higgs, T., & Carter, A. J. (2015) Autism spectrum disorder and sexual offending: Responsivity in forensic interventions. *Aggression and Violent Behavior*, 22, 12–119. https://doi.org/10.1016/j.avb.2015.04.003

Ingamells, B., & Morrissey, C. (2014). *I can feel good: Skills training for people with intellectual disabilities and problems managing emotions*. Hove: Pavilion Publishing & Media Ltd.

Kerns, C. M, Roux, A. M., Connell, J. M., & Shattuck, P. T. (2016). Adapting cognitive behavioural techniques to address anxiety and depression in cognitively able emerging adults on the autism spectrum. *Cognitive and Behavioural Practice*, 23, 329–340. https://doi.org/10.1016/j.cbpra.2016.06.002

Langdon, P. E., Murphy, G. H., Clare, I. C. H., Palmer, E. J., & Rees, J. (2013). An evaluation of the EQUIP program with men who have intellectual or other developmental disabilities. *Journal of Applied Research in Intellectual Disability*, 26(2), 167–180. https://doi.org/10.1111/jar.12004

Lewis, A., Pritchett, R., Hughes, C., & Turner, K. (2015). Development and implementation of autism standards for prison. *Journal of Intellectual Disabilities and Offending Behaviour*, 6(2), 68–80. https://doi.org/10.1108/JIDOB-05-2015-0013

Luke, L., Clare, I. C. H., Ring, H., Redley, M., & Watson, P. (2011). Decision making difficulties experienced by adults with autism spectrum conditions. *Autism*, 16(6), 612–621. https://doi.org/10.1177/1362361311415876

MacDonald, S., Clarbour, J., Whitton, C., & Rayner, K. (2017). The challenges of working with sexual offenders who have autism in secure services. *Journal of Intellectual Disabilities and Offending Behaviour*, 8(1), 41–54. https://doi.org/10.1108/JIDOB-10-2016-0020

Mann, B., Matias, E., & Allen, J. (2014). Recovery in forensic services facing the challenge. *Advances in Psychiatric Treatment*, 20, 125–131. https://doi.org/10.1192/apt.bp.113.011403

Mazefsky, C., Herrington, J., Siegel, M., Scarpa, A., Maddox, B., Scahill, L. & White, S. (2013). The role of emotion regulation in autism spectrum disorder. *Journal of the American Academy of Child and Adolescent Psychiatry*, 52(7), 679–688. doi: 10.1016/j.jaac.2013.05.006

Mesibov, G. B., Shea, V., & Schopler, E. (2004). *The TEACCH approach to autism spectrum disorders* (1st ed.). New York: Springer. doi: 10.1007/978-0-306-48647-0

Mezey, G. C., Kavuma, M., Turton, P., Demetriou, A., & Wright, C. (2010). Perceptions, experiences and meanings of recovery in forensic psychiatric patients. *The Journal of Forensic Psychiatry and Psychology*, 21(5), 683–696. https://doi.org/10.1080/14789949.2010.489953

Milton, D. E. (2012). On the ontological status of autism: The 'double empathy problem'. *Disability & Society*, 27, 883–887. https://doi.org/10.1080/09687599.2012.710008

Misra, P., Patel, M., & Edwards, J. (2013). The need for specialist service for offenders with autistic spectrum disorder in high secure psychiatric care. *European Psychiatry*, 28 (Supplement 1), 1–1. https://doi.org/10.1016/S0924-9338(13)76798-1

Moloney, N., & Gulati, G. (2019). Autism spectrum disorder and Irish prisoners. *Irish Journal of Psychological Medicine*, 26, 1–3. https://doi.org/10.1017/ipm.2019.30

Morrissey, C., Geach, N., Alexander, R., Chester, V., Devaproam, J., Duggan, C., Langdon, P. E., Lindsay, B., McCarthy, J., & Walker, D. (2017). Researching outcomes from forensic services for people with intellectual or developmental disabilities: A systematic review, evidence synthesis and expert and patient/carer consultation. *Health Services and Delivery Research*, 5.3. doi: 10.3310/hsdr05030

Murphy, D., & Allely, C. S. (2019). Autism Spectrum Disorders in high secure psychiatric care: A review of literature, future research and clinical directions. *Advances in Autism*, 6(1), 17–34. http://dx.doi.org/10.1108/AIA-10-2018-0044

Murphy, D., & McMorrow, K. (2015). View of autism spectrum conditions held by staff working in a high secure psychiatric hospital. *Journal of Forensic Practice*, 17(3), 231–240. https://doi.org/10.1108/JFP-01-2015-0005

Murphy, D., & Mullens, H. (2017). Examining the experiences and quality of life of patients with an autism spectrum disorder detained in high secure psychiatric care. *Advances in Autism*, 3(1), 3–14. doi: 10.1108/AIA-02-2016-0006

Murphy, D., Bush, E. L., & Puzzo, I. (2017). Incompatibilities and seclusions among individuals with an autism spectrum disorder detained in high secure psychiatric care. *Journal of Intellectual Disabilities and Offending Behaviour*, 8(4) 188–200. doi: 10.1108/JIDOB-05-2017-0007

Murphy, V., Kelleher, M. J., & Gulati, G. (2017). Autism awareness training for An Garda Siochana (Letter to the Editor). *Irish Journal of Psychological Medicine*. https://doi.org/10.1017/ipm.2017.31

Nadeau, J., Sulkowski, M. L., Ung, D., Wood, J. J., Lewin, A. B., Murphy, T. K., May, J. E., & Storch, E. A. (2011). Treatment of comorbid anxiety in autism spectrum disorders. *Neuropsychiatry (London)*, 1(6), 567–578. doi: 10.2217/npy.11.62

National Autistic Society. (2007). *Youth justice: The next steps? A response from the National Autistic Society*. National Autistic Society.

National Autistic Society. (2013a). *Passport to individual autism support*. The National Autistic Society. Retrieved from: www.derbyshire.gov.uk/site-elements/documents/pdf/social-health/adult-care-and-wellbeing/disability-support/autism/passport-to-individual-autism-support-the-national-autistic-society.pdf

National Autistic Society. (2013b). *Strategies and interventions – SPELL*. Retrieved from: www.autism.org.uk/advice-and-guidance/topics/strategies-and-interventions/strategies-and-interventions/spell

National Autistic Society. (2020). *Criminal justice – A guide for police officers and professionals*. Retrieved from: www.autism.org.uk/advice-and-guidance/topics/criminal-justice/criminal-justice/professionals

National Autistic Society. (2021). *Autism accreditation*. Retrieved from: www.autism.org.uk/what-we-do/best-practice/accreditation

National Institute for Health and Care Excellence. (2012) *Autism spectrum disorder in adults: Diagnosis and management, Clinical Guidance* (CG142). Retrieved from: www.nice.org.uk/guidance/cg142

Nelson, K., & Fivush. R. (2020). The development of autobiographical memory, autobiographical narratives, and autobiographical consciousness. *Psychological Reports*, 123(1), 71–96. https://doi.org/10.1177%2F0033294119852574

Nimmo-Smith, V., Heuvelman, H., Dalman, C., Lundberg, M., Idring, S., Carpenter, P., Magnusson, C., & Rai, D. (2020). Anxiety disorders in adults with autism spectrum disorder: A population-based study. *Journal of Autism and Developmental Disorders*, 50, 308–318. https://doi.org/10.1007/s10803-019-04234-3

Norris, J. E., Crane, L., & Maras, K. (2020). Interviewing autistic adults: Adaptations to support recall in police, employment, and healthcare interviews. *Autism*, 24(6) 1506–1520. doi: 10.1177/1362361320909174

Peeteers, T., & Jordan, R. (2010). What makes a good practitioner in the field of autism? *Good Autism Practice*, 14–15.

Robertson, C. E., & McGillivray, J. A. (2015). Autism behind bars: A review of the research literature and discussion of key issues. *The Journal of Forensic Psychiatry & Psychology*, 26(6), 719–736. https://doi.org/10.1080/14789949.2015.1062994

Royal College of Psychiatrists. (2006). *Psychiatric services for adolescents and adults with Asperger syndrome and other autistic-spectrum disorders* (Council Report CR136).

Royal College of Speech and Language Therapists. (2013). *Five good communication standards.* London: RCSLT.

Royal College of Speech and Language Therapists. (2018). *The box communication help for the justice system.* Version 1 [E-Learning]. Retrieved from: www.rcslt.org/learning/the-box-training/

Shively, R. (2004). Treating offenders with mental retardation and developmental disabilities. *Corrections Today*, 66, 84–87.

Ward, T. (2002). Good lives and the rehabilitation of sexual offenders: Promises and problems. *Aggression and Violent Behavior*, 7, 513–528. https://doi.org/10.1016/S1359-1789(01)00076-3

Weiss, J. A., & Fardella, M. A. (2018). Victimization and perpetration experiences of adults with autism. *Frontiers in Psychiatry*, 9, 203–213. https://doi.org/10.3389/fpsyt.2018.00203

Wing, L. (1981). Asperger's syndrome: A clinical account. *Psychological Medicine*, 11(1), 115 –129. doi: 10.1017/s0033291700053332

Wing, L. (1997). Asperger's syndrome: Management requires diagnosis. *Journal of Forensic Psychiatry*, 2(8), 253–257. https://doi.org/10.1080/09585189708412008

Worthington, R. (2016). What are the key skills that staff require to support adults on the autism spectrum effectively? *Forensic Update. A compendium of the main articles in issues 121 122 & 123*, 61–69.

Zolyomi, A., Begel, A., Waldern, J. F., Tang, J., Barnett, M., Cutrell, E., McDuf, D., Andrist, S., & Morris, M. R. (2019). Managing stress: The needs of autistic adults in video calling. *Proceedings of the ACM on Human-Computer Interaction.* 3 (CSCW), 1–29. https://doi.org/10.1145/3359236

What support interventions are helpful for families and carers of autistic people in the criminal justice system?

11

Rachel Worthington

Needs of families/carers and staff

This chapter critically analyses the existing evidence base surrounding what interventions and supports are helpful for families/carers and staff of people with autism involved in the criminal justice (CJS) and forensic mental health systems (FMHS), primarily focused on the UK, and provides practitioners with recommendations about how these groups can be supported in clinical practice.

A Rapid Evidence Assessment (REA) approach was used to review the extant literature and ensure informed conclusions could be made following critical appraisal of the evidence base (Ganann et al., 2010). Databases searched included PsychINFO, OVID (including MedLine and Embase), Scopus, Google Scholar and MetSearch, returning 258 papers. Following abstract screening, 41 papers were assessed for eligibility. Nineteen papers reported direct research with family members/carers (eight papers) or staff (eleven papers) supporting adults with autism in the criminal justice system (CJS). These broadly reflected (i) family and staff experiences and identified difficulties, and (ii) supportive interventions.

Experiences and identified difficulties

A lack of support services was identified as a common difficulty for both staff and family/carers. They described feeling isolated in the CJS (Rogers, 2019; Lazaratou et al., 2016) with a lack of systemic professional services to provide both preventative support (Tidball, 2017) and following the person's involvement with the CJS (Burch & Rose, 2020; Berryessa, 2016). All papers noted the desire for more support which extended to once the person moved back into the community (Myers, 2004). This lack of support was noted to cause

emotional (Tidball, 2017; MacDonald et al., 2017), financial and practical difficulties (Man & Kangas, 2019; Tint et al., 2017).

An absence of appropriate training was identified for both staff and parent/
carers. Whilst some participants had received training, it was noted that this
did not match their needs (Chown, 2010; Berryessa, 2014a) in that, whilst it
provided basic information about autism, it did not give them training on how
to apply this knowledge in their role. For example, staff stated they lacked training in how to use communication tools (such as Augmentative and Alternative
Communication [AAC]), interviewing skills and how to manage behaviours
of concern. Participants also over-estimated their skills in comparison to their
actual knowledge and abilities (Chown, 2010; Murphy & McMorrow, 2015).

Exposure to aggression was identified as an area where support was
needed for both family/carers and staff, especially with dealing with the
complex emotions and ethical concerns arising from being responsible for
supporting the person with autism in the CJS whilst having been a victim
of aggression themselves (Rogers, 2019; Berryessa, 2014a; Raggi et al., 2013).
Recognition that the family member/carer may also or instead be a perpetrator of abuse was included (Lazaratou et al., 2016; Tidball, 2017). Compassion
fatigue was noted by staff who struggled to remain empathetic because a lack
of empathy in some of the clients meant they would describe their offences
without consideration to the victim (MacDonald et al., 2017).

The relational dynamics of family members/carers to the CJS were also
observed, with some identifying how they felt a responsibility (or were expected)
to advocate for their family member, causing anxiety (Zummo, 2013; Man &
Kangas, 2019; Tidball, 2017). A lack of communication about the CJS process
was also a contributing factor to anxiety (Crane et al., 2016) as was the stigma
associated with being involved in the CJS (Tidball, 2017; Berryessa, 2014b).

Identified supportive interventions

Nine papers suggested that having professional specialists in autism to offer
support and access to autism specific services would help both family mem-
bers/carers and staff (e.g., Man & Kangas, 2019) particularly to assist families
to understand the needs of the person they supported (Lazaratou et al., 2016)
and how to provide advice on preventative intervention strategies to families
(Lazaratou et al., 2016; Zummo, 2013). Accessing systemic specialist provision in a co-ordinated way through Multi-Disciplinary Teams (MDTs; Man
& Kangas, 2019), specific crisis intervention teams (Tint et al., 2017) and the
implementation of the Care Programme Approach (CPA; Myers, 2004) was
suggested as a way to support assessment, intervention and consideration of
how CJS professionals directed the sentence pathway (Berryessa, 2014b).

Eight papers identified ways in which improved training could act as a supportive intervention (these are considered later in the section on 'Supporting staff'). Other supportive interventions included providing reflective practice/supervision for staff to process their experiences and consider ways of working (MacDonald et al., 2017) and improving communication between family members/carers and staff (Rogers, 2019). Two papers identified the need for more research on understanding the role of expert testimony for people with autism to help staff consider the impact of autism on *mens rea* for Judges (Berryessa, 2014a), and the role of media perceptions of people with autism and the potential influence on juror decision making (Berryessa, 2014b).

Recommendations for supporting families/carers and staff

The findings are summarised in terms of (i) supporting families/carers and (ii) supporting staff.

Supporting families/carers

Professional specialist support

Parents/carers described being exposed to behaviours of concern from their children but finding support in the community to manage these was either unavailable or inadequate (Zummo, 2013; Lazaratou et al., 2016; Tidball, 2017). Lazaratou et al. (2016) identified a lack of social, educational and psychiatric support and Zummo (2013) noted that when educational social care was available, funding complexities caused prolonged difficulties. Turcotte et al. (2016) referred to this as the 'service cliff' with a lack of resources for people with autism and their families. Man and Kangas (2019) suggest multidisciplinary approaches, such as crisis intervention teams (Franz & Borum, 2011), could fill the gaps in social care. Support should be compassionate to the challenges the family member/carer may have experienced.

In the UK, the National Autistic Society (NAS) offers families and carer support groups which provide practical advice, training and support in the community; this could be extended to include family members in the CJS. The National Prisoners' Families Helpline does not currently provide specialist help for parents/carers of those with autism. Thus, a task force should be designed to identify specific support for family members and carers of people who are involved in the CJS.

Victimisation

The complex dynamic that family/carers experienced as a result of being both victim and advocate for the person was also highlighted when family members/carers had been exposed to violence from their family member. Escaping this violence was difficult due to a sense of loyalty to the person, feeling guilty for 'letting their child down' and 'failing them' (Zummo, 2013), and fearing that no alternative placement would be available (other than prison/hospital/secure settings), so that parents/carers described feeling trapped in a violent relationship and unable to leave (Tidball, 2017; Zummo, 2013).

Family members/carers and staff may therefore become direct and indirect victims and would benefit from access to support and interventions that other victims of abuse may be offered. For example, information on specialist support services for victims of intra-familial family aggression could be provided in police stations, courts and prisons. The NAS provides a 24-hour parent to parent telephone helpline as well as local family support groups, which could be added to police awareness leaflets.

People with autism may also be at risk of emotional or other forms of victimisation and require safeguarding, including within their family/care settings, with complex dual potential for abuse within parent–child settings (e.g., Wilcox, 2012). The routine use of tools to explore victimisation is indicated. These should avoid using abstract concepts (e.g., 'have you ever been bullied?') and instead ask the person if they have been exposed to a comprehensive list of behaviours (e.g., Direct and Indirect Prisoner Behaviour Checklist [DIPC-R] or the Direct and the Indirect Patient Behaviour Checklist – Hospital Version Revised [DIPC-HR] – Ireland et al., 2009).

Communication: Encouraging advocacy and building trust

Sadly, some parents/carers in the studies described being made to feel that they were being difficult, feeling ignored and having to 'fight to be heard' (Zummo, 2013) and in some cases by the time they were consulted it was too late (Tidball, 2017). The invaluable knowledge parents/carers have should be captured by ensuring that their views are actively included in assessment and treatment (Man & Kangas, 2019). Furthermore, the complex dynamic that a parent/carer faces when their child is being supported by 'experts' should also be attended to. For example, contact with the CJS may result in their child suddenly being provided with support by paid professionals. Families/carers may have supported their child and endured significant life changes as a result; whilst some may find the provision of formal support reassuring, others may perceive this as offensive or an under-estimation of their knowledge. Parents/carers also described experiencing indirect victimisation as a result of their child's involvement with the CJS in terms of how they may be viewed in society (Tidball, 2017) thus compounding a sense of guilt and isolation. Ali et al. (2012) noted that family members are often blamed for a person's disability (family stigma) and may also experience affiliate stigma (e.g., experiencing negative emotions and cognitions about their parenting) which subsequently may increase their risk of victimisation by responses such as withdrawal.

Families and carers can provide a wealth of information in relation to how to best to support the person (Helverschou et al., 2018). Their input and advice should be sought at all stages of the process. The most effective ways of improving understanding of the person's needs can be achieved through using Person-Centred Planning (PCP; Franklin & Sanderson, 2013) where the person with autism is at the centre of the process and family and friends are involved (Sanderson et al., 2000). Use of formalised PCP approaches by CJS/FMHS (forensic mental health systems) staff with family members/carers to identify how best to support the person with autism would capture valuable knowledge and improve trust and communication with staff.

In terms of overcoming stigma, Wong et al. (2016) suggest that self-compassion (a type of emotional regulation strategy) can act as an internal coping resource. Positive outcomes have also been reported for online mindfulness with guided telephone support with families of people with intellectual disabilities. These represent potential strategies for supporting parents/carers of people with autism in the CJS and FMHS.

Building resiliency and reducing anxiety

Several studies noted how delays in the CJS process contributed to family/carer stress (Crane et al., 2016; Myers, 2004; Tidball, 2017), for example: the length of time from arrest to attending court; cancellations of court dates; waiting for intermediaries; a lack of clarity/explanation from police and the courts; and waiting for discharge plans from hospital to less secure settings. These would be stressful for any person; however, given the nature of difficulties for someone with autism in terms of coping with ambiguity it is perhaps not surprising that these were noted to cause additional stress for families and carers. Some aspects of the timing of CJS processes are difficult to specify (e.g., when the trial may be listed) because of the multiple factors involved. However, systems could be put in place to reduce some of the stress, such as ensuring that family members/carers receive regular communication from liaison officers, and prioritising cases so that cancellations are avoided wherever possible. In addition, information could be provided about the CJS process including visual support formats of the routines, rules and expectations which could be given to the person and their family member/carer. This could support the family member/carer to better prepare the person for what to expect and reduce anxiety. Referral for brief anxiety interventions may help them manage whilst they wait for a trial, as well as support the person in the community following the

CJS process. Coping with Uncertainty in Everyday Situations (Adult) [CUES-A©] programme may represent one option (Rodgers et al., 2017). Specialised MDTs could also provide advice on alternative strategies for supporting the family with discharge from FMH hospitals into the community.

Supporting staff

Training and practical guidance

Eight of the ten papers involving staff identified further training as a support need. Whilst staff had sometimes received autism awareness training, they felt they lacked sufficient training on how to support someone with autism in the CJS. Suggested improvements included having different methods of delivery; involving experts by experience (Chown, 2010); covering information on autism and the environment; Positive Behavioural Support (PBS); dual diagnosis; individualised care planning; physical health care; health promotion (Burke & Cocoman, 2020); and risk management (Murphy & McMorrow, 2015; Berryessa, 2014a). Other suggested interventions included teaching staff mindfulness and resiliency skills (MacDonald et al., 2017; Burch & Rose, 2020).

The National Autistic Society (NAS; 2012) states that "effective training is essential to the development of best practice and to good outcomes in autism" (p. 5). However, at the same time they note that most autism training is unregulated (NAS, 2012). In addition, improved training in health and social care settings were noted in the *Autism Act* (2009) by the Department of Health (2015) and NICE Guidance (2016). Recommendations included that training should be mandatory, include refresher sessions, be supported by the organisation through facilitating time for training and, where possible, training should be co-produced and delivered by people with autism. The success of any training should be measured based on the outcomes for people with autism using those CJS facilities/services (Murphy & Broyd, 2019) rather than participant self-report (Murphy & McMorrow, 2015).

The Core Capabilities Framework for Supporting Autistic People (Department of Health and Social Care, 2019) outlines the skills and knowledge that health and social care workers need to deliver high-quality care and support for people with autism. Specifically, training should cover five domains:

A. Understanding autism;
B. Personalised support;
C. Physical and mental health;
D. Risk, legislation and safeguarding;
E. Leadership and management, education and research.

For each domain there are different tiers of training that should be provided depending on the role of the person:

- Tier 1 – those who require a general understanding of autism.
- Tier 2 – people with responsibility for providing care and support for people with autism but who could seek support from others for complex management or decision making.
- Tier 3 – for health, social care and other professionals with a high degree of autonomy, able to provide care and support in complex situations and/or who lead services for people with autism.

Every CJS setting and FMHS supporting people with autism should establish which Tier of training their staff need and ensure they are adequately trained. The guidance also states that staff working with clients with autism in residential/secure settings should have access to a specially trained consultant who is trained to the standards of the Core Competency Frameworks for Applied Behavioural Analysis (ABA) and Positive Behavioural Support (PBS) as well as a specialised postgraduate qualification in autism. This is also consistent with NICE Guidance.

In addition, mental health difficulties may manifest differently in people with autism and as such it is important that health professionals also receive specific training. For example, they could be supported to use specialised tools for assessing psychopathology (see Chapter 2 on comorbid mental health needs) and to develop specific 'Health Action Plans' (Department of Health, 2009) in relation to factors such as dental care, mental health, diet, medication, immunisations, mobility, etc. Examples of free templates to assist with this can be found online (e.g., easyhealth.org).

For staff actively supporting people in CJS living environments (e.g., prisons, hospitals or hostels) additional training in Person-Centred Planning (PCP), Positive Behavioural Support (PBS) and Active Support may be beneficial in line with NICE Guidance (Worthington, 2016).

PCP places the person with autism at the centre of the process; family and friends are involved. The plan shows what is important to a person now and for the future; includes the person as part of a community; and includes what the person wants out of life (Sanderson et al., 2000). Examples of formalised PCP approaches include the McGill Action Planning System (MAPS) (Vandercook et al., 1989). In the UK there are also template tools recommended by the Department of Health (2010):

1) One page profile;
2) All about me;
3) Relationships circle;
4) Communication charts;
5) Matching staff;

6)   Important to/important for me;
7)   What's working/What's not working.

PCP could be used to establish which staff may be best matched to support the person, what they feel is working and not working in their environment and how they would like people to communicate with them. In addition, the communication checklist for PCP (Grove & McIntosh, 2005) provides some prompts for questions that CJS professionals may ask a family or carer of someone with autism which would help to capture their knowledge of how best to support the person.

Karger et al. (2018) found that PBS assisted staff to identify the functions of a person's behaviour and associated risks. Thus, PBS can help CJS staff to better support someone with autism to meet their needs and improve their quality of life through alternative ways and reducing behaviours of concern (such as harm to self and others).

Active Support has also been shown to improve quality of life (Mansell & Beadle-Brown, 2012) and in particular in increasing participation in daily life, social and community activities, as well as increasing people's skills, adaptive behaviour and choice, and reducing challenging behaviour (Bradshaw et al., 2004). Training CJS/FMHS staff in Active Support could also enable them to improve the person's independence and skills for life and promote desistance.

Recruitment

MacDonald et al. (2017) and Murphy and Broyd (2019) noted the importance of ensuring the right staff are recruited to support people with autism in CJS settings. Worthington et al. (2018) also noted that whilst certain skills could be taught to staff, values-based recruitment should also be considered when selecting staff. Staff who worked positively with people with autism were identified as: approachable; reflective/self-aware; empathetic; benevolent; empowering; confident; able to follow plans; resilient; and respectful. In addition, where possible such staff should be selected by an interview panel that includes service users with autism to ensure an inclusive person-centred approach.

Lack of support services

A lack of professional support and access to services was identified as a need whereby staff in the studies reported that they had training in autism but did not know how to apply this with the individual they were supporting, how to identify the specific needs of the individual and what to do practically to better support the person. CJS staff should therefore have access to professionals such as Occupational Therapists (OTs) for advice on sensory needs and Speech and Language Therapists (SLTs) for advice on communication. These practitioners should be part of the specialist autism multidisciplinary team (MDT) and should be available in CJS services even if the service is not a specialised autism unit.

CJS staff struggling to access professionals could access free alternative tools whilst waiting for formal assessments. For example, the Sensory Assessment Checklist (Autism Education Trust, n.d.) is readily available online and acts as a sensory screening checklist which could be used with adults to highlight sensory preferences or challenges. The NAS also offers 'quick tips' on communicating with people with autism as well as visual emotions cards to help the person express how they feel. The Do-IT profiler (Kirby & Saunders, 2015) has also been used within prisons and only takes approximately 30 minutes to complete. The screening tool has individualised modules which specifically map onto autism needs with separate versions for people in the community and people in prisons/hospitals. Whilst these tools do not seek to replace professional assessments, they could be used to provide CJS professionals with guidance for how to better support someone with autism in the absence of more comprehensive assessments.

Building resiliency

Several papers described how staff reported experiencing compassion fatigue as a result of being exposed to direct and indirect victimisation from the people they supported. Raggi et al. (2013) found staff were exposed to physical harm but felt a sense of helplessness or vulnerability due to their inability to exit this relationship without losing their job. MacDonald et al. (2017) also discussed the effects of indirect victimisation (false allegations and explicit accounts of the person's offending) as a result of supporting people with autism.

MacDonald et al. (2017) suggested that reflective practice and supervision was imperative when working with this client group. Critical reflection is considered to be one of the main learning domains by the World Health Organization (2010). Thus, it would be helpful for staff (at all levels) in CJS/FMHS settings to have access to reflective practice and supervision if they are supporting someone with autism. In addition, the use of forensic case formulation (Shine & Cooper-Evans, 2016) would also assist CJS/FMHS staff to better identify and formulate risks and offence-paralleling behaviours, identify treatment needs and improve pro-social coping.

Conclusion

There is a lack of research on the experiences of families/carers and staff supporting people with autism in the CJS. It is of specific concern that no papers identified the needs of those supporting people with autism who are victims of crime. Future research should attend to this absence. However, from the available research, recommendations could be made and these are summarised in Table 11.1.

Table 11.1 Support interventions

Experienced difficulty		Identified support intervention
Family Members/ Carers	Lack of Support Services	• Create MDTs to fill the gaps in preventative and CJS-related support for family members/carers in line with *The Care Act* (2014). • Crisis Intervention Teams. • Creation of a government task force to identify specific support for family members and carers.
	Victim of Aggression	• Police should provide advice and support to family members/carers on how to access victim support strategies if they are a victim of aggression. • Police Awareness leaflets should provide information on how to access the National Autistic Society (NAS) parent to parent helpline and family support groups.
	Perpetrator of Aggression	• Police and staff in the CJS (probation, prison) should ensure people with autism are safeguarded from potential victimisation from family members/carers by undertaking direct assessments at the point of contact. Consider tools such as the DIPC.
	Lack of Trust and Communication	• Invite family members/carers to contribute to Person-Centred Planning (PCP). • Outcomes from MDT clinician input should be communicated to family members/carers (where consent is given).
	Stigma	• Offer access to mindfulness and self-compassion interventions.
	Anxiety	• Regular communication from liaison officers regarding the legal process. • CJS settings should provide information about the process including visual support format of routines, rules and expectations to enable preparation. • Offer anxiety interventions (e.g., Coping with Uncertainty in Everyday Situations (Adult) [CUES-A©]) to help them manage pre and post legal process. • Services such as the National Prisoners' Families helpline should include specialist advice for parents/carers of people with autism.

Staff	Inadequate Training	• CJS staff should be trained in line with the Core Capabilities Framework for Supporting Autistic people (Department of Health and Social Care, 2019).
		• Access to a consultant in autism with postgraduate qualification in autism and trained to the standards of the Core Competency Frameworks for Applied Behavioural Analysis (ABA) and Positive Behavioural Support (PBS) [NICE Guidance].
		• Specific training for health professionals on manifestation of mental health difficulties in autism.
		• CJS health professionals should use specific screening tools for health and develop 'Health Action Plans' (Department of Health, 2009) e.g., for dental care, mental health, diet, medication, immunisations, mobility, etc.
		• Success of training should be measured based on the outcomes for people with autism using those CJS facilities/services rather than participant self-report.
		• Training should be: mandatory; include refresher training; have organisational support/time; co-produced and delivered by people with autism.
		• Staff in prisons/approved premises/hospitals should receive additional training in Person-Centred Planning (PCP), Positive Behavioural Support (PBS) and Active Support [NICE Guidance].
		• Staff recruitment should be values-based, use 'staff matching' tools and people with autism on interview panels wherever possible.
	Lack of Support Services	• Access to an MDT trained in supporting people with autism.
		• CJS staff should use freely available autism friendly tools from organisations such as the National Autistic Society (NAS) and the Autism Education Trust.
		• Services should consider using tools such as the Do-IT profiler to identify the needs of people with autism and access information materials to help the person understand the CJS setting.
		• Use of quality assurance systems such as the National Autistic Society (NAS) accreditation scheme.
	Compassion Fatigue	• Access to supervision and reflective practice facilitated by someone with expertise in autism.
		• Use of forensic case formulation to identify/formulate risks and offence-paralleling behaviours, identify treatment needs and improve pro-social coping.

References

Ali, A., Hassiotis, A., Strydom, A., & King, M. (2012). Self stigma in people with intellectual disabilities and courtesy stigma in family carers: A systematic review. *Research in Developmental Disabilities*, 33(6), 2122–2140. doi: 10.1016/j.ridd.2012.06.013

Autism Act. (2009). London: HMSO. Retrieved from: www.legislation.gov.uk/ukpga/2009/15/pdfs/ukpga_20090015_en.pdf

Autism Education Trust. (n.d.). *Sensory autism checklist*. Retrieved from: www.aettraininghubs.org.uk/wp-content/uploads/2012/05/37.2-Sensory-assessment-checklist.pdf

Berryessa, C. M. (2014a). Judicial perceptions of media portrayals of offenders with high functioning autistic spectrum disorders. *International Journal of Criminology and Sociology*, 3, 46–60. doi: 10.6000/1929-4409.2014.03.04

Berryessa, C. M. (2014b). Judiciary views on criminal behaviour and intention of offenders with high-functioning autism. *Journal of Intellectual Disabilities and Offending Behaviour*, 5(2), 97–106. doi: 10.1108/JIDOB-02-2014-0002

Berryessa, C. M. (2016). Brief report: Judicial attitudes regarding the sentencing of offenders with high functioning autism. *Journal of Autism and Developmental Disorders*, 46(8), 2770–2773. doi: 10.1007/s10803-016-2798-1

Bradshaw, J., McGill, P., Stretton, R., Bradshaw, J., Kelly-Pike, A., Moore, J., Macdonald, S., Eastop, Z., & Marks, B. (2004). Implementation and evaluation of active support. *Journal of Applied Research in Intellectual Disabilities*, 17(3), 139–148. doi.org/10.1111/j.1468-3148.2004.00190.x

Burch, E., & Rose, J. (2020). The subjective experiences of liaison and diversion staff who encounter individuals with autism. *Journal of Criminological Research, Policy and Practice*, 6(2), 137–150. doi: 10.1108/JCRPP-11-2019-0067

Burke, D., & Cocoman, A. (2020). Training needs analysis of nurses caring for individuals an intellectual disability and or autism spectrum disorder in a forensic service. *Journal of Intellectual Disabilities and Offending Behaviour*, 11(1), 9–22. doi: 10.1108/JIDOB-10-2019-0024

The Care Act (2014). London: HMSO.

Chown, N. (2010). 'Do you have any difficulties that I may not be aware of?' A study of autism awareness and understanding in the UK police service. *International Journal of Police Science and Management*, 12(2), 256–273. doi :10.1350/ijps.2010.12.2.174

Crane, L., Maras, K. L., Hawken, T., Mulcahy, S., & Memon, A. (2016). Experiences of autism spectrum disorder and policing in England and Wales: Surveying police and the autism community. *Journal of Autism and Developmental Disorders*, 46(6), 2028–2041. doi: 10.1007/s10803-016-2729-1

Department of Health. (2009). *Health Action Planning and Health Facilitation for people with learning disabilities: Good practice guidance*. Retrieved from: www.dh.gov.uk/publications

Department of Health. (2010). *Personalisation through person-centred planning*. www.bl.uk/collection-items/personalisation-through-personcentred-planning

Department of Health. (2015). *Adult autism strategy: Supporting its use*. www.gov.uk/government/publications/adult-autism-strategy-statutory-guidance

Department of Health and Social Care. (2019). *Core capabilities framework for supporting autistic people*. Retrieved from: https://skillsforhealth.org.uk/wp-content/uploads/2020/11/Autism-Capabilities-Framework-Oct-2019.pdf

Franklin, S., & Sanderson, H. (2013). *Personalisation in practice: Supporting young people with disabilities through the transition to adulthood*. London and Philadelphia: Jessica Kingsley Publishers.

Franz, S., & Borum, R. (2011). Crisis intervention teams may prevent arrests of people with mental illnesses. *Police Practice and Research: An International Journal*, 12(3), 265–272. doi: 10.1080/15614263.2010.497664

Ganann, R., Ciliska, D., & Thomas, H. (2010). Expediting systematic reviews: Methods and implications of rapid reviews. *Implementation Science*, 5(56). https://doi.org/10.1186/1748-5908-5-56

Grove, N., & McIntosh, B. (2005). *Communication for person centred planning*. London: Foundation for People with Learning Disabilities. Retrieved from: www.learningdisabilities.org.uk/learning-disabilities/publications/communication-person-centred-planning

Helverschou, S. B., Steindal, K., Nøttestad, J. A., & Howlin, P. (2018). Personal experiences of the criminal justice system by individuals with autism spectrum disorders. *Autism*, 22(4), 460–468. doi: 10.1177%2F1362361316685554

Ireland, J. L., Power, C. L. Bramhall, S., & Flowers, C. (2009). Developing an attitude towards bullying scale for prisoners: Structural analyses across adult men, young adults and women prisoners. *Criminal Behaviour and Mental Health*, 19(1), 28–42. doi: 10.1002/cbm.722

Karger, G., Davies, B., Jenkins, R., & Samuel, V. (2018). Staff perceptions of positive behavioural support in a secure forensic adult mental health setting. *Journal of Forensic Practice*, 20(2), 42–53. doi: 10.1108/JFP-10-2017-0044

Kirby, A., & Saunders, L. (2015). A case study of an embedded system in prison to support individuals with learning difficulties and disabilities in the criminal justice system. *Journal of Intellectual Disabilities and Offending Behaviour*, 6(2), 112–124. doi:10.1108/JIDOB-09-2015-0036

Lazaratou, H., Giannopoulou, I., Anomitri, C., & Douzenis, A. (2016). Case report: Matricide by a 17-year old boy with Asperger's syndrome. *Aggression and Violent Behavior*, 31, 61–65. doi: 10.1016/j.avb.2016.07.007

MacDonald, S., Clarbour, J., Whitton, C., & Rayner, K. (2017). The challenges of working with sexual offenders who have autism in secure services. *Journal of Intellectual Disabilities and Offending Behaviour*, 8(1), 41–54. doi: 10.1108/JIDOB-10-2016-0020

Man, J., & Kangas, M. (2019). Service satisfaction and helpfulness ratings, mental health literacy and help seeking barriers of carers of individuals with dual disabilities. *Journal of Applied Research in Intellectual Disabilities*, 32(1), 184–193. doi:10.1111/jar.12520

Mansell, J., & Beadle-Brown, J. (2012). *Active support: Enabling and empowering people with intellectual disabilities*. London and Philadelphia: Jessica Kingsley Publishers.

Murphy, D., & Broyd, J. G. (2019). Evaluation of autism awareness training provided to staff working in a high secure psychiatric care hospital. *Advances in Autism*, 6(1), 35–47. doi:10.1108/AIA-06-2019-0017.

Murphy, D., & McMorrow, K. (2015). View of autism spectrum conditions held by staff working within a high secure psychiatric hospital. *Journal of Forensic Practice*, 17(3), 231–240. doi:10.1108/JFP-01-2015-0005

Myers, F. (2004). *On the borderline? People with learning disabilities and/or autistic spectrum disorders in secure forensic and other specialist settings*. Scottish Executive Social Research.

National Autistic Society (NAS). (2012). *Good practice in autism training: A code of practice*. London: National Autistic Society.

NICE Guidance. (2016). *Autism spectrum disorder in adults: Diagnosis and management Clinical guideline [CG142]*. Retrieved from: www.nice.org.uk/guidance/cg142

Raggi, C., Xenitidis, K., Moisan, M., Deeley, Q., & Robertson, D. (2013). Adults with autism spectrum disorder and learning disability presenting with challenging behaviour: How tolerant should we be? *Journal of Intellectual Disabilities and Offending Behaviour*, 4(1/2), 41–52. doi: 10.1108/jidob.2013.55404aaa.001

Rodgers, J., Hodgson, A., Shields, K., Wright, C., Honey, E., & Freeston, M. (2017). Towards a treatment for intolerance of uncertainty in young people with autism spectrum disorder: Development of the coping with uncertainty in everyday situations (CUES©) programme. *Journal of Autism and Developmental Disorders*, 47(12), 3959–3966. doi: 10.1007/s10803-016-2924-0

Rogers, C. (2019). Just mothers: Criminal justice, care ethics and "disabled" offenders. *Disability and Society*, 35(6), 926–948. doi: 10.1080/09687599.2019.1655711

Sanderson, H., Kilbane, J., & Gitsham, N. (2000). *Person-centred planning (PCP): A resource guide*. Retrieved from: www.nwtdt.com/Archive/pdfs/pcp.pdf

Shine, J., & Cooper-Evans, S. (2016). Developing an autism specific framework for forensic case formulation. *Journal of Intellectual Disabilities and Offending Behaviour*, 7(3), 127–139. doi:10.1108/JIDOB-04-2015-0006

Tidball, M. (2017). *The governance of adult defendants with autism through English criminal justice policy and criminal court practice*. Unpublished doctoral dissertation, University of Oxford.

Tint, A., Palucka, A. M., Bradley, E., Weiss, J. A., & Lunsky, Y. (2017). Correlates of police involvement among adolescents and adults with autism spectrum disorder. *Journal of Autism and Developmental Disorders*, 47(9), 2639–2647. doi: 10.1007/s10803-017-3182-5

Turcotte, P., Mathew, M., Shea, L. L., Brusilovskiy, E., & Nonnemacher, S. L. (2016). Service needs across the lifespan for individuals with autism. *Journal of Autism and Developmental Disorders*, 46(7), 2480–2489. doi: 10.1007/s10803-016-2787-4

Vandercook, T., York, J., & Forest, M. (1989). The McGill Action Planning System (MAPS): A strategy for building the vision. *The Journal of the Association for Persons with Severe Handicaps*, 14(3), 205–215. doi:10.1177/154079698901400306

Wilcox, P. (2012). Is parent abuse a form of domestic violence? *Social Policy and Society*, 11(2), 277. doi: 10.1017/S1474746411000613

Wong, C. C., Mak, W. W., & Liao, K. Y. H. (2016). Self-compassion: A potential buffer against affiliate stigma experienced by parents of children with autism spectrum disorders. *Mindfulness*, 7(6), 1385–1395. doi: 10.1007/S12671-016-0580-2

World Health Organization. (2010). *World health statistics 2010*. World Health Organization.

Worthington, R. (2016). What are the key skills that staff require to support adults on the autism spectrum effectively? *Forensic Update*, (121), 122.

Worthington, R., Patterson, C., & Halder, N. (2018). Working with intellectually disabled autistic individuals–a qualitative study using repertory grids. *Journal of Intellectual Disabilities and Offending Behaviour*, 9(1), 22–21. doi: 10.1108/JIDOB-08-2017-0017

Zummo, S. (2013). To save a son. *Odyssey: New Directions in Deaf Education, 14*, 78–81.

Women and autism

12

Verity Chester, Bethany Driver and Regi T. Alexander

Introduction

Early autism conceptualisations were largely developed from work with males by Leo Kanner and Hans Asperger (see Pearce, 2005). Autism occurs at a 4:1 male:female ratio, 2:1 among those with intellectual disability (ID) and 10:1 without ID (Barnard-Brak et al., 2019). Whether these ratios stem from real differences or diagnosis gender bias is unclear (Carpenter et al., 2019). Diagnostic criteria, screening and assessment tools that have been developed on males do not capture the difficulties experienced by females, and therefore lack validity (Carpenter et al., 2019; Gould & Ashton-Smith, 2011). Consequently, the autistic profile recognised is male, and females do not typically fit (Happé et al., 2006). Autistic females without ID are particularly overlooked (Zener, 2019). Parent-reported emotional/behavioural problems increase the probability of diagnosis, suggesting that autism is more likely to be recognised in girls who present with more difficulties (Duvekot et al., 2017).

Receiving a timely diagnosis can provide essential validation and education (Zener, 2019). Females have their autism diagnosed later in life, or missed altogether (Gould & Ashton-Smith, 2011) reducing the likelihood of earlier intervention (Daley, 2004). Pathways to diagnosis differ, and include having a family member/partner being diagnosed then identifying signs in themselves, recognising personal traits in accounts by autistic women, following employment difficulties or burnout (Zener, 2019). Females may be more negatively affected by adolescence/adulthood, through encountering difficulties without understanding that these are autism related (Zener, 2019). Knowledge of the female autistic profile could increase the ability of clinicians to recognise autism among women within forensic settings, and better direct the rehabilitation pathway (Alexander et al., 2016). Table 12.1 highlights the characteristics of autistic women, adapted from Driver and Chester (2021).

DOI: 10.4324/9781003036722-15

Table 12.1 The female autistic profile

Social communication and social interaction	Restricted, repetitive patterns of behaviour, interests or activities (RBRIs)
• Fewer/less obvious socio-communication issues. • Tendency to "camouflage"/"mask" social difficulties. • More reciprocal behaviour than boys, but less than neurotypical peers, "flitting" between solitary time and peer group sidelines.	• Less obvious, more female oriented RRBIs. • More compulsive, sameness, restricted and self-injurious behaviour. • Increased sensory issues.

Women in forensic settings

Women represent 5% of the prison population (Prison Reform Trust, 2011). Between 8–19% of admissions to secure services are women (Coid et al., 2000; Dent, 2006). This minority status means women are marginalised within a system largely designed by men for men (Corston, 2007). Clinical assessments within forensic psychiatric settings are not adequately tailored to the backgrounds of women (Aitken, 2006). Studies report that women within forensic settings have more complex psychiatric psychopathology than men, with higher rates of previous psychiatric admissions, depression, anxiety, phobias and Borderline Personality Disorder (BPD) (Coid et al., 2000). Alcohol/drug misuse is higher than in men, affecting approximately one third of women, alongside eating disorders (Davenport, 2004). Women are more likely to have self-harm histories (Coid et al., 2000), childhood sexual abuse and abusive adulthood relationships (Fish, 2013; Lindsay et al., 2004). Women have fewer convictions, being more likely to have transferred from less secure settings following non-criminalised behaviour disorders (Coid et al., 2000). The conceptualisation of being "different" can further stigmatise and problematise women (Aitken & Noble, 2001), rather than facilitate gender-specific treatment approaches. Despite having lower and less severe criminal offences than men, women are viewed as presenting challenges, due to high levels of aggression and self-harm (Fish, 2000), and subject to negative labelling, e.g., "attention seeking" or "volatile" (Crawford et al., 2001).

Autistic female offenders

Prevalence and characteristics

Prevalence research with autistic females is limited to cohort studies within forensic settings, and no studies describe sociodemographic, clinical or forensic characteristics of females relative to males, though a number of case studies provide contextual information (see Table 12.2). Eaton and Banting (2012) describe a woman with an unstable/traumatic developmental history, low

Table 12.2 Research including female autistic offenders

Authors	Study type	Country	Forensic setting/ population	Autism diagnosis	Details
Eaton & Banting (2012)	Case	United Kingdom	Low secure hospital.	Pathological demand avoidance	Female case.
Gómez-Durán et al. (2013)	Case	Spain	Two siblings charged with matricide because of failure to act, following the death of their mother.	Autism	One female.
Kumar et al. (2017)	Case series	India	Five individuals with a history of abnormal sexual behaviours which led to legal cognizance.	Asperger syndrome	One female.
Aral et al. (2018)	Case	Turkey	Adolescent girl charged with possession/ sharing of child pornography.	Asperger syndrome	Female case.
Markham (2019)	Case	England	Medium secure psychiatric hospital.	ASD	Female inpatient.
Ashworth et al. (2020)	Case	England	Medium secure ID hospital.	ASD	Female inpatient.
Hare et al. (1999)	Cohort	England	Three special hospitals.	ASD	In the autistic group, 29 (93.5%) were male and two (6.5%) were female. In the uncertain group there were 28 (90.3%) males and three (9.7%) females.
Soderstrom et al. (2004)	Cohort	Sweden	100 perpetrators of violent crimes admitted under court order to undergo forensic psychiatric investigation.	ASD	One of eight females had ASD, vs. 18 of 92 men.

(Continued)

Authors	Study type	Country	Forensic setting/ population	Autism diagnosis	Details
Anckarsäter et al. (2008)	Cohort	Sweden	Forensic psychiatry populations: 1 a hospital where patients have typically been convicted of serious crimes, sentenced and referred for highly specialised inpatient treatment; 2 violent or sexual offenders undergoing pre-trial investigation.	ASD. Patients with autistic features as part of a more complex psychiatric picture or atypical autism not included in this study.	Case series of 42 with ASD: 1 four diagnosed with ASD, two female. 2 18 were autistic, and three were women.
Woodbury-Smith et al. (2005; 2010).	Cohort	England	21 offenders.	ASD without intellectual impairment	Three women.
Enayati et al. (2008)	Cohort	Sweden	Offenders referred for forensic psychiatric assessment.	Autism/Aspergers	Of 15 autistic arsonists, two were female, and of 69 autistic violent offenders, seven were female.
Mouridsen et al. (2008)	Cohort	Denmark	313 former child psychiatric inpatients, compared with 933 general population matched controls.	PDD (Pervasive Developmental Disorders) – three subgroups (childhood autism, atypical autism and Asperger syndrome)	Females had a much lower rate of convictions than males in the comparison sample, however, females with PDD had similar risk of being convicted.
Kumagami & Matsuura (2009)	Cohort	Japan	Family courts, where juvenile delinquents are tried by law.	PDD	Of 28 defendants with PDD, two were female.
Långström et al. (2009)	Cohort	Sweden	31 individuals hospitalised following violent or sexual offenses.	Autistic disorder or Asperger syndrome	Two female.

Authors	Study type	Country	Forensic setting/ population	Autism diagnosis	Details
Kawakami et al. (2012)	Cohort	Japan	36 individuals with a prior history of criminal behaviours.	ASD	Six female.
Søndenaa et al. (2014)	Cohort	Norway	Forensic examinations involving violent or sexual crime (n = 33) over a ten-year period.	ASD	Five were female, and all were convicted of violent, not sexual crimes.
Helverschou et al. (2015)	Cohort	Norway	Forensic psychiatric service (n = 48).	ASD	Seven female.
Esan et al. (2015)	Cohort	England	Forensic ID hospital (n = 138).	ASD (n = 42)	Six female.
Griffiths et al. (2018)	Cohort	United Kingdom	Low/medium secure services (n = 347).	Asperger syndrome (n = 34)	Four female.
Helverschou et al. (2018)	Cohort	Norway	Nine individuals with experience of the CJS.	ASD	One female.
Hill et al. (2019)	Cohort	England	100 patients admitted to secure forensic adolescent hospital.	PDD	Of 39 females, one had PDD.
Bosch et al. (2020)	Cohort	Netherlands	Forensic psychiatric patients (n = 32)	ASD	Three female.

cognitive ability and complex diagnostic profile with multiple past diagnoses. It is unclear whether the patient received any formal convictions, however, there were extensive reports of "offending-like" behaviour; a concept introduced to capture offending behaviour displayed by those with ID which is not processed by the criminal justice system (CJS) (Alexander et al., 2006).

Aral et al. (2018) reported a female case who had been chatting via social media with an unknown person, who asked her to send pictures of naked people, which she did without question. The stranger then wanted her to send naked child pictures, which she did. She explained that everybody is curious about naked people, and that she thought downloading and sharing naked child pictures was legal, given that they were on the internet, and the photos could not have been taken against children's will. The authors felt circumscribed interests, and insufficient understanding of social moral rules were key factors in this case.

Markham (2019) reported the case of a female detained in a secure unit following injuring a male colleague with a knife. During this admission, she was diagnosed with autism. The clinical history noted that during university, concerns were raised about her obsessional tendencies, emotional difficulties and preoccupation with work to the exclusion of eating. Prior to the index offence, she felt that her doctor was not responding appropriately to the distress she was reporting. The offence was described as a last resort to obtain help, which clinicians felt reflected unusual logical reasoning processes.

Ashworth et al. (2020) reported a female with a difficult upbringing, mental health difficulties and an extensive history of assaultative behaviour, which resulted in "upwards referral" through mental health services of increasing security to a medium secure service. Her autism was only recognised and diagnosed at this time, alongside ID. The authors provided a formulation including predisposing, precipitating and perpetuating factors of her problem behaviours, many of which were autism-related, such as sensory overload, interpersonal conflict and a lack of role models due to social isolation and limited relationships.

Forensic issues

Assessment

Few forensic settings have formal autism screening or diagnostic programmes. Research among autistic males has suggested that many only receive their diagnosis once within the forensic system (Billstedt et al., 2017; Kawakami et al., 2012). The case studies suggest this issue also affects females. This could affect assessments of criminal responsibility (Markham, 2019).

Women within forensic settings typically experience clinical comorbidity. Undiagnosed autistic women often seek support for mental health difficulties (Zener, 2019), but autism is not considered as an underlying cause (Carpenter et al., 2019). Any difficulties are then attributed to the initial diagnosis, known as diagnostic overshadowing (Lai et al., 2015). The initial diagnosis may be incorrect or comorbid. The most common comorbid or differential diagnoses are Borderline Personality Disorder (BPD), Anxiety, Depression, Eating Disorders, Obsessive Compulsive Disorder, Attention Deficit Hyperactivity Disorder, or Gender Dysphoria (Driver & Chester, 2021). As mental health diagnoses can overshadow autism, autism can overshadow mental health diagnoses. Autistic people are more vulnerable to mental ill health (Sedgewick et al., 2020), and autism can complicate presentation, via communication impairments, therapeutic relationship difficulties or emotional introspection difficulties.

Within forensic settings, the most common initial diagnosis of females is BPD; a reflection of high rates of attachment difficulties, abuse and trauma. In some instances, women who later go on to be diagnosed with autism have been treated according to a BPD diagnosis for years within forensic services, with minimal improvement in presentation. In undiagnosed autism, the initial diagnosis is either an incorrect fit, or insufficient in capturing the patient's difficulties. The BPD label can be very entrenched, even in light of a differential or additional diagnosis of autism. However, correctly identifying autism can prompt the viewing of a person through an "autistic lens", supporting more effective formulation, treatment and management. In addition, patients can be diagnosed with both autism and trauma related psychiatric diagnoses, and the autistic population are at increased risk of maltreatment (Kuhl-Meltzoff Stavropoulos et al., 2018) and victimisation (Kock et al., 2019). Rydén et al. (2008) reported that 15% of those with BPD had autism, and those with this dual diagnosis had higher suicidality, and lower adaptive functioning. Differentiating autism from trauma related diagnoses can be difficult in practice, due to symptom overlap, and a lack of training on the female autistic profile compounds this.

Management and treatment

There are numerous studies showing that autistic women within forensic settings display challenging behaviours, including violence to others and self-harm (Anckarsäter et al., 2008; Ashworth et al., 2020; Eaton & Banting, 2012). Dudas et al. (2017) noted that establishing the function of self-harming is important, as autistic self-harm is associated with sensory overload, compared to interpersonal conflict/emotional dysregulation in BPD. Restrictive practices may be put in place to manage risk.

Minimal research has explored the experiences of autistic women within forensic settings. Holloway et al. (2020) examined the experiences of two autistic adults (one female) during the custody process. Negative experiences identified included communication barriers and sensory demands (small spaces, noise and lighting). The authors highlighted the need for autism training, emotional support and more accessible forms of information.

Interpersonal difficulties are very common. Markham (2019) describes relational difficulties with patient peers, including a lack of understanding of others' perspectives, inflexibility in pursuit of goals and low awareness of how she might appear to others (e.g., not realising she presented as angry when anxious). Furthermore, there was an expectation of others to understand why something would have upset her when it related to an idiosyncratic need that others would be unlikely to be aware of. Sedgewick et al. (2020) reported that autistic women find it harder to interpret social situations, more relationship difficulties, fewer and more intense relationships than non-autistic women. Difficulties between autistic females and peers within forensic services can stem from accusations of "copying", which can be a form of camouflaging (Lai et al., 2017). These points are illustrated in the case study in this chapter.

Few descriptions of treatment programmes exist for autistic women within the CJS. Two case studies have described personally tailored treatment programmes, based on the assessed needs of the individual. Ashworth et al. (2020) described a 22-week Cognitive Behaviour Therapy intervention which aimed to improve understanding of autistic traits, thinking styles and behavioural patterns. Eaton and Banting (2012) employed Positive Behaviour Support strategies, attempting to understand the function of, and reduce challenging behaviour. Both studies reported equivocal findings post-intervention, highlighting the current difficulties in providing treatment to this population.

In the context of lack of research, autistic women are being offered "treatment as usual" within forensic settings (e.g., Dialectical Behaviour Therapy, anger management and offence-specific therapies). One of the main psychological treatments offered to autistic male offenders is the Equipping Youth to Help One Another Programme (EQUIP) (Langdon et al., 2013), which aims to address moral reasoning delays, distorted cognitions and social skills. Whether any of these treatments are suitable for autistic female offenders is unclear, and further research is therefore required.

Box 12.1   Case study: Krista

Krista was admitted to a low secure service following numerous incidents of violence within the family home, one of which resulted in the assault of an attending police officer, and committing arson after moving into supported living. Krista was diagnosed with BPD following admission. However, Krista had no experiences of neglect, attachment issues or trauma, and nursing staff noted she was "different" to other patients on the ward. While other patients' behavioural incidents had an element of predictability (i.e., identifiable triggers and worsening affect), Krista consistently presented as very amenable, with a permanent fixed smile, and incidents were noted to "erupt" with no observable antecedents. Krista was also known for making a high volume of complaints, using the services' internal processes, to advocates and commissioners.

An autism assessment highlighted that Krista presented with many autism signs (e.g., difficulties modulating eye contact, rigid thinking and behavioural patterns, and a lack of reciprocal conversation), though

Krista's autistic presentation was relatively subtle. A diagnosis of Pervasive Developmental Disorder – Not Otherwise Specified was made.

Her offences were reformulated based on the autism classification, which indicated that she had engaged in violence following considerable disruption to her living situation and routine. Her arson offence was committed in the context of an intense emotional response to a perceived unfairness in placement rules, and a punishment for breaking these rules. Krista's difficulties with emotional regulation and lacking social problem solving skills exacerbated this situation.

Regarding management in the ward environment, the psychology team suggested an approach of proactively "checking in" with Krista to inquire about her feelings that moment and whether she had any problems. Previously, staff had assumed Krista was not in need of any support due to her amenable presentation and fixed smile. Krista would tell staff her problems when prompted, which meant issues were picked up and resolved quickly. However, challenges remained, as not all staff believed in the autism diagnosis and retained negative attitudes towards Krista, such as that she received preferential treatment. Despite this, Krista progressed well; she received psychology input for emotional recognition and regulation, offence-specific sessions and a social problem solving programme. She moved into the community after approximately two years of treatment.

Conclusion

The prevalence of offending behaviour in autistic females, or the prevalence of autistic females in offender populations, is unknown. It is recommended that prevalence studies investigate this. Few studies have examined the characteristics of this population, and knowledge is based on a small number of case studies, which suggests that, similar to male offenders, comorbid mental disorders or emotional difficulties, late diagnosis of autism and social problem solving factors can predispose offending behaviour. The evidence base on male autistic offenders began with case studies and it is possible that cases could be of benefit in developing an initial understanding of autistic female offenders. The low numbers of autistic women within forensic settings could make cohort studies challenging; multi-site studies will be required.

In the context of underdeveloped screening pathways, low clinician awareness of autistic females, a lack of female-sensitive tools and diagnostic challenges, it is possible that autistic women remain unidentified within forensic settings. Undiagnosed autism can mean females' formulations, and subsequent assessment and treatment pathways are an incorrect fit. The views of the female being assessed should be incorporated within the diagnostic process (Markham, 2019), as autistic women often reveal their social difficulties in self-report, rather than difficulties being directly observable (Lai et al., 2017). Nowell et al. (2019) recommended that clinicians familiarise themselves with the interests of similar aged neurotypical females when assessing autism in women. Where diagnosis is equivocal, testing an autism-based management approach can be helpful. Increasing focus on females within autism training programmes can support awareness (Tromans et al., 2019).

Further issues include the provision of effective forensic rehabilitation, considering the lack of evidence base to guide practice. Until this situation is resolved, it is recommended that autistic females are treated according to their individually assessed needs. Markham (2019) highlighted that typical indicators of therapeutic progress (e.g., stable behaviour) may not adequately capture clinical progress for autistic patients. Future research should evaluate treatment outcomes for autistic females within forensic settings, in comparison to those without autism.

References

Aitken, G. (2006). Women and secure settings. *The Psychologist*, 19(12), 726–729.

Aitken, G. & Noble, K. (2001). Violence and violation: Women and secure settings. *Feminist Review*, 68(1), 68–88. https://doi.org/10.1080/01417780110042400

Alexander, R. T., Crouch, K., Halstead, S., & Piachaud, J. (2006). Long-term outcome from a medium secure service for people with intellectual disability. *Journal of Intellectual Disability Research*, 50(4), 305–315. https://doi.org/10.1111/j.1365-2788.2006.00806.x

Alexander, R., Langdon, P. E., Chester, V., Barnoux, M., Gunaratna, I., & Hoare, S. (2016). Heterogeneity within autism spectrum disorder in forensic mental health: The introduction of typologies. *Advances in Autism*, 2(4), 201–209. https://doi.org/10.1108/AIA-08-2016-0021

Anckarsäter, H., Nilsson, T., Saury, J.-M., Råstam, M., & Gillberg, C. (2008). Autism spectrum disorders in institutionalized subjects. *Nordic Journal of Psychiatry*, 62(2), 160–167. https://doi.org/10.1080/08039480801957269

Aral, A., Say, G. N., & Usta, M. B. (2018). Distinguishing circumscribed behavior in an adolescent with Asperger syndrome from a pedophilic act: A case report. *Dusunen Adam*, 31(1), 102–106. https://doi.org/10.5350/DAJPN2018310111

Ashworth, S., Bamford, J., & Tully, R. (2020). The effectiveness of a CBT-based intervention for depression symptoms with a female forensic inpatient with cognitive disability and autism. *The Journal of Forensic Psychiatry & Psychology*, 31(3), 432–454. https://doi.org/10.1080/14789949.2020.1754445

Barnard-Brak, L., Richman, D., & Almekdash, M. H. (2019). How many girls are we missing in ASD? An examination from a clinic- and community-based sample. *Advances in Autism*, 5(3), 214–224. https://doi.org/10.1108/AIA-11-2018-0048

Billstedt, E., Anckarsäter, H., Wallinius, M., & Hofvander, B. (2017). Neurodevelopmental disorders in young violent offenders: Overlap and background characteristics. *Psychiatry Research*, 252, 234–241. https://doi.org/10.1016/j.psychres.2017.03.004

Bosch, R., Hummelen, K., & Chakhssi, F. (2020). Inpatient aggression in forensic psychiatric patients with autism spectrum disorder: The role of risk and protective factors. *Journal of Intellectual Disabilities and Offending Behaviour*, 11(2), 93–100. https://doi.org/10.1108/JIDOB-05-2019-0008

Carpenter, B., Happé, F., & Egerton, J. (2019). *Girls and autism: Educational, family and personal perspectives*. Routledge. https://doi.org/10.1080/09585180050142525

Coid, J., Kahtan, N., Gault, S., & Jarman, B. (2000). Women admitted to secure forensic psychiatry services: I. Comparison of women and men. *Journal of Forensic Psychiatry*, 11(2), 275–295. https://doi.org/10.1080/09585180050142525

Corston, J. (2007). *The Corston Report: A review of women with particular vulnerabilities in the criminal justice system*. London, UK. Retrieved from: https://webarchive.nationalarchives.gov.uk/ukgwa/20130206102659/http://www.justice.gov.uk/publications/docs/corston-report-march-2007.pdf

Crawford, T. N., Cohen, P., & Brook, J. S. (2001). Dramatic-erratic personality disorder symptoms: I. Continuity from early adolescence into adulthood. *Journal of Personality Disorders*, 15(4), 319–335. https://doi.org/10.1521/pedi.15.4.319.19182

Daley, T. C. (2004). From symptom recognition to diagnosis: Children with autism in urban India. *Social Science & Medicine*, 58(7), 1323–1335. https://doi.org/10.1016/S0277-9536(03)00330-7

Davenport, S. (2004). A gender-sensitive therapeutic environment for women. In P. Campling, S. Davies, & G. Farquharson (Eds.), *Toxic institutions to therapeutic environments*. London, UK: Gaskell.

Dent, E. (2006). The safer sex. *Health Service Journal*, 116, 24–26.

Driver, B., & Chester, V. (2021). The presentation, recognition and diagnosis of autism in women and girls. *Advances in Autism* (ahead-of-print). https://doi.org/10.1108/AIA-12-2019-0050

Dudas, R. B., Lovejoy, C., Cassidy, S., Allison, C., Smith, P., & Baron-Cohen, S. (2017). The overlap between autistic spectrum conditions and borderline personality disorder. *PLOS ONE*, 12(9), e0184447. https://doi.org/10.1371/journal.pone.0184447

Duvekot, J., van der Ende, J., Verhulst, F. C., Slappendel, G., van Daalen, E., Maras, A., & Greaves-Lord, K. (2017). Factors influencing the probability of a diagnosis of autism spectrum disorder in girls versus boys. *Autism*, 21(6), 646–658. https://doi.org/10.1177/1362361316672178

Eaton, J., & Banting, R. (2012). Adult diagnosis of pathological demand avoidance – subsequent care planning. *Journal of Learning Disabilities and Offending Behaviour*, 3(3), 150. https://doi.org/10.1108/20420921211305891

Enayati, J., Grann, M., Lubbe, S., & Fazel, S. (2008). Psychiatric morbidity in arsonists referred for forensic psychiatric assessment in Sweden. *Journal of Forensic Psychiatry & Psychology*, 19(2), 139–147. https://doi.org/10.1080/14789940701789500

Esan, F., Chester, V., Gunaratna, I. J., Hoare, S., & Alexander, R. (2015). The clinical, forensic and treatment outcome factors of patients with autism spectrum disorder treated in a forensic intellectual disability service. *Journal of Applied Research in Intellectual Disabilities*, 28(3), 193–200. https://doi.org/10.1111/jar.12121

Fish, R. M. (2000). Working with people who harm themselves in a forensic learning disability service: Experiences of direct care staff. *Journal of Learning Disabilities*, 4(3), 193–207. https://doi.org/10.1177/146900470000400302

Fish, R. (2013). Women who use secure services: Applying the literature to women with learning disabilities. *Journal of Forensic Practice*, 15, 192–205. https://doi.org/10.1108/JFP-09-2012-0016

Gómez-Durán, E. L., Martin-Fumadó, C., Litvan, L., Campillo, M., & Taylor, P. J. (2013). Matricide by failure to act in autism. *Journal of Autism and Developmental Disorders*, 43(2), 495–497. https://doi.org/10.1007/s10803-012-1590-0

Gould, J., & Ashton-Smith, J. (2011). Missed diagnosis or misdiagnosis? Girls and women on the autism spectrum. *Good Autism Practice*, 12(1), 34–41.

Griffiths, C., Roychowdhury, A., & Girardi, A. (2018). Seclusion: The association with diagnosis, gender, length of stay and HoNOS-secure in low and medium secure inpatient mental health service. *Journal of Forensic Psychiatry and Psychology*, 29(4), 656–673. https://doi.org/10.1080/14789949.2018.1432674

Happé, F., Ronald, A., & Plomin, R. (2006). Time to give up on a single explanation for autism. *Nature Neuroscience*, 9, 1218–1220. https://doi.org/10.1038/nn1770

Hare, D. J., Gould, J., Mills, R., & Wing, L. (1999). *A preliminary study of individuals with autistic spectrum disorders in three special hospitals in England*. Retrieved from: www.researchgate.net/profile/Dougal-Hare/publication/335149129_A_preliminary_study_of_individuals_with_autistic_spectrum_disorders_in_three_special_hospitals_in_England/links/5d52f4c5458515304072d2c0/A-preliminary-study-of-individuals-with-autistic-spectrum-disorders-in-three-special-hospitals-in-England.pdf

Helverschou, S. B., Rasmussen, K., Steindal, K., Søndanaa, E., Nilsson, B., & Nøttestad, J. A. (2015). Offending profiles of individuals with autism spectrum disorder: A study of all individuals with autism spectrum disorder examined by the forensic psychiatric service in Norway between 2000 and 2010. *Autism*, 19(7), 850–858. https://doi.org/10.1177/1362361315584571

Helverschou, S. B., Steindal, K., Nøttestad, J. A., & Howlin, P. (2018). Personal experiences of the criminal justice system by individuals with autism spectrum disorders. *Autism*, 22(4), 460–468. https://doi.org/10.1177/1362361316685554

Hill, S. A., Chamorro, V., Hosking, A., & Ferreira, J. (2019). Characteristics and personality profiles of first 100 patients admitted to a secure forensic adolescent hospital. *Journal of Forensic Psychiatry and Psychology*, 30(2), 352–366. https://doi.org/10.1080/14789949.2018.1547416

Holloway, C. A., Munro, N., Jackson, J., Phillips, S., & Ropar, D. (2020). Exploring the autistic and police perspectives of the custody process through a participative walkthrough. *Research in Developmental Disabilities*, 97, 103545. https://doi.org/10.1016/j.ridd.2019.103545

Kawakami, C., Ohnishi, M., Sugiyama, T., Someki, F., Nakamura, K., & Tsujii, M. (2012). The risk factors for criminal behaviour in high-functioning autism spectrum disorders (HFASDs): A comparison of childhood adversities between individuals with HFASDs who exhibit criminal behaviour and those with HFASD and no criminal histories. *Research in Autism Spectrum Disorders*, 6(2), 949–957. https://doi.org/10.1016/j.rasd.2011.12.005

Kock, E., Strydom, A., O'Brady, D., & Tantam, D. (2019). Autistic women's experience of intimate relationships: The impact of an adult diagnosis. *Advances in Autism*, 5(1), 38–49. https://doi.org/10.1108/AIA-09-2018-0035

Kuhl-Meltzoff Stavropoulos, K., Bolourian, Y., & Blacher, J. (2018). Differential diagnosis of autism spectrum disorder and post traumatic stress disorder: Two clinical cases. *Journal of Clinical Medicine*, 7(4), 71. https://doi.org/10.3390/jcm7040071

Kumagami, T., & Matsuura, N. (2009). Prevalence of pervasive developmental disorder in juvenile court cases in Japan. *Journal of Forensic Psychiatry & Psychology*, 20(6), 974–987. https://doi.org/10.1080/14789940903174170

Kumar, S., Devendran, Y., Radhakrishna, A., Karanth, V., & Hongally, C. (2017). A case series of five individuals with asperger syndrome and sexual criminality. *Journal of Mental Health and Human Behaviour*, 22(1), 63. https://doi.org/10.4103/0971-8990.210703

Lai, M. C., Lombardo, M. V, Auyeung, B., Chakrabarti, B., & Baron-Cohen, S. (2015). Sex/gender differences and autism: Setting the scene for future research. *Journal of the American Academy of Child and Adolescent Psychiatry*, 54, 11–24. https://doi.org/10.1016/j.jaac.2014.10.003

Lai, M.-C. C., Lombardo, M. V., Ruigrok, A. N., Chakrabarti, B., Auyeung, B., Szatmari, P., … & MRC AIMS Consortium. (2017). Quantifying and exploring camouflaging in men and women with autism. *Autism*, 21(6), 690–702. https://doi.org/10.1177/1362361316671012

Langdon, P. E., Murphy, G. H., Clare, I. C. H., Palmer, E. J., & Rees, J. (2013). An evaluation of the EQUIP treatment programme with men who have intellectual or other developmental disabilities. *Journal of Applied Research in Intellectual Disabilities*, 26(2), 167–180. https://doi.org/10.1111/jar.12004

Långström, N., Grann, M., Ruchkin, V., Sjöstedt, G., & Fazel, S. (2009). Risk factors for violent offending in autism spectrum disorder: A national study of hospitalized individuals. *Journal of Interpersonal Violence*, 24(8), 1358–1370. https://doi.org/10.1177/0886260508322195

Lindsay, W. R., Smith, A. H. W., Quinn, K., Anderson, A., Smith, A., Allan, R., & Law, J. (2004). Women with intellectual disability who have offended: Characteristics and outcome. *Journal of Intellectual Disability Research*, 48(6), 580–590. https://doi.org/10.1111/j.1365-2788.2004.00627.x

Markham, S. (2019). Diagnosis and treatment of ASD in women in secure and forensic hospitals. *Advances in Autism*, 5(1), 64–76. https://doi.org/10.1108/AIA-09-2018-0027

Mouridsen, S. E., Rich, B., Isager, T., & Nedergaard, N. J. (2008). Pervasive developmental disorders and criminal behaviour: A case control study. *International Journal of Offender Therapy and Comparative Criminology*, 52(2), 196–205. https://doi.org/10.1177/0306624X07302056.

Nowell, S. W., Jones, D. R., & Harrop, C. (2019). Circumscribed interests in autism: Are there sex differences? *Advances in Autism*, 5(3), 187–198. https://doi.org/10.1108/AIA-09-2018-0032

Pearce, J. M. S. (2005). Kanner's infantile autism and Asperger's syndrome. *Journal of Neurology, Neurosurgery & Psychiatry*, 76(2), 200-205. http://dx.doi.org/10.1136/jnnp.2004.042820

Prison Reform Trust. (2011). *Reforming women's justice: Final report of the Women's Justice Taskforce*. London.

Rydén, G., Rydén, E., & Hetta, J. (2008). Borderline personality disorder and autism spectrum disorder in females: A cross-sectional study. *Clinical Neuropsychiatry: Journal of Treatment Evaluation*, 5(1), 22–30.

Sedgewick, F., Leppanen, J., & Tchanturia, K. (2020). Gender differences in mental health prevalence in autism. *Advances in Autism*, 7(3), 208-224. doi: 10.1108/AIA-01-2020-0007

Soderstrom, H., AK, S., Carlstedt, A., Forsman, A., Jodin, A., Carlstedt, A., & Forsman, A. (2004). Adult psychopathic personality with childhood-onset hyperactivity and conduct disorder: A central problem constellation in forensic psychiatry. *Psychiatry Research*, 121(3), 271–280. https://doi.org/10.1016/s0165-1781(03)00270-1.

Søndenaa, E., Helverschou, S. B., Steindal, K., Rasmussen, K., Nilsson, B., & Nøttestad, J. A. (2014). Violence and sexual offending behavior in people with autism spectrum disorder who have undergone a psychiatric forensic examination. *Psychological Reports*, 115(1), 32–43. https://doi.org/10.2466/16.15.PR0.115c16z5.

Tromans, S., Chester, V., Kapugama, C., Elliott, A., Robertson, S., & Barrett, M. (2019). The PAAFID project: Exploring the perspectives of autism in adult females among intellectual disability healthcare professionals. *Advances in Autism*, 5(3), 157–170. https://doi.org/10.1108/AIA-09-2018-0033

Woodbury-Smith, M. R., Clare, I. C. H., Holland, A. J., Kearns, A., Staufenberg, E., & Watson, P. (2005). A case-control study of offenders with high functioning autistic spectrum disorders. *Journal of Forensic Psychiatry and Psychology*, 16(4), 747–763. https://doi.org/10.1080/14789940500302554

Woodbury-Smith, M., Clare, I., Holland, A. J., Watson, P. C., Bambrick, M., Kearns, A., & Staufenberg, E. (2010). Circumscribed interests and "offenders" with autism spectrum disorders: A case-control study. *Journal of Forensic Psychiatry & Psychology*, 21(3), 366–377. https://doi.org/10.1080/14789940903426877

Zener, D. (2019). Journey to diagnosis for women with autism. *Advances in Autism*, 5, 2–13. https://doi.org/10.1108/AIA-10-2018-0041

Victimisation experiences of autistic people and restorative practice approaches to repairing harm

13

Sarah Cooper and
Lisa Whittingham

Victimisation and autistic individuals

Autistic people are more likely to be victims of interpersonal violence, including child maltreatment, intimate partner violence, workplace aggression, and bullying than non-autistic people (Weiss & Fardella, 2018). Autistic adults also appear to be at greater risk than individuals without autism of sexual assaults, exploitation, workplace bullying, and emotional abuse (Weiss & Fardella, 2018). Increased attention has been paid to understanding newer forms of victimisation towards autistic people including cyber victimisation and hate crimes, of which they may be at greater risk and less is known about the impact in their lives (Chaplin & Mukhopadhyay, 2018; Holfeld et al., 2019). Incidents of victimisation involving autistic people may be underreported due to individual impairments and social conditions that may hinder ability or willingness to report incidents (Sevlever et al., 2013).

Vulnerabilities contributing to victimisation for autistic people

Victimisation is the result of "the interplay between the complex factors that may contribute towards being disproportionately targeted and does not seek to pathologise situational or social vulnerability without taking into account societal contributions" (Pearson et al., 2020, p.3).

DOI: 10.4324/9781003036722-16

Individual characteristics

Autistic people exhibit specific traits and behavioural profiles that may increase victimisation. Autistic people who do not have intellectual disability have reported experiencing higher rates of bullying than individuals with the diagnosis of intellectual disability alone (Jawaid et al., 2012). Impairments of *executive functioning* can lead to difficulties in controlling emotions and behaviours, and poor problem-solving skills, which in turn reduces the ability to find adaptive solutions to challenges in social situations and increases proneness to impulsive behaviours that lead others to exclude them and increases risks of bullying by peers (Kloosterman et al., 2014).

Deficits in *theory of mind* generate challenges in reading important social cues, such as context or facial expression, increasing risk of victimisation if people cannot recognise contextual clues, signalling an unsafe situation (Gökçen et al., 2016). Further, autistic people may be slower to recognise and detect deception by others (van Tiel et al., 2020).

Impairments in communication and social skills are associated with an increased risk of victimisation, regardless of the individual's intellectual abilities (Jawaid et al., 2012). Such impairments include decreased use of pragmatic language, inability to follow social norms, and compromised understanding of physical and social boundaries (Forster & Pearson, 2019). Autistic people who exhibit impairments in communication and social skills tend to have smaller peer networks and challenges making friends, both protective factors against bullying and victimisation (Zeedyk et al., 2014). Difficulty understanding abstract or ambiguous social cues and communication may also increase the risk of cyberbullying and online abuse (e.g., phishing) (Forster & Pearson, 2019).

Social characteristics

Structural and societal factors, including social isolation and loneliness, increased contact with care providers, and social exclusion may also contribute to the experiences of victimisation of autistic people (Forster & Pearson, 2019).

Autistic people are more likely to experience social isolation and loneliness due to challenges in making and maintaining friendships (Finke et al., 2019). Accounts by adults with autism who have experienced abuse identified that a desire to be perceived positively by others had led to avoiding confrontation or not reporting abuse (Fardella et al., 2018; Pearson et al., 2020). Further, their desire to be liked and to sustain their (possibly few) relationships left them too trusting, normalising abuse, and accepting one-sided relationships (Pearson et al., 2020).

Autistic people with high support needs may come into contact with a multitude of care providers throughout their lives, which may put them at risk from opportunistic perpetrators or normalised poor boundaries and reinforced compliance (Chandler et al., 2019; Pearson et al., 2020). They may also be selected as victims because their abusers believe that they will not disclose or lack the necessary skills to report the incident (Forster & Pearson, 2019). However, good support relationships may also be protective by providing the opportunity for supervision, advocacy, and trusted feedback (Sevlever et al., 2013).

Autistic people are more likely to experience marginalisation and barriers to social inclusion, including stigma, dehumanisation, and lack of access to the accommodations and resources for inclusion. These societal and structural barriers create the conditions in which victimisation can occur (Fardella et al., 2018). For example, an autistic person facing workplace harassment may remain in their job because of difficulties securing another post.

Addressing the victimisation of autistic people

Autistic people who have been victimised have an elevated risk of mental disorders including anxiety, depression, and post-traumatic stress disorder (PTSD) (Taylor & Gotham, 2016). The cumulative effects of unresolved trauma and mental disorders can result in significant behavioural changes (e.g., aggression) and outcomes including suicidality and offending behaviour (Kildahl et al., 2019). It is therefore imperative that autistic people have access to both preventative and responsive interventions.

Adults with autism have identified that education and training, promoting support and advocacy, and increased opportunities for social inclusion are critical for addressing victimisation (Fardella et al., 2018). To date, most interventions have focused on education and training in social skills (Miltenberger et al., 2017), recognising abuse (Ledbetter-Cho et al., 2016), and improving socio-sexual knowledge (Sala et al., 2019). Increasingly, both individual and group-based cognitive behaviour therapy (CBT) is being used to address trauma and victimisation in individuals with autism, demonstrating small to medium effect sizes with outcomes depending on target behaviours selected for intervention and the ability of the individual to participate (Weston et al., 2016). Using creative means to engage individuals with autism including dance/movement (Takahashi et al., 2019) or drama (Feniger-Schaal & Orkibi, 2020) may enhance the impact of CBT.

Agencies supporting autistic people should also adopt a *trauma-informed* framework that "emphasize[s] safety, trustworthiness, choice, collaboration, and empowerment" and "acknowledges the pervasiveness of trauma" (Keesler, 2014, p.37). While accepted as a positive approach to supporting individuals with autism, more evidence is needed for best practice and how to incorporate it into services (Truesdale et al., 2019).

Restorative practice

In recognition that autistic people may have been victimised in the past and continue to be exposed to similar events in forensic settings, restorative practices (RP) emphasise a holistic approach to understanding their past and current experiences. It is a process in which victims (individuals harmed) and perpetrators (harmers) come together in a safe and controlled environment to talk about a wrongdoing (Restorative Justice Council, 2020). Described by Braithwaite (1989) as *reintegrative shaming*, this practice holds the harmer accountable, provides an opportunity for reflection and learning about the impact of their actions, and reintegrates them back into their community. It also enables the person harmed to tell the harmer about the impact of their act and to assert their need for at least some reparation to be possible (Hafemeister et al., 2012). Positive outcomes include improved victim outcomes (Angel et al., 2014) and satisfaction, reduced reoffending rates, and cost savings in services (Shapland et al., 2008; Strang et al., 2013). The application of RP to forensic mental health is recent (Drennan et al., 2015). Cook and colleagues (2015) were the first to demonstrate the remarkable impact that this approach could have for patients and staff in UK forensic mental health settings. Similar programmes have been developed in other regions of the UK (Drennan & Cooper, 2018), the Netherlands (van Denderen et al., 2020), and Australia (Power, 2017).

Participation in RP requires that all participants have the capacity to engage in reciprocal dialogue and experience empathy; lacking awareness of others' feelings may lead to negative outcomes (Levy, 1999). Potentially stigmatising assumptions regarding the interpersonal skills of autistic people may influence beliefs about their 'fit' with RP. Traditionally, research has suggested that autistic people experience deficits in empathy, leading to difficulties in recognising complex emotions, reading vocal intonation and body language (Baron-Cohen, 2009), and pedantic speech (Tager-Flusberg, 1993). 'Double empathy', an alternative conceptualisation of empathy in individuals with autism, suggests that autistic individuals experience the world differently and may respond in different, unexpected ways to their communication partners, leading to a breakdown in mutual understanding (Milton, 2012).

Fletcher-Watson and Bird (2020) observe that individuals with autism "are simply not following the same response-script as a neurotypical person" (p.3); and may be overwhelmed by emotional empathy, needing longer to process cognitive aspects of empathy and sensory information (Forster & Pearson, 2019; Elcheson et al., 2018). Evaluation of the capacity of autistic people to engage in RP is at an early stage (van Denderen et al., 2020) and one case study has encouraging outcomes (Tapp et al., 2020).

Building a restorative culture in a forensic mental health service

Understanding that the most critical function of RP is to restore and build relationships (Wachtel, 2013), the first author (SC) identified its potential to address violations experienced in a low secure inpatient unit for adult male offenders with intellectual disability, many of whom presented with complex needs including autism, mental illness, and personality disorders (Cooper & Inett, 2018). Building on available guidance (National Offender Management Service, 2013; Restorative Justice Council, 2011), a procedure was developed to ensure safe practices, safeguarding processes, and collaboration with the police where needed. Twelve members from the multidisciplinary team completed an accredited four-day facilitator training, allowing them to offer restorative conferences to patients and staff.

Box 13.1   Case study: Mathew[1]

Mathew had a history of verbal and physical aggression against staff. He had rigid and fixed rules about what others 'should' and 'shouldn't' do, leading him to use threatening and intimidatory behaviour to reassert control in situations when his expectations were thwarted. He frequently externalised blame and appeared to present with little or no remorse. Individual therapy revealed he experienced significant, intolerable shame. It was formulated that Mathew responded to his shameful feelings by attacking others. This response, coupled with a fixed belief that staff working in forensic settings were impervious to harm, exacerbated his propensity to minimise their experiences.

Restorative conferences can trigger intense emotional responses, leading to transformative change (Cook, 2019; Drennan, 2018) and Mathew needed a way to sit with difficult and painful feelings of shame

---

before participating in a conference. Incorporating restorative principles with an integrated therapeutic approach achieved a feeling of safety and containment, while facilitating opportunities for him to process these feelings. Therapeutic processes enabled Mathew to become an active agent for positive change in his life by understanding, labelling, and normalising his emotional response to shame. He wanted to learn and develop his understanding of staff needs, and his ability to accept responsibility in causing harm gradually shifted.

Work with Mathew remains ongoing and he has requested to meet in person with those he harmed, to enable him to learn more about how they were affected. Concerns remain about his capacity to tolerate honest feedback without returning to patterns of externalised shame. Using a 'victim by proxy' could enable Mathew to process the experiences of health care workers without personal connection and enhance his capacity to recognise harm (Drennan, 2018). A restorative conference with those he harmed could be considered if Mathew is able to safely engage using this approach.

Developing a culture of restorative wards

As with the general population, Mathew's case demonstrates that it is not always appropriate or safe to move forward with a conference. It also represents the diverse needs and levels of readiness of individuals and the need to develop meaningful and creative ways to safely engage them in restorative dialogue. As such, the concept of the 'restorative ward' (Table 13.1) was born and a pilot project was trialled for six months (Cooper et al., in preparation). All unit staff attended a two-day training programme on implementing informal RP and fortnightly supervision sessions created opportunities for reflection and skills development. Table 13.1 shows how the pilot used the approaches described in the restorative continuum (Wachtel, 2013) to achieve Dekker's (2018) three goals of restorative justice. Restorative approaches were extended to include a collection of proactive processes that build connections, develop relationships and a sense of community, and prevented wrongdoings (Wachtel, 2013).

When informal RP are part of everyday life, they have the cumulative impact of creating an environment that fosters awareness, empathy, and responsibility, in addition to providing opportunities to develop more effective emotional regulation (McCold & Wachtel, 2001). This approach has been largely successful in schools and residential units for children with complex emotional needs and behavioural difficulties (Littlechild, 2011; Preston, 2015) and shows promise in forensic services and for individuals with autism. The pilot, described here, demonstrated improvements approaching statistical significance in measures of therapeutic hold, patient cohesion, and experienced safety, as well as reduction in harms experienced on the unit (Cooper et al., in preparation).

Table 13.1 Restorative wards

Moral Engagement Supporting patients to focus on the right thing to do	Restorative circles build relationships and support while developing perspective-taking and empathy. Non-threatening discussions about events and experiences allow participants to observe in a safe space that others hold different views (Wachtel, 2013).

• Voluntary attendance.
• Held four days a week.
• 15 minutes, following a structured format.
• Patients and staff sit in a circle; the face of every participant seen, emphasising equality and collective responsibility (Boyes-Watson & Pranis, 2015).
• Everyone has an equal voice and opportunity to be heard (Costello et al., 2010).
• Everyone permitted to say 'pass' when they do not wish to comment.

Peter, diagnosed with autism and paranoid schizophrenia, experienced significant mistrust of others and avoided all group programmes. Knowing that autistic people may experience social gatherings as overwhelming or distressing (Baron-Cohen, 2009), the team was not confident Peter would attend the circles. The predictable and structured format of the circle enabled Peter to become a regular circle attendee, at first listening, and soon finding the confidence to voice his views. Though autistic people may face challenges in maintaining social relationships, connection with others and a sense of belonging are a basic need and valued by all (Muller et al., 2008).

Affective statements (Rosenberg, 2003) provide feedback about positive and harmful behaviours including clear communication about:

• Behaviours observed, without judgement or evaluation.
• Our feelings.
• How our feelings are connected to our needs.
• Our requests.

Affective statements are helpful in building therapeutic rapport by building on patient strengths and engaging those who are not ready to converse with restorative conversations.

To help embed RP into the ward, patient care plans and positive behaviour supports incorporate restorative approaches. Staff are supported to adopt restorative language and approaches in clinical reviews and case conferences.

(Continued)

Emotional Processing

Supporting patients to process feelings and build trust

Restorative questions and impromptu restorative conversations validate victim experiences, and enable harmers to learn about the impact of actions in a safe and non-judgemental manner, whilst beginning to identify ways to repair some of the harm.

Questions for harmer	**Questions for harmed**
What happened?	What happened?
What were you thinking at the time?	What were your thoughts at the time?
What have you thought since?	
Who has been affected? How have they been affected?	What have you thought since?
	How has this affected you and others? What was the hardest thing for you?
What needs to happen to make things right?	
	What do you think needs to happen next?

Chris was threatened by another patient and subsequently transferred to another ward. It was not safe to engage the harmer with a restorative conference, so a restorative conversation was facilitated with Chris. The process, using restorative questions, afforded him the opportunity to share his account of what happened and its impact, have his experiences validated, and collaboratively develop a plan to maintain his sense of safety.

Reintegration

Supporting patients to reintegrate with their ward and wider community

Restorative circles address harms that have happened on the ward, but only where a safe space had been established.

Restorative conferences, shuttle conferences, and restorative letters (Restorative Justice Council, 2020) support patients and staff in rebuilding relationships, by engaging in safe and structured dialogues, in a manner most responsive to their needs.

Referral	*John engaged in a series of incidents putting everyone's safety at risk. Heather, a health care worker, reported an incident to the nurse-in-charge.*
	John called her a 'snitch' and ignored all her subsequent requests. Heather became anxious supporting John in the community, concerned for his safety, and her capacity to manage risk. Both reported a good working relationship until the incident.
Risk assessment and preparation	*John understood he was challenging Heather, although did not recognise she had been affected [limited understanding of others]. John missed having some enjoyable banter with Heather [learned routines of positive social interaction].*

The following were described and explored with John:

- *The conference format;*
- *Questions he would be asked;*
- *Reflections on what Heather might say [rehearsal of a novel situation].*

John was able to process emotionally challenging information in a safe and contained manner and worked through what he wanted to communicate [support with emotional regulation, enabling time to process cognitive aspects of empathy].

Heather wanted to use the conference to develop John's understanding about the impact of his actions and to repair the damage to their relationship [developing John's perspective taking and problem-solving skills]. Heather thought about what she wanted to share with John, while avoiding over-disclosure in her professional role.

Heather was advised that John might laugh and smile at inappropriate times during the conference when he felt embarrassed and ashamed [limited ability to manage social behaviour]. Heather's expectations could be managed and allowed for discussions about the nature of John's needs, their possible impact in the conference, and how they would be managed [increased mutual understanding, 'double empathy'].

Restorative conference

When John smiled with his head down, his feelings were acknowledged [validation from a shared understanding]. Helping John anticipate what would happen put him at ease. As the conference progressed, he increased eye-contact and showed more congruent facial expressions [self-managing emotional aspects of empathy].

John gave an honest account of what happened, describing his thoughts at the time of the incident and since [sequencing and consequential thinking supported]. Language was adapted to suit John's needs and time was provided for him to formulate his responses [responsive to communication needs].

John listened to Heather share how she had been affected by his actions and what she found hardest. They agreed how to move forward, reaffirming Heather's responsibility in reporting concerns [collaborative problem solving].

Reintegration

After the conference, with genuine concern, John asked Heather, "Were you really affected by what I did?" and she responded affirmatively [increased awareness into others' needs].

In separate follow-up meetings, both reported an improvement in their relationship. Heather felt confident supporting John in the community, stating he was responsive to her requests, and appeared to have greater insight into their interactions. Heather commented, "it [RP] really does work".

Conclusion

Autistic people are at greater risk of victimisation and require creative, innovative interventions. One opportunity to acknowledge the history of victimisation in persons with autism in forensic settings is the inclusion of RP. Hafemeister and colleagues (2012) argued that the presence of a mental, intellectual, or developmental disorder should not be a basis for exclusion from RP. The pilot project described here demonstrates that when the needs of an individual are understood and adequate steps are taken to ensure the safety of all parties, opportunities exist for restorative engagement. Whilst more research is needed to understand the complex interplay between RP and the needs of autistic people, the case studies in this chapter demonstrate that positive outcomes can be achieved and point towards the importance of including this already marginalised group in restorative processes.

Learning points

- Autistic people are at greater risk of experiencing victimisation than their neurotypical peers and experience numerous individual and social factors that contribute to the likelihood of victimisation.
- Most interventions addressing the risk of victimisation have focused on teaching preventative skills to autistic people and more attention is needed for trauma-informed approaches.
- RP has been shown to support the needs of both victims and harmers, by bringing them together in a safe and supportive environment.
- Until now, autistic people have largely been excluded from RP, limiting their opportunities for healing and learning.
- Early indications from a pilot project using RP processes in a low secure forensic unit revealed individuals with autism were able to participate in and benefit from RP.

Note

1 All names and identifying information have been changed.

References

Angel, C. M., Sherman, L. W., Strang, H., Ariel, B., Bennett, S., Inkpen, N., Keane, A., & Richmond, T. S. (2014). Short-term effects of restorative justice conferences on post-traumatic stress symptoms among robbery and burglary victims: A randomized controlled trial. *Journal of Experimental Criminology*, 10, 291–307. https://doi.org/10.1007/s11292-014-9200-0

Baron-Cohen, S. (2009). Autism: The empathizing–systemizing (ES) theory. *Annals of the New York Academy of Sciences*, 1156(1), 68–80. doi: 10.1111/j.1749-6632.2009.04467.x

Boyes-Watson, C., & Pranis, K. (2015). *Building a restorative school community*. St. Paul, MN: Living Justice Press, Institute for Restorative Initiatives.

Braithwaite, J. (1989). *Crime, shame and reintegration*. New York, NY: Cambridge University Press.

Chandler, R. J., Russell, A., & Maras, K. L. (2019). Compliance in autism: Self-report in action. *Autism*, 23(4), 1005–1017. doi: 10.1177/1362361318795479

Chaplin, E., & Mukhopadhyay, S. (2018). Autism spectrum disorder and hate crime. *Advances in Autism*, 4(1), 30–36. https://doi.org/10.1108/AIA-08-2017-0015

Cook, A. (2019). Restorative practice in a forensic mental health service: Three case studies. *The Journal of Forensic Psychiatry & Psychology*, 30(5), 876–893. doi: 10.1080/14789949.2019.1637919

Cook, A., Drennan, G., & Callanan, M. M. (2015). A qualitative exploration of the experience of restorative approaches in a forensic mental health setting. *The Journal of Forensic Psychiatry and Psychology*, 26(4), 510–531. doi: 10.1080/14789949.2015.1034753

Cooper, S. L., & Inett, A. C. (2018). Staff support procedures in a low-secure forensic service. *Journal of Forensic Practice*, 20(3), 191–201. https://doi.org/10.1108/JFP-09-2017-0034

Cooper, S. L., Craster, L., & Inett, A. (in preparation). Implementing a restorative ward in a low secure forensic unit for individuals with intellectual disabilities.

Costello, B., Wachtel, J., & Wachtel, T. (2010). *Restorative circles in schools: Building community and enhancing learning*. Bethlehem, PA: International Institute for Restorative Practices.

Dargis, M., Newman, J., & Koenigs, M. (2016). Clarifying the link between childhood abuse history and psychopathic traits in adult criminal offenders. *Personality Disorders: Theory, Research, and Treatment*, 7(3), 221–228. doi: 10.1037/per0000147

Dekker, S. (2018). *Restorative just culture checklist*. Retrieved from: https://safetydifferently.com/wp-content/uploads/2018/12/RestorativeJustCultureChecklist-1.pdf

Drennan, G. (2018). Restorative justice applications in mental health settings: Pathways to recovery and restitution. In J. Adlam, T. Klutting, & B. X. Lee (Eds.). *Violent states and creative states* (Vol. 2). London: Jessica Kingsley Press.

Drennan, G., & Cooper, S. (2018). Restorative practice in mental health – Gathering momentum. *Resolution*, 63, 12–13. Retrieved from: https://restorativejustice.org.uk/sites/default/files/resources/files/Resolution%20%2363%20Autumn%202018.pdf

Drennan, G., Cook, A., & Kiernan, H. (2015). The psychology of restorative practice in forensic mental health recovery. In T. Gavrielides (Ed.). *The psychology of restorative justice: Managing the power within* (pp. 127–142). Surrey, England: Ashgate Publishing Ltd.

Elcheson, J., Stewart, C., Lesko, A., Willey, L. H., Craft, S., Purkis, Y., & Campbell, M. (2018). *Spectrum women: Walking to the beat of autism*. London: Jessica Kingsley Press.

Fardella, M. A., Burnham Riosa, P., & Weiss, J. A. (2018). A qualitative investigation of risk and protective factors for interpersonal violence in adults on the autism spectrum. *Disability & Society*, 33(9), 1460–1481. doi: 10.1080/09687599.2018.1498320

Feniger-Schaal, R., & Orkibi, H. (2020). Integrative systematic review of drama therapy intervention research. *Psychology of Aesthetics, Creativity, and the Arts*, 14(1), 68–80. https://doi.org/10.1037/aca0000257

Finke, E. H., McCarthy, J. H., & Sarver, N. A. (2019). Self-perception of friendship style: Young adults with and without autism spectrum disorder. *Autism & Developmental Language Impairments*, 4, 1–16. doi: 10.1177/2396941519855390

Fletcher-Watson, S., & Bird, G. (2020). Autism and empathy: What are the real links? *Autism*, 24(1), 3–6. doi: 10.1177/1362361319883506

Forster, S., & Pearson, A. (2019). "Bullies tend to be obvious": Autistic adults' perceptions of friendship and the concept of 'mate crime.' *Disability & Society*, 35, 1103–1123. doi: 10.1080/09687599.2019.1680347

Gökçen, E., Frederickson, N., & Petrides, K. V. (2016). Theory of mind and executive control deficits in typically developing adults and adolescents with high levels of autism traits. *Journal of Autism and Developmental Disorders*, 46(6), 2072–2087. doi: 10.1007/s10803-016-2735-3

Hafemeister, T. L., Garner, S. G., & Bath, V. E. (2012). Forging links and renewing ties: Applying the principles of restorative and procedural justice to better respond to criminal offenders with a mental disorder. *Buffalo Law Review*, 60, 147–224.

Holfeld, B., Stoesz, B., & Montgomery, J. (2019). Traditional and cyber bullying and victimization among youth with autism spectrum disorder: An investigation of the frequency, characteristics, and psychosocial correlates. *Journal on Developmental Disabilities*, 24(2), 61–76.

Jawaid, A., Riby, D. M., Owens, J., White, S. W., Tarar, T., & Schulz, P. E. (2012). 'Too withdrawn' or 'too friendly': Considering social vulnerability in two neuro-developmental disorders. *Journal of Intellectual Disability Research*, 56(4), 335–350. doi: 10.1111/j.1365-2788.2011.01452.x

Keesler, J. M. (2014). A call for the integration of trauma-informed care among intellectual and developmental disability organizations. *Journal of Policy and Practice in Intellectual Disabilities*, 11(1), 34–42. https://doi.org/10.1111/jppi.12071

Kildahl, A. N., Bakken, T. L., Iversen, T. E., & Helverschou, S. B. (2019). Identification of posttraumatic stress disorder in individuals with autism spectrum disorder and intellectual disability: A systematic review. *Journal of Mental Health Research in Intellectual Disabilities*, 12(1–2), 1–25. https://doi.org/10.1080/19315864.2019.1595233

Kloosterman, P. H., Kelley, E. A., Parker, J. D., & Craig, W. M. (2014). Executive functioning as a predictor of peer victimization in adolescents with and without an autism spectrum disorder. *Research in Autism Spectrum Disorders*, 8(3), 244–254. https://doi.org/10.1016/j.rasd.2013.12.006

Ledbetter-Cho, K., Lang, R., Davenport, K., Moore, M., Lee, A., O'Reilly, M., Watkins, L., & Falcomata, T. (2016). Behavioral skills training to improve the abduction-prevention skills of children with autism. *Behavior Analysis in Practice*, 9(3), 266–270. doi: 10.1007/s40617-016-0128-x

Levy, K. S. (1999). The Australian juvenile justice system: Legal and social science dimensions. *Qunnipiac Law Review*, 18, 521–551.

Littlechild, B. (2011). Conflict resolution, restorative justice approaches and bullying in young people's residential units. *Children and Society*, 25, 47–58. https://doi.org/10.1111/j.1099-0860.2009.00259.x

McCold, P., & Wachtel, T. (2001). Restorative justice in everyday life. In J. Braithwaite & H. Strang (Eds.). *Restorative Justice and Civil Society* (pp. 114–129). Cambridge, UK: Cambridge University Press.

Miltenberger, R. G., Zerger, H. M., Novotny, M., & Livingston, C. P. (2017). Behavioral skills training to promote social behavior of individuals with autism. In *Handbook of Social Skills and Autism Spectrum Disorder* (pp. 325–342). New York, NY: Springer.

Milton, D. E. (2012). On the ontological status of autism: The 'double empathy problem'. *Disability & Society*, 27, 883–887. https://doi.org/10.1080/09687599.2012.710008

Muller, E., Schuler, A., & Yates, G. B. (2008). Social challenges and supports from the perspective of individuals with Asperger syndrome and other autism spectrum disabilities. *Autism*, 12(2), 173–190. doi:10.1177/1362361307086664

National Offender Management Service. (2013). *Wait 'til Eight. An essential start up guide to MONS RJ Scheme implementation*. Retrieved from: www.justice.gov.uk/downloads/publications/policy/moj/wait-til-eight-guide.pdf

Pearson, A., Rees, J., & Forster, S. (2020). *Experiences of interpersonal victimisation in autistic and non-autistic adults*. Pre-print. https://doi.org/10.31219/osf.io/amn6k

Power, M. (2017). International innovations in restorative justice in mental health – Next steps for Australia [PowerPoint presentation]. Retrieved from: www.griffith.edu.au/__data/assets/

pdf_file/0019/107443/Michael-Power-Churchill-Fellowship-Restorative-Approaches-in-Mental-Health-V2.pdf

Preston, N. (2015). Restorative practices, affect script psychology and the social and emotional aspects of learning. In T. Gavrielides (Ed.). *The psychology of restorative justice: Managing the power within* (pp. 65–81). Surrey, England: Ashgate Publishing Ltd.

Restorative Justice Council. (2011). *Best practice guidance for restorative practice*. Restorative Justice Council. Retrieved from: https://restorativejustice.org.uk/sites/default/files/resources/files/Best%20practice%20guidance%20for%20restorative%20practice%202011.pdf

Restorative Justice Council. (2020). *Restorative practice guidance 2020*. Restorative Justice Council. Retrieved from: https://restorativejustice.org.uk/resources/rjc-practice-guidance-2020-0

Rosenberg, M. B. (2003). *Nonviolent communication: A language of life*. Encinitas, CA: Puddledancer Press.

Sala, G., Hooley, M., Attwood, T., Mesibov, G. B., & Stokes, M. A. (2019). Autism and intellectual disability: A systematic review of sexuality and relationship education. *Sexuality and Disability*, 37(3), 353–382. https://doi.org/10.1007/s11195-019-09577-4

Sevlever, M., Roth, M. E., & Gillis, J. M. (2013). Sexual abuse and offending in autism spectrum disorders. *Sexuality and Disability*, 31(2), 189–200. doi: 10.1007/s11195-013-9286-8

Shapland, J., Atkinson, A., Atkinson, H., Dignan, J., Edwards, L., Hibbert, J., Howes, M., Johnstone, J., Robinson, G., & Sorsby, A. (2008). *Restorative justice: Does restorative justice affect reconviction. The fourth report from the evaluation of three schemes*. Ministry of Justice Research Series 10/08. London: Ministry of Justice. Retrieved from: https://restorativejustice.org.uk/sites/default/files/resources/files/Does%20restorative%20justice%20affect%20reconviction.pdf

Strang, H., Sherman, L., Mayo-Wilson, E., Woods, D. J., & Ariel, B. (2013). Restorative Justice Conferencing (RJC) using face-to-face meetings of perpetrators and victims: Effects on perpetrator recidivism and victim satisfaction. A systematic review. *Campbell Systematic Reviews*, 9(1), 1–59. https://doi.org/10.4073/csr.2013.12

Tager-Flusberg, H. (1993). What language reveals about the understanding of minds in children with autism. In S. Baron-Cohen, H. Tager-Flusberg, & D. J. Cohen (Eds.). *Understanding other minds: Perspectives from autism*. Oxford University Press.

Takahashi, H., Matsushima, K., & Kato, T. (2019). The effectiveness of dance/movement therapy interventions for autism spectrum disorder: A systematic review. *American Journal of Dance Therapy*, 41(1), 55–74. https://doi.org/10.1007/s10465-019-09296-5

Tapp, J., Moore, E., Stephenson, M., & Cull, D. (2020). "The image has been changed in my mind": A case of restorative justice in a forensic mental health setting. *The Journal of Forensic Practice*, 22(4), 213–222. doi: 10.1108/JFP-05-2020-0023

Taylor, J. L., & Gotham, K. O. (2016). Cumulative life events, traumatic experiences, and psychiatric symptomatology in transition-aged youth with autism spectrum disorder. *Journal of Neurodevelopmental Disorders*, 8(1), 28. doi: 10.1186/s11689-016-9160-y

Truesdale, M., Brown, M., Taggart, L., Bradley, A., Paterson, D., Sirisena, C., Walley, R., & Karatzias, T. (2019). Trauma-informed care: A qualitative study exploring the views and experiences of professionals in specialist health services for adults with intellectual disabilities. *Journal of Applied Research in Intellectual Disabilities*, 32(6), 1437–1445. https://doi.org/10.1111/jar.12634

van Denderen, M., Verstegen, N., de Vogel, V., & Feringa, L. (2020). Contact between victims and offenders in forensic mental health settings: An exploratory study. *International Journal of Law and Psychiatry*, 73, 101630. https://doi.org/10.1016/j.ijlp.2020.101630

van Tiel, B., Deliens, G., Geelhand, P., Murillo Oosterwijk, A., & Kissine, M. (2020). Strategic deception in adults with autism spectrum disorder. *Journal of Autism and Developmental Disorders*, 51(1), 255–266. https://doi.org/10.1007/s10803-020-04525-0

Wachtel, T. (2013). *Defining restorative*. International Institute for Restorative Practices. Retrieved from: www.iirp.edu

Weiss, J. A., & Fardella, M. A. (2018). Victimization and perpetration experiences of adults with autism. *Frontiers in Psychiatry*, 9, 203–213. https://doi.org/10.3389/fpsyt.2018.00203

Weston, L., Hodgekins, J., & Langdon, P. E. (2016). Effectiveness of cognitive behavioural therapy with people who have autistic spectrum disorders: A systematic review and meta-analysis. *Clinical Psychology Review*, 49, 41–54. https://doi.org/10.1016/j.cpr.2016.08.001

Zeedyk, S. M., Rodriguez, G., Tipton, L. A., Baker, B. L., & Blacher, J. (2014). Bullying of youth with autism spectrum disorder, intellectual disability, or typical development: Victim and parent perspectives. *Research in Autism Spectrum Disorders*, 8(9), 1173–1183. https://doi.org/10.1016/j.rasd.2014.06.001

Part IV

Future directions

Future directions for research and practice

14

Anne Sheeran and Nichola Tyler

This chapter draws together some of the key themes from the volume and sets out some key areas for development in research, policy, and practice, with a focus on the voices of autistic people and drawing from interviews completed by one of the authors as part of a co-produced service improvement project with autistic patients. Areas of omission from this volume are highlighted, including themes of diversity.

Introduction

> Everyone's not special, people are human and people should be treated how human beings should be treated – people who have autism and people who haven't got autism – they are equal.
>
>   (Male, 30s, inpatient in a forensic intellectual disabilities service, 2020)

The assumption of equal rights for autistic people is found in position statements (e.g., in the US, the Autism Society National Position Statement, n.d.) and the protection of these rights within legislation (e.g., in the UK, *Equality Act*, 2010). Within the Forensic Mental Health System (FMHS) and the Criminal Justice System (CJS), it is now recognised that identification of autistic individuals is crucial in order to provide appropriate support and the reasonable adjustments required to meet the specific needs. Nevertheless, the absence of systematic screening and assessment in many services continues to hinder this process; for example, the UK National Probation Service identified in 2020 that "there are no national data on the number of people under probation service in the community who have autism" (Public Health England, 2020). Patients in hospital also identified that staff who are new to the service may not know that there are autistic people in the service; one patient commented:

> When new bank [temporary] staff open up the notes, it should tell them at the very beginning.
>
>   (Male, 20s, inpatient in forensic intellectual disabilities service, 2020)

DOI: 10.4324/9781003036722-18

Recognition of an autistic person's needs within FMHS/CJS relates not only to factors such as the reasonable adjustments to environments and systems required to support equal access to justice and person-centred approaches to treatment and care. There is a need, highlighted in different chapters throughout this volume, for mental health (and CJS) professionals to formulate how autism fits into the "picture of criminal culpability for a particular individual in respect of particular conduct at a particular time" (Freckelton, 2013, p.170). Beyond the courts, into prisons, hospitals, and community forensic settings, approaches to risk management, intervention, and treatment and care for autistic people also require an approach to formulation that draws on clinical understanding of the individual, as well as an evidence-based framework. The need for increased awareness and iterative training for practitioners is clear. The limited availability of valid and reliable outcome measures for autistic adults is recognised (e.g., Brugha et al., 2015) and development of an evidence base for measures to evaluate outcomes within FMHS/CJS should be prioritised.

Terminology

I don't accept it's going to ruin my life – it's just going to be there.
(Male, 30s, FMH inpatient, 2020)

Autism-related stigma may lead some to adopt camouflaging strategies; both cause and response can contribute to mental health difficulties. (e.g., Perry et al., 2022). The use of identity-first language – "autistic people" – is seen by some as a way of highlighting autism as a part of a person's identity and as a way of being, rather than a focus on the medicalised concept of a 'disorder' or deficit – consistent with the concept of 'neurodiversity', in which autism is considered as "one form within the diversity of human minds" (Kenny et al., 2016, p.443). Kenny et al.'s UK study highlighted the endorsement of the term 'autistic' by a large percentage of autistic adults and family/friends, whereas professionals were more likely to endorse person-first language such as 'person with autism', and that there was currently no universally accepted way to describe autism within the community. A more recent Australian study (Bury et al., 2020) found a preference for person-first language by people who reported a diagnosis of autism.

The semantic issues in this field are evolving and contentious; we recognise that this extends to all aspects of the narrative around autism, especially the use of the term 'disorder' or 'condition', with its inherent connotations of medicalised diagnostic criteria based in behaviour and deficits. This is problematic, in that it reflects the current perspectives of professionals and a neurotypical narrative, rather than one led by autistic people who are experts by experience. In recognition of this changing context, for the purpose of this volume, the editorial decision was made that both identity-first and person-first terms would be used, but that the use of 'condition' and 'disorder' would be excluded unless with specific reference to texts or psychiatric discourse. Future policy, research, and interventions in FMHS and CJS will need to take account of the emerging terminologies.

Self-advocacy

> People are different from other people – people with autism work differently to other things, they spot things out, recognise things more than others [without autism]. We work different.
>
> (Male, 40s, inpatient in FMHS, 2020)

> Learning from other people's experience and knowing I'm not the only one here. And knowing this diagnosis is nothing, just something that's there with us – people with autism – a normal person – doesn't make me different to any other people.
>
> (Male, inpatient in forensic intellectual disabilities service, 2020)

The uniqueness of individuals – whether or not they have a diagnosis of autism – is often stressed by autistic people in recognition of both the differences and commonalities of their experiences. Autobiographical accounts by autistic people of their experiences, including as prisoner (Attwood, 2018) and as police officer (Buchan, 2022), provide detailed contextual perspectives which can inform the practice of staff in the CJS. There is emerging literature from autistic mental health practitioners who set out both barriers and enablers conferred by the manifestations of autism and the contexts of their experiences (e.g., Hawker, 2017). The need to involve the autistic community and prioritise research areas relevant to autistic people is clear (e.g., Pellicano et al., 2014). A US research study which surveyed views of autistic participants and family members concluded that autistic people's insights derived from lived experience could confer expertise and suitability for training others, and that identifying how autistic people think about autism is important in developing research relevant to their interests and needs (Gillespie-Lynch et al., 2017).

Extrapolation from wider research on FMHS and CJS – and more systematic approaches to scoping and understanding the experiences of autistic people within these systems to inform improved services – are emerging, as exemplified in a study in a UK region of the experiences and recommendations by people with intellectual disability and/or autism who have been through hospital and/or prison (NHS England and Pathways Associates, 2019). The findings included that people who had been through these systems wanted to contribute to improving services for others: "We want to do something positive – such as training or being an expert by experience – so that the system learns and other people are treated better than we were" (p.6). Such comments were echoed by service users interviewed in 2020 by one of the editors. One young man with autism identified a number of areas he thought could contribute to improving support offered by staff and clinicians, including the provision of experiential information:

> You can do a leaflet about what autism is, and give to each member of staff here. Or a meeting – get professionals to tell staff what autism is all about. But also one of us patients with autism can sit in the meeting, then they see a patient in the room with autism and can ask questions.
>
> (Male, 20s, inpatient in a forensic service, 2020)

He was subsequently able to follow this through by planning and participating in a panel discussion with other autistic people about their experiences – in daily life and in the service – as part of a new induction programme for staff, and co-delivering the session on autism.

The involvement of autistic people in leading research and development in the criminal justice system is also emerging. For the impact of such initiatives to gain momentum, embedding strategic objectives of a truly collaborative approach to engagement of autistic people in research and development within CJS and FMHS will be required. This will need to encompass the development of alternatives to the current provision – for example, exploration of the use of community options such as the provision of intervention programmes tailored to the needs of autistic people, not only targeted upon offending behaviour but also enhancement of mental health and wellbeing, to reduce the risks and vulnerabilities. In the UK, the use of Mental Health Treatment Requirements (MHTRs) was introduced in 2005 as a sentencing option for people whose offences do not meet the custodial threshold and who do not require treatment in secure mental health services. Numerous barriers to their implementation have been identified (e.g., National Offender Management Service, 2014) which have resulted in very limited use (e.g., Molyneaux et al., 2021).

Diversity

Future policy, practice, and research will need to address the perspectives of autistic people not as a homogenous group but recognising the different experiences of autistic people from diverse communities and with diverse identities. There is evidence that the perceptions of autism are socially constructed in different cultures (e.g., Kim, 2012; Matson et al., 2017) and greater understanding of the impact of different perspectives will need to inform research and service provision. Jones and Mandell (2020) note that the impact of systemic racism in the sciences affects autism research and that Black autistic people have been historically underrepresented in autism research. They make recommendations to address these disparities. While this is from a US perspective, it is likely that the underrepresentation of diverse groups is replicated in other cultures. A UK study by the National Autistic Society on the experiences of families from Black and Minority Ethnic (BAME) backgrounds identified that there were additional challenges, including missed identification of autism, and lack of cultural competence of some professionals leading to misunderstanding of parents and carers, and increased isolation for families who have poor experiences of services. The report makes recommendations for strategy and commissioning of services, including consulting families from BAME communities about their specific needs, and funding for research to improve diagnostic and support services (National Autistic Society, 2014). The overrepresentation of BAME people in prisons in the UK (e.g., Halliday, 2021) and elsewhere (e.g., Canada – Owusu-Bempah et al., 2021) suggests that there will be significant numbers of autistic people of colour whose needs may go unrecognised and unmet.

Autism is no longer conceptualised as a predominantly male phenomenon and the presence and needs of autistic women are increasingly becoming recognised. However, it is argued that current research and clinical practice tend to conflate sex and gender, with a binary approach to gender (Strang et al., 2020). Recent research suggests that there may be co-occurrence between autism or self-reported autistic traits and trans- or gender-diverse identity (Warrier et al., 2020), or autism and gender-dysphoria, as defined in DSM-5 (American Psychiatric Association, 2013; Van Der Miesen et al., 2016).

Hospitals and prison services typically have a rigid binary system for housing service users; strategies to meet the needs of gender-diverse people in such services reflect the limitations within such binary settings of the attempts to strike the balance between protecting people's rights of equality of access to care and to freedom of gender expression, and management of the potential vulnerabilities/risks for themselves or others (e.g., Bright, 2020). Detailed discussion of these issues is beyond the scope of this book, however, see Richards and Barrett (2020a, 2020b) for summaries of key issues for gender-diverse people in prison, and for gender-diverse autistic people. Strang et al. (2020) argue for advancement of research and practice in the intersection between sex, gender, and autism through a more diversified approach and a focus on lived experience. Policy and practice in this area should also reflect the needs and views of autistic gender-diverse individuals in FMHS/CJS.

Future directions for research

As highlighted across the various chapters in this volume, there is a paucity of research on the prevalence, needs, and experiences of autistic people and their families in contact with criminal justice and forensic mental health systems, limiting the guidance available for practitioners and policy makers. However, it is apparent that the impacts on autistic people who come into contact with these systems necessitate an increased research focus to improve the recognition, identification, and support available for people with autism and their families within these contexts. While momentum has increased considerably in recent years, a number of recurring themes are highlighted throughout the preceding chapters as still requiring research focus, including:

- Understanding the experiences of autistic people and their families – with the inclusion of people from diverse groups – of the criminal justice and forensic mental health systems, to identify what works well and what does not from their perspectives and to identify gaps in provision.
- Identifying and measuring positive outcomes for autistic people and their families based on a collaborative understanding on what 'good outcomes' mean at an individual, familial, and systemic (e.g., criminal justice) level.
- Developing a deeper understanding of the complex interplay between traits of autism, comorbid conditions, and offending behaviours; as well as the interplay between these factors and risk of victimisation.
- Developing a more accurate understanding of the representation and diversity of autistic people within criminal justice and forensic mental health settings, and appropriate training, identification, and/or screening approaches to support staff to recognise autism and appropriately support those in their care.
- Examining the effectiveness of recommended support strategies for autistic people within forensic settings including, but not limited to, autism advocacy/peer support, the use of appropriate adults, registered intermediaries, positive behavioural support planning, and restorative practices.
- Developing and exploring the effectiveness of offence-focused interventions in producing positive outcomes for autistic people, utilising high quality research designs.

These research priorities broadly map on to those identified through surveys with the wider autism community (for a detailed review see Roche et al., 2021), suggesting that some of these questions are of wider concern than the criminal justice context. However, further research in these areas will hopefully enable the co-production and development and/or adaptation of effective screening, training, risk assessment approaches, interventions, and support strategies that can be tailored to the unique context of the CJS and FMHS and therefore improve the experiences and outcomes for those individuals who may find themselves in contact with these services.

While it is important to generate empirical evidence to guide the development and/or adaptation of appropriate assessment, support, and intervention protocols, it is critical that any research agenda is co-produced with input from autistic researchers and those with lived experience of the CJS and FMHS. Large scale international surveys with members of the autism community have highlighted that research ideas and funding priorities do not always mirror those of the autism community and their self-identified needs (Pellicano et al., 2014; Roche et al., 2021). Furthermore, the autism community is itself diverse. Thus, consultation with the wider autism and justice involved communities will be important for progressing research in the area. Given the unique contextual, organisational, and environmental features of forensic settings, involving individuals with lived experience of these settings will be of particular importance for prioritising research topics, as well as designing and conducting new research and ensuring that diverse perspectives are represented (rather than being confined to those who choose to participate in research). Such input not only represents best practice in applied research but has also been suggested to inform the development of more acceptable services (Spiers et al., 2005; Völlm et al., 2017).

As noted earlier, co-production and involvement of experts by experience is of both importance and benefit when designing research, education, and care services. Active involvement of experts by experience may include contributing to the design of research, participating in steering and monitoring groups, reviewing and designing research materials, supporting with recruitment of participants, involvement in data collection as a member of the research team, disseminating findings, and involvement in translating findings into practice (i.e., implementation) (National Institute for Health Research, 2021; Völlm et al., 2017). Given the nature of forensic settings, there are often additional challenges to navigate to involve people with lived experience in research and service design. Völlm et al. (2017) helpfully outline some key considerations when engaging individuals with lived experience of forensic services in research, beyond identifying research priorities, including: ensuring meaningful engagement and not tokenistic involvement, considering the risks of consultation fatigue (e.g., not always drawing on the expertise of the same individuals), maintaining awareness of and mitigating power imbalances (e.g., existing and/or creating these between researchers, experts by experience, and potential participants); wider staff relationships; and practical difficulties (e.g., navigating organisational, policy, and practice restrictions). While requiring additional time and effort, such engagement is likely to be of particular value to researchers, practitioners, and, most importantly, those who come into contact with these services.

Conclusion

Advancements have been made in recent years to improve support for autistic people involved with the CJS and FMHS; however, there is still much progress to be made. Developing and delivering specialist services that recognise and respond to the diverse needs of autistic people and their families, and provide positive outcomes, require further attention from a research, policy, and practice perspective. Co-production of training, research, and services with members of the autism community and those who have lived experience of the CJS and FMHS is central to this aim. Such an approach is needed to ensure that the criminal justice and forensic mental health systems can recognise and respond effectively to the needs of autistic people who come into contact with these services. Perhaps this comment from a former patient of forensic services should serve as an underlying principle:

> It's more important to understand myself, even more than staff understanding anger – releasing it all – because I was hurting other people. The most important thing is to give people all the information so they know.
>
> (Male, 40s, former patient, 2020)

Acknowledgements

Thank you to the service users who agreed to share their time and experiences with us for the purpose of this chapter. Your generosity and insight have been invaluable.

References

American Psychiatric Association. (2013). *Diagnostic and Statistical Manual of Mental Disorders: Diagnostic and Statistical Manual of Mental Disorders*, Fifth Edition. Arlington, VA.

Attwood, W. (2018). *Asperger's Syndrome and Jail: A Survival Guide*. London: Jessica Kingsley Publishers.

Autism Society. (n.d.). *National Position Statement on Human Rights*. Retrieved from: www.autism-society.org/public-policy/national-position-statements/national-position-statement-human-rights/

Bright, K.L. (2020). Gender identity and prisons in England and Wales: the development of rights and rules; checks and balances. In: *Law in Motion: 50 years of legal change*. Eds: Claydon, Devy & Ajevski. Milton Keynes: The Open University.

Brugha, T.S., Doos, L., Tempier, A., Einfeld, S. & Howlin, P. (2015). Outcome measures in intervention trials for adults with autism spectrum disorders: a systematic review of assessments of core autism features and associated emotional and behavioural problems. *International Journal of Methods in Psychiatric Research*, 24 (2), 99–115. doi: 10.1002/mpr.1466

Buchan, A. (2020). *Autism and the Police: Practical Advice for Officers and Other First Respond-ers*. London: Jessica Kingsley Publishers.

Bury, S.M., Jellett, R., Spoor, J.R. & Hedley, D. (2020). "It defines who I am" or "It's something I have": what language do [autistic] Australian adults [on the autism spectrum] prefer? *Journal of Autism and Developmental Disorders*. doi: 10.1007/s10803-020-04425-3

Equality Act. (2010). London: HMSO. Retrieved from: www.legislation.gov.uk/ukpga/2010/15. Accessed 28.03.21.

Freckelton, I. (2013). Forensic issues in autism spectrum disorder: learning from court deci-sions. In *Recent Advances in Autism Spectrum Disorders* Volume II. Ed: Michael Fitzgerald. IntechOpen. doi: 10.5772/55400

Gillespie-Lynch, K., Knapp, S., Brooks, P.J., Pickens, J. & Schwartzman, B. (2017). Whose exper-tise is it? Evidence for autistic adults and critical autism experts. *Frontiers in Psychology*, 438(8). doi: 10.3389/fpsyg.2017.00438

Halliday, M. (2021). *Bromley Briefings Prison Factfile: Winter 2021*. Prison Reform Trust. Retrieved from: www.prisonreformtrust.org.uk/Portals/0/Documents/Bromley%20Brief-ings/Winter%202021%20Factfile%20final.pdf

Hawker, D. (2017). Practising clinical psychology on the autistic spectrum. *Clinical Psychology Forum*, 294, 9–13.

Jones, D.R. & Mandell, D.S. (2020). To address racial disparities in autism research, we must think globally, act locally. *Autism*, 24(7) 1587–1589. https://doi.org/10.1177/1362361320948313

Kenny, L., Hattersley, C., Molins, B., Buckley, C., Povey, C. & Pellicano, E. (2016). Which terms should be used to describe autism? Perspectives from the UK autism community. *Autism*, 20(4), 442–462. doi: 10.1177/1362361315588200

Kim, H.U. (2012). Autism across cultures: rethinking autism. *Disability & Society*, 27(4), 535–545. doi: 10.1080/09687599.2012.659463

Matson, J.L., Matheis, M., Burns, C.O, Esposito, P., Venuti, P., Pisula, A., Misiak, E., Kalyva, V., Kamio, Y., Ishitobi, M. & Goldin, R.L (2017). Examining cross-cultural differences in autism spectrum disorder: A multinational comparison from Greece, Italy, Japan, Poland, and the United States. *European Psychiatry*, 42, 70–76. https://doi.org/10.1016/j.eurpsy.2016.10.007

Molyneaux, E., San Juan, N.V., Brown, P., Lloyd-Evans, B. & Oram, S. (2021). A pilot programme to facilitate the use of mental health treatment requirements: Professional stakeholders' expe-riences. *British Journal of Social Work*, 51, 1041–1059. Advance Access Publication October 14, 2020. doi: 10.1093/bjsw/bcaa111

National Autistic Society. (2014). *Diverse Perspectives. The challenges for families affected by autism from Black, Asian, and Minority Ethnic communities*. Retrieved from: https://s3.chorus-mk.thirdlight.com/file/1573224908/63849355948/width=-1/height=-1/for-mat=-1/fit=scale/t=445333/e=never/k=7c17beeb/Diverse-perspectives-report.pdf

National Institute for Health Research (NIHR). (2021). *Briefing notes for researchers – public involvement in NHS, health and social care research*. Retrieved from: www.nihr.ac.uk/docu-ments/briefing-notes-for-researchers-public-involvement-in-nhs-health-and-social-care-research/27371

National Offender Management Service. (2014). *Mental Health Treatment Requirements Guid-ance on Supporting Integrated Delivery*. Retrieved from: https://assets.publishing.service.gov.uk/government/uploads/system/uploads/attachment_data/file/391162/Mental_Health_Treatment_Requirement_-_A_Guide_to_Integrated_Delivery.pdf

NHS England and Pathways Associates. (2019). *Beyond the High Fence*. Retrieved from: www.england.nhs.uk/wp-content/uploads/2019/02/beyond-the-high-fence.pdf

Owusu-Bempah, A., Jung, M., Shai, F., Wilton, A.S. & Kouvoumdjian, F. (2021). Race and incarceration: the representation and characteristics of black people in provincial correctional facilities in Ontario, Canada. *Race and Justice*. Available online before print 8 April 2021. doi. org/10.1177/21533687211006461

Pellicano, E., Dinsmore, A. & Charman, T. (2014). What should autism research focus upon? Community views and priorities from the United Kingdom. *Autism*, 18(7), 756–770. doi: 10.1177/1362361314529627

Perry, E., Mandy, W., Hull, L. & Cage, E. (2022). Understanding camouflaging as a response to autism-related stigma: A social identity theory approach. *Journal of Autism and Developmental Disorders*, 52, 800–810. https://doi.org/10.1007/s10803-021-04987-w

Public Health England. (2020). *Health and social care needs assessment of adults under probation service supervision in the community*. Retrieved from: https://assets.publishing.service.gov. uk/government/uploads/system/uploads/attachment_data/file/875279/Probation_HSNA_ Guidance.pdf

Richards, C. & Barrett, J. (2020a). Supporting trans and non-binary people in forensic settings. In: *Trans and Non-binary Gender Healthcare for Psychiatrists, Psychologists, and Other Health Professionals* (pp. 61–69). Cambridge: Cambridge University Press. doi: 10.1017/9781108628419.006

Richards, C., & Barrett, J. (2020b). Autistic spectrum conditions and intellectual disability. In: *Trans and Non-binary Gender Healthcare for Psychiatrists, Psychologists, and Other Health Professionals* (pp. 70–80). Cambridge: Cambridge University Press. doi: 10.1017/9781108628419.007

Roche, L., Adams, D. & Clark, M. (2021). Research priorities of the autism community: a systematic review of key stakeholder perspectives. *Autism*, 25(2), 336–348. doi: 10.1177/1362361320967790

Spiers, S., Harney K. & Chilvers, C. (2005). Editorial: Service user involvement in forensic mental health: Can it work? *Journal of Forensic Psychiatry and Psychology*, 16(2), 211–220. doi: 10.1080/14789940500098137

Strang, J.F., van der Miesen, A.I.R., Caplan, R., Hughes, C., daVanport, S. & Lai, M-C. (2020). Both sex- and gender-related factors should be considered in autism research and clinical practice. *Autism*, 24(3), 539–543. https://doi.org/10.1177/1362361320913192

Van Der Miesen, A.I.R., Hurley, H. & De Vries, A.L.C. (2016). Gender dysphoria and autism spectrum disorder: a narrative review. *International Review of Psychiatry*, 28(1), 70–80. doi: 10.3109/09540261.2015.1111199

Völlm, B., Foster, S., Bates, P. & Huband, N. (2017). How best to engage users of forensic services in research: Literature review and recommendations. *International Journal of Forensic Mental Health*, 16(2), 183–195. doi: 10.1080/14999013.2016.1255282

Warrier, V., Greenberg, D.M., Weir, E., Buckingham, C., Smith, P., Lai, M-C., Allison, C. & Baron-Cohen, S. (2020). Elevated rates of autism, other neurodevelopmental and psychiatric diagnoses, and autistic traits in transgender and gender-diverse individuals. *Nature Communications*, 11, 3959. doi: 10.1038/s41467-020-17794-1

Index

Note: **Bold** page numbers refer to tables; *italic* page numbers refer to figures.

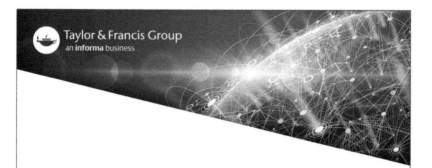

Taylor & Francis eBooks

www.taylorfrancis.com

A single destination for eBooks from Taylor & Francis
with increased functionality and an improved user
experience to meet the needs of our customers.

90,000+ eBooks of award-winning academic content in
Humanities, Social Science, Science, Technology, Engineering,
and Medical written by a global network of editors and authors.

TAYLOR & FRANCIS EBOOKS OFFERS:

A streamlined
experience for
our library
customers

A single point
of discovery
for all of our
eBook content

Improved
search and
discovery of
content at both
book and
chapter level

REQUEST A FREE TRIAL
support@taylorfrancis.com